Woman Without A Name

A Wisdom Tale

To Sharon
for being Wisdom's
living invitation
and for supporting
this work -
Karen
Nov. 2010

Karen Mitchell

Outskirts Press, Inc.
Denver, Colorado

Woman Without A Name
A Wisdom Tale
All Rights Reserved.
Copyright © 2010 Karen Mitchell
v2.0

Cover image © 2010 by Linda Beeuwsaert. All rights reserved. Used with permission.

Outskirts Press, Inc.
http://www.outskirtspress.com

ISBN: 978-1-4327-6074-8

Outskirts Press and the "OP" logo are trademarks belonging to Outskirts Press, Inc.

PRINTED IN THE UNITED STATES OF AMERICA

For my husband, Kent Mitchell,
who has supported me in so many
ways throughout the writing process

and

for my sister, Linda Beeuwsaert
who provided important feedback
and the image for the cover of this book.

I.

Of Streams and Falling Stars

Chapter One

S ophia was waking up.

I was having that same disturbing dream again, she thought. *I'm glad I didn't sleep any longer.* She noticed a slight, pleasant pressure about her head. Curious, she opened her eyes and found herself looking at the round, freckled face of a young girl less than an arm's length away. The girl's eyebrows shot up and her open, upraised hand quickly made a fist. Sophia smiled, realizing that she had been woken by the young girl's pushing against the loose and flying strands of her always unruly hair. Smiling back, the girl lowered her hand, placing it on the narrow, rough-hewn table that separated them. "I told you not to bother her."

Sophia turned toward the scolding voice and saw a taller, sterner-looking girl and recognized her as the older sister. The older girl was holding some of Sophia's wrapped goat cheese up to her nose. Carefully she set the cheese back down, and then without making eye contact with Sophia, asked if she had seen Jeremiah.

"He should be here by now. He has to tell us the story," the younger whined.

Sophia straightened up and rolled her head around, trying to get the stiffness out of her neck while keeping the earnest faces of the two girls in view. "He'll be here," she said. "He's probably here already." Sophia craned her neck and looked out over the crowd as if she suspected Jeremiah was close by.

"Come on," the older one commanded the younger, grabbing at her sleeve. "Let's go look some more." The young one pushed the older one's hand away and took off, running. The older shouted a quick, "Good day," to Sophia and tried to catch up with her sister. Sophia, shielding her eyes with her hands from the bright sun, watched as they darted through the crowd. It was Saturday and market day and Midsummer's Eve was only a few days away. A few hundred people, nearly the entire population of the village, were milling about. People were buying, selling, bartering, exchanging news and making plans for the Midsummer's celebration. There were many visitors from the valley who had also come, drawn by the village's reputation for fine craftsmanship and healthy animals.

Sophia stood up to stretch. She was short, strong-looking and solid, resembling in shape and countenance roughly squared and weather-beaten stone. Her rolled-up sleeves showed muscled forearms, thick wrists, broad hands and thick, bent fingers. She was still looking at the sisters when the younger came to an abrupt halt, pointed at something, and began shouting. The din of raised voices and the cackling, baying, and bleating of so many animals made it impossible to make out her words. A boy ran past Sophia's table yelling, "Jeremiah's here! He's come!" Children were shouting, and running from all directions toward the smithy.

Sophia's good friend, the village's storyteller, came into view. Jeremiah was walking barefoot, as was his summer habit. He was short, only a little taller than Sophia herself, and not much taller than the children who clutched at his threadbare sleeves and the back of his shirt like beggars desperately hungry. Jeremiah had been telling the same story on the market day before Midsummer's Eve for twenty years. While most adults found his story about their village merely entertaining, the children believed summer was not summer without it.

Sophia watched as a broad-shouldered, bony man gave Jeremiah an arm up onto an empty cart, after first leveling it. Sophia recognized him as her neighbor, a good-natured farmer who would let her board her two goats in his barn in the harsh winter months. Once Jeremiah was in the cart he moved about, finding a good position. Then he looked out at his audience. With his assured air and generous gaze, Sophia thought he looked more like a visiting prince than the beggar he actually was.

Jeremiah closed his eyes, held out his arms palms up and tilted his head back as if he were drinking the sun. The children stirred in their seats and then slowly settled down. Lowering his head and opening his eyes, Jeremiah smiled appreciatively at his audience. "Breathe in," he told the children and those adults who were also listening. "Take everything around you into yourself." He extended his arms, then drew them back toward himself until his hands rested over his chest. It was as if he was indeed taking everything in. The children imitated him. Many would insist, later, that they became bigger and taller when they did this, just as Jeremiah seemed to do.

"Now, breathe out," Jeremiah said. "Give the world your thankfulness and love." He moved his hands away from his chest, stretching out his arms and hands in a gesture of offering. Again, the children followed his example and tasted a sweetness many would remember till their old age.

"Very good," he said as if they had accomplished a great deed. "Now, how many of you have gone to the ruins in the forest?"

Many hands went up.

"Wonderful! Those who haven't seen them must see them soon. And how many of you know why we live here, high up on a hill, even though the growing season is shorter and the winters much colder?"

"Because it's so beautiful up here," an older girl blurted out. "We have meadows and a river and the big forest."

"Ah, thank you. You're right, of course. It *is* beautiful, up here. And who knows why we love beauty so much?"

"You tell us," the children shouted.

Jeremiah waved an arm aloft and when Sophia waved an arm back, he locked eyes with her and smiled. The children turned around and Sophia felt many pairs of eyes staring at her. It was all part of the ritual. When they turned again to look at Jeremiah, he put his hand to his throat and opened his mouth, acting as if despite his good intentions and his best effort, he was suddenly too parched to go on.

"He's thirsty," one of the older children said. "He needs something to drink."

Sophia, on cue, bent down, then raised two cups in the air, one filled with water and another with goat's milk. Jeremiah pointed to Sophia and clapped his hands. The children moved for her as she approached the cart. First, she handed the cup of water to Jeremiah. He took it and held it gratefully before draining it. He placed the emptied cup at his feet and then Sophia handed him the cup of goat's milk. Again, he took it appreciatively, holding the cup in his hands for a moment before he drank. Winking at Sophia, he handed both cups back to her and said aloud, "Ah, now, I am ready. We must thank Sophia for her gift." Jeremiah bowed to her and the children clapped. Some of the older ones whistled. A young boy found her a small bench. Sophia knew that Jeremiah had told the children that he wanted her close, because when his friend was near his stories would always come out better. Sophia slowly took her seat on the bench – her knees were not what they used to be.

"I feel better. Thank you, everyone. And now I will answer my own question by telling you a story. This is a wonderful story; it will make you see how special you all are and how special this village is." Jeremiah closed his eyes and waited for the children to quiet down again. When they did, he opened his eyes and began.

"Long time ago, our ancestors lived in the forest. One day they were inspired to build a city among the trees. Now, they had never built anything so big before and did not know how to go about it. So they began paying attention to what was around them: the animals, plants, birds, sun, wind, stars, the earth and the moon, water, fire, and stones; and all these beings, seeing how our ancestors respected them, agreed to teach them. And so did the angels. The angels would come and visit our ancestors like our relatives come and visit us today. They would tell our ancestors what heaven was like. They said that in heaven everyone worked together for the common good. Our ancestors learned from the angels too, and were very appreciative; they always treated the angels hospitably. Slowly, the city they were building grew and the people felt good living there. Everyone was paid attention to and treated with great courtesy and kindness. Adults respected children, and children reminded the older folk to play. Everyone used the gifts God had given them and all gifts were appreciated. Nearly every week there was a celebration for a special occasion, and our ancestors would all dance and sing and eat their favorite foods.

"The city got bigger and bigger and filled with things. The animals did not come around as much and there wasn't room for all the plants and trees. Soon, people started to forget all that the earth and its creatures had taught them. They were very busy and hurried and felt that they didn't have time to entertain the angels any more. And so the angels, who had always been on the borders of vision, became invisible. Unfortunately our ancestors also began to see animals only as food or as slaves that did their work for them, and so they began to fear them. Nearly every man and woman forgot how they had once spoken with the angels and with all earth's creatures. And because they forgot this, the elders began teaching the young that it was they who had built the city and that they had done it without any help. They said that the city was theirs; it belonged to them; and if they did not protect it, it would not last.

"Our ancestors started building huge, towering walls with strong, thick gates. These walls blocked out the sun, the moon, and the stars, scared off the animals, and made the angels feel even more unwelcome. So much time was spent repairing walls that there was very little time left for building anything new. So the city stopped growing and inside it everything began collapsing and breaking down. The people replaced what had fallen down and what had been broken with things that were ugly and looked the same and didn't work. This was because they did not care any more.

"For many years, the change was felt by only a few, so slowly did it happen, but eventually everyone became very sad and angry, though they didn't know why, and kindness was rarer. However, whenever kindness was shown, it would remind people of how things once had been. That kept hope from dying completely, and that hope made our ancestors restless. Hundreds of years passed and one day they had had enough. They stopped working and abandoned the city, scattering themselves to the four winds. All that is left of the city now are the ruins we see in the forest.

"Our ancestors went everywhere – all over the earth. They went searching for something, but they didn't know what they were looking for; they didn't know what would fill the emptiness in their hearts. But they believed that some day their hearts would be full again, and for thousands of years their children and their children's children roamed the earth, always looking, always hoping, even though they suffered many hardships.

"One Midsummer's Eve long ago, many of our ancestors arrived at this place. Some had come over the hills and some had come up from the valley. They were surprised that they had come to the same place at the same time, and they were happy because they recognized each other and knew they were all somehow related. When they saw the forest and the ruins of the once-great city, it stirred up memories, grief, and a great longing. And when they looked around and saw the meadows, the creeks, and the river, with all the animals and birds, they realized that what they had been looking for all along was Beauty – Beauty in Her earthly form.

"Our ancestors caught a glimpse of Beauty on this hill. And some even had glimpses of Her working to build another city, a city with room enough for everything — even for heaven itself — a city even God would like to live in. Those who saw Beauty building Her city – even for a moment – never forgot it.

"Our great-great-great-great-grandmothers and grandfathers put down strong and stubborn roots here so that nothing would ever force them to go away. Though they rarely saw Beauty for more than a few moments, and even more rarely saw Her making Her new city, they knew She was with them and was using all that they saw and touched and heard to make something wonderful. They began paying close attention to everything again: the plants and animals, the moon and the stars. They could smell, touch, and taste many things — and sometimes they could even hear the angels. All this helped our ancestors create this village. Beauty's presence has protected us and made us strong, strong enough to survive droughts, fires, floods, sicknesses, and wars. Nothing has been able to destroy us. And because we have loved Beauty, Beauty has given us many gifts and talents. Our village is known for its crafts; we have many men and women who can make beautiful things. That is why even people who do not live in our village come from very far away to be with us on market day."

Jeremiah paused, "So where is Beauty building Her city?"

Sophia and many of the children swept their arms in front of them. "Yes…very good," Jeremiah said, smiling. His arm also swept the space in front of him. "She is right here, working, right in our own village — though we can't see Her. And what an amazing city it will be: full of light like shining jewels. There will be treasure to find everywhere! We will know and feel things and move in ways we can't imagine now. Everything will sing and dance together. And we will listen very carefully to each other, because we will see how each being knows a special secret about God. In Beauty's city, we will draw up joy from all its wells and when we drink it, it will make us feel as if there was a light inside of us. And what will make us happiest of all is seeing how God loves Beauty and how much Beauty loves God. Their love will be the new sun that will shine upon us and the new fire that will warm and brighten us at night.

"Even now, all of you can catch a glimpse of Beauty's city if you banish ugliness from your thoughts, if you pay attention as best you can to everything and everyone around you, and if you try to do your work with care. These are very wonderful things, and they please Beauty very much. These things make Her smile, and when Beauty smiles at you, you will see yourself as She sees you. You will see how lovely and strong you are and how dear to Her and to everything." The children sighed, knowing the story was over. Some were sure they had seen the city Beauty was making as Jeremiah was talking, while others were begging him for more details. When the sun began setting, parents and grandparents stepped in to collect their offspring. Sophia and a young boy named Aaron moved the bench she had been sitting on next to the cart. Jeremiah stepped down and Sophia congratulated him warmly on captivating his audience once again. He declined her invitation to join her for supper, but agreed to take the goat cheese she offered. It was one of his favorite things to eat.

Chapter Two

Since Jeremiah had decided not to join her for supper after market day, Sophia made her way back home alone. She lived in a small cottage on the edge of the forest, a little north of the main part of the village. The story still circulating in the village was that she had come to visit a relative nearly 40 years ago, and finding her relative deceased, she had decided not to leave and had instead remained in her relative's house. No one knew why. Some said that she had done wicked deeds wherever she had come from and wished to put the past behind her. The more common opinion was that she had fled something: a great sorrow or threat, perhaps an abusive husband. But this was all speculation; Sophia never said anything about her motives.

She seemed to have no family. No one in the village had heard of any relative coming to visit her. She kept mostly to herself, but appeared to enjoy the company of Father Lawrence, the village priest, and of Jeremiah. The villagers found her friendship with the priest inexplicable because Sophia rarely set foot inside the church. And as for her affinity for Jeremiah, that too was incongruous, for Sophia was known to be a no-nonsense, hard-working type of person, a sometimes forgetful woman, but certainly not one given to flights of fancy that rendered people like Jeremiah unfit. In fact, it was well-known in the village that at one time, Sophia had been a masterful weaver. Her beautiful rugs were still being passed from mothers to daughters as wedding presents. When her hands became too bent and crippled to ply her demanding craft, she spent more time tending the sick. No one knew more about the healing powers of plants and how to combine them than Sophia, and she was never stingy with what she knew. She would teach anyone who was truly willing to learn. She had won the villagers' respect; they recognized she had an important part to play in their lives despite her solitary nature. If the full truth be told, however, it must be mentioned that their respect would, on occasion, border on fear. This was due to the fact that Sophia was very free in giving her opinion, and it was also because she evoked sensations and feelings in the villagers similar to the ones they experienced when they wandered about the old ruins, particularly at the twilight hour.

When Sophia arrived home she ate a meager meal of a thin vegetable soup and bread, and was tidying up. On a typical mild summer evening, she would have taken her two chairs outside; sitting on one and putting her feet up on another, she would have enjoyed listening to the forest and watching the stars make their appearance — for although her health was not good, her hearing and eyesight were still excellent. Sophia, however, was more tired than usual and decided to go right to bed — she had not slept well for many nights because of the disturbing dream she had been having every night for nearly a week. After a concentrated effort she would wake herself up from it, but then was never able to go back to sleep.

Soon after going to bed Sophia fell asleep, and as she feared might happen, she found herself back in the same dream.

She was sitting on the ground with her legs stretched out in front of her. She felt something rough scraping against her back and knew she was leaning against a tree. A woman wailed nearby; the piercing sound of the woman's despair, grief, and longing penetrated deep inside of Sophia like a hook and yanked her full attention. Sophia moved her head, hoping to locate the woman, but it was too dark to make out anything. "Where are you?" Sophia cried out. "Are you badly hurt?"

And then she remembered she was dreaming and that she, Sophia, was the one badly wounded. The unendurable wailing she had heard had been her own. She tried to force herself awake at this point, as she had been able to do previously. But tonight it was different. Tonight, her dream's course was set by another's will. She very clearly heard these words:

"Your pain is part of my labor."

Sophia knew it was a woman who had spoken to her but could not identify her, even though the voice was strangely familiar and beloved. She was about to ask who she was, when she noticed that her own hands were wet and sticky and jittered on her lap like flaying fish. The need to know what had happened to them was so urgent and pressing that she forgot to ask the woman her name.

"Why can't I move my hands?" Sophia had a vague memory of being told something horrible. "Why did the healer say I couldn't have children?"

"You *will* have a child," the woman said.

Sophia was irritated because the woman did not answer her

questions and had said something absurd instead. The woman laughed as if she knew Sophia's thoughts, and her laughter was like water, undulating.

"Stand up," she commanded.

Fortified by the authority in the woman's voice, Sophia stood up immediately and looked up at the night sky. The darkness was blooming and then it was breathing in and out in every direction through a multitude of stars. Everywhere she looked she sensed life: pregnant, laboring, pushing. Her pain was forgotten and wonder replenished her. She watched as a single star plucked itself from night's quiver and shot itself across the dark sky, blazing a trail of fire.

"Catch it, then let it go," the woman said.

Though she was afraid, Sophia stretched out her hands to catch the fiery arrow and realized she was waking up.

When she opened her eyes, Sophia saw the clean light of the moon shining through an unshuttered window. She stared at it for a long while until wakefulness and dream slowly disentangled themselves. When she realized she had to relieve herself, and sat up in bed, she felt a trembling in her belly and a contracting and releasing in her heart and knew what it portended. Soon, she was nothing more than a loom upon which grief and longing, like weft and warp, were being woven once again. However, though the grief and longing were familiar, she felt a new pattern was being created, a pattern she had not planned and was incapable of imagining. Tears came, copious tears. They ran down the deep creases in her cheeks and after they stopped she felt lighter. She did not have any idea how much time had passed.

A child! Why did she say a child? It's not possible.... It can't be. I'm over sixty — too old to be entertaining such things. How could I raise a child? What do I know? And why am I still thinking about it? Weak-mindedness is pitiful and dangerous. I need to get moving.

She took a deep breath and got out of bed, shocked by how steady she felt. She blew her nose, wiped her eyes, and dried her face. Grabbing her staff, she dragged the chamber pot out from underneath the bed with it. While she was using it, she looked about the room, entranced. Everything appeared unspoiled in the moon's light: the jug by her bed, the small table, her old shawl hanging on its hook. The stark shadows of all these familiar objects accentuated their innocence — and hers as well.

Afterward, she thought about going back to bed, but decided she was too restless for sleep. She shuffled to the window. In the fine, cool air, the stars blinked at her as if startled by her existence, and she blinked back. Feeling dazed, she reached for one of her two skirts and put it on; taking her shawl off a hook, she wrapped it about her shoulders. She decided she would check on her goats, reasoning that a chore might distract her for a little while and help her keep her feet on the ground.

Malena and Maxine, the goats she had had since they were weaned, possessed an unfortunate talent for sensing the most direct routes to the finest and least protected of the village gardens. Whenever they got loose, Sophia knew she had to move quickly before they consumed some treasured plant or an eagerly awaited harvest. The villagers, even the more forgiving, were getting fed up with their incorrigible ways and had begun warning Sophia of the likelihood of their early demise. She could not fault them for being frustrated and angry, or for not understanding her long-tested loyalty to them.

When Sophia got to the post where she had tied them up,

she was not surprised to find only two frayed rope ends. She tied them up only at night, and only because they had broken out of their makeshift pen so many times that any more repairing was an exercise in futility. They needed a sturdier pen. But the tethering was no guarantee, either. She had caught Malena and Maxine chewing on their ropes just the other day. Now, she cursed them and cursed herself for failing to obtain new rope in time, but it was mostly in jest; inwardly she was not so very peeved. Now she had a reasonable explanation for wandering about at night if she ran into anyone. She started walking toward the village.

Light from the moon and stars trickled through the trees and struck the ground in some places, but the path was mostly invisible. She knew the way, however, having walked along the same track for over 40 years. She knew where the ground was uneven, where she had to lean more heavily on her staff. She knew where the trees were and what families they came from: birch, spruce, fir, pine, and a few willows. Something scurried in the bushes, an owl hooted, a branch slowly cracked under a deer's tentative hoof. Coming to a large clearing, she looked up, expecting she would see a falling star.

"What am I doing? That was a dream...this is waking. I'm muddling everything up."

"Sophia! *Who* are you talking to?"

She heard the voice, but it was as if someone she didn't know was calling someone else. She kept looking at the sky.

"It's me, David...I'm with Anna."

Sophia lowered her gaze. She had difficulty focusing on the pair before her.

"Are you all right?"

"What do you mean 'am I all right'?"

"I don't want to offend you, Sophia, but you looked very strange just now and you were talking to yourself. Anna and I were worried. When my grandmother was…"

Sophia held up a hand. "Spare me. No grandmother stories tonight."

"But…"

"No buts. When has a comparison ever pleased anyone?"

"All right, Sophia…. Don't be angry. I didn't mean to offend – but why are you out?"

"Business…*my* business…but if you must know, I'm looking for my goats."

"We can help."

"No…I'm grateful for your offer, but you've got better things to do. Anna, you haven't said anything. Are you enjoying yourself? Is he treating you well?"

"Oh yes, Sophia! It's a wonderful night, isn't it?"

"It is. Good, then. You two have more important things to do…certainly more pleasurable…so stop badgering old women and get on with it." She clucked and motioned them away with her hand.

David bowed hastily toward Sophia, and grabbing Anna's hand, fled into the darkness between the trees.

"Who was that?"

Sophia recognized the voice immediately: Jeremiah was nearby. She was delighted. But as she sometimes did, she pretended she felt quite differently.

"Is *everyone* out tonight?" she asked, trying to sound irritated.

Jeremiah stepped into the clearing and the moon immediately shone on him, greeting him like a lover. He lived in the forest surrounding the village and frequently spent the night keeping the moon company. He was dark-haired and slender, his head and hands large for his body. And he smelled. That smell, a pungent reminder of the world's ubiquitous decay, had always been disagreeable to her, but she considered it a small price to pay for so generous a friend.

"I'm *sure* it was David and Anna! The rumors are true!"

"Don't be spreading any stories and causing them more trouble than they already have. There's a saying, 'poets are respected by the wise, but gossips, only by fools.'"

"I've heard that before, many times, but only from you. Have you been quoting yourself?"

"What of it?"

"You know I don't want to start trouble."

"You never *intend* harm…but you'll take something like this and put it into one of your poems and everyone knows who you're talking about. You don't have to name names." Sophia's irritation at this point was genuine.

Jeremiah raised a hand high in the air and put the other over his heart. "I vow, utter, and swear complete silence concerning what I have seen here tonight, and I call upon my good friends Sophia and the queen of the night sky," he pointed toward the moon, "to be my witnesses. Does that satisfy you?"

Sophia snorted. "How many times have you promised already? What good are such promises when you don't remember making them? Oh, never mind. Where've you been?"

"In the village. I was walking near Angela's house when she happened to look out and we started talking. She told me she couldn't sleep because none of the teas you made for her had worked. When I said I was sorry to hear that, she laughed and said, 'I'm all right. Insomnia won't kill me. I think insomnia is really God's way of inviting us to jubilate with the stars.' What a phrase! How did Angela come up with something like that? She's so ordinary-looking."

Sophia tried to bite her tongue, but was too late. "A humble appearance is something poets seem to have in common."

Jeremiah backed up a few steps toward the trees. Sophia immediately regretted her words. She often pricked his vanity, teased him for it, usually in a good-natured, affectionate, amused sort of way, but tonight her words sounded cruel to her own ears. And she knew how sensitive he was. *Why did I say that? There's no excuse.*

"I'm a mean, cranky old woman. Why do you put up with me?"

He stepped toward her again, slowly moving side to side on the balls of his feet. Wisps of untrimmed beard blew before his face, catching the moonlight.

"I put up with you, Sophia, because you put up with me. That's what friends do. About what you said about appearing ordinary… how could anyone who celebrates with the stars not be beautiful even though an ordinary physical appearance may veil that beauty?"

"You're right. You and Angela are certainly beautiful."

While Jeremiah seemed to invite flattery, when a compliment knocked on his door, it was not his habit to let it in. He said nothing in response to Sophia's statement, as if he had not heard it.

"After I left Angela's, I walked in the forest, and a passage came to me: 'When the morning stars sang together, and all the sons of God shouted for joy.' Have you heard that line before, Sophia?"

Sophia was relieved. She had been forgiven. Jeremiah was in

— 18 —

one of his rapturous moods. They always made him impervious to her needling.

"I don't remember. Say those words again."

"'When the morning stars sang together, and all the sons of God shouted for joy.' Can you feel what's in those few words, the bliss that's making them burst open? There are no other words like that in the Bible, Sophia. I believe they are older than anything else written there, older than anything else I've ever heard. I'm sure of it. I've been repeating them to myself for hours. The morning stars were singing *together* and *all* the sons of God were shouting for joy. I can almost hear them." Jeremiah closed his eyes and swayed as if he indeed heard something.

"Now, tell me, what do *you* hear?"

"Um," she grunted, making it sound as if she had nothing to say.

Jeremiah opened his eyes. "Why do you always begin by pretending you're a stone?"

Sophia closed her eyes and cocked her head for effect, and Jeremiah repeated the words a third time. Thinking was not something she wanted to do, but she felt herself being swept up by her friend's enthusiasm.

Off the top of her head, and surprised by her own curiosity, she asked, "Who are the morning stars?"

Jeremiah jumped and clapped his hands. "Perfect! That's the question. Venus is the morning star. So why *did* the poet say morning stars as if there were many?" He appeared to be thinking. "Maybe in some early time women knew they were not separate from Her — from the goddess of Love and Beauty. So when they sang, Venus was singing in them. And the sons of God were the men, of course. Yes…that's it! When the men heard the women singing, they shouted for joy because in the sound of the women's voices they knew the light of heaven was dawning on earth. The men listened with the whole of themselves. The listened with love and through their love, they understood they were also great beings. And that also made them shout with joy. Ah, Sophia, how much we could see and hear then! How deeply we felt!" Sophia had wanted to tell Jeremiah about her dream, but knew if she said anything at all, she would be interrupting something important. He was taking in something that required all his attention. Keeping still for his sake, she felt a sharp pang and realized it came from Jeremiah naming a joy she had glimpsed once and had almost forgotten.

In an ecstatic rush, Jeremiah continued. "But then pain came between men and women. We grew divided from each other and that was the first sign of earth's fall into darkness. When such joy exists between men and women again, it will be a new dawn on earth."

He looked up at the sky and said no more. *For all his fine words, I wonder if he has ever passionately loved a woman, and if he has, did he ever find the courage to tell her?* As Sophia asked herself this she suddenly felt warmth coursing throughout her body and abandoned her separating thought. *I am so fond of him. His raptures and his wounds — they are mine.*

She noticed he was shaking, and then whatever was moving him made him twirl round and round with his arms extended, palms held upward toward the sky. Sophia knew it was too late to tell him about her dream; he needed to be alone.

"Sophia..."

"I have things to do," she said as if he was disturbing her and not the other way around.

"Thank you, my friend."

She limped away from him and headed toward a grove of trees.

"Look up, Sophia."

Looking at the sky, she caught the briefest glimpse of a falling star. She said nothing, and did not turn around and look at Jeremiah, but she raised her staff in acknowledgment before continuing on.

When she came to the base of a slight hill, she rested before climbing to the top. From the crest she could see nearly the whole village. Only a few glimmering candles and the steadier light of a couple of lanterns punctuated the darkness. Tendrils of smoke rose into the moonlit sky from untended fires. She looked down toward the village church. It seemed to be crouching like some fearful thing in the hill's shadow. Sophia knew the mortar between the stones of its walls was crumbling, and she remembered hearing that there were places where the roof leaked. She was still looking at the church when she saw a tall man — well over six feet — leave the church and start climbing the little hill. Neither his size nor his priestly robes hid the hesitant and deliberate grace of a young deer that had not yet found its legs. *On this special night I will be able to speak with both of my friends,* she thought.

"Good evening, Father Lawrence," Sophia called down.

"Sophia!" The priest stopped and raised his head with its shock of thick, dark, unruly hair and his dark beard.

"Why are you coming up here, tonight, Father? What's your purpose? There are no lost sheep on the top of this hill, just an old woman looking for her goats."

He had stopped his climb. Sophia heard him chuckling. It was a low, pleasant, comforting sound, like his speaking voice. She never tired of hearing either.

"You know me, I need to be useful. Can I help you find them?"

"No. You know how *they* are…skittish. But I *would* like the company."

When Father Lawrence reached the top of the hill, he stood at Sophia's side. Together, they looked out over the village, enjoying a companionable silence.

"Why aren't you in bed, Father?"

"I could ask you the same question. As for me, I thought some perspective might make things clearer…simpler."

"Nothing's simple, Father. Simplicity is a dream we are always waking from."

Father Lawrence gave a snort that was like a laugh.

"So you are having another one of those nights," Sophia said.

"I am…or was…until I heard you." Father Lawrence paused for a while before going on. "I was remembering how I carved out Christ's words on the wall above my bed at home. The words were: *I have come to cast fire on the earth.* When I was a boy, I wanted to do such great things. I shared my desire with my father and I remember telling him many times that it felt as if there was a fire inside of me. He never scoffed at me, never told me that the feeling would pass. He said I should be grateful for it. He said that the inner fire was the sign and presence of a noble destiny. My father believed everyone was destined to something wonderful, something beyond their comprehension."

"Your father was a remarkable man."

"He was. But boys aren't meant to see the world through their father's eyes forever. I had to see with my own eyes eventually and my eyes couldn't take in all that my father's could. I knew that, and to compensate, I tried seeing the world through the eyes of my friends and other men. That was usually disheartening. It was rare to find another man, young or old, who knew about that inner fire and had reverence for it like my father had. I lost that reverence for awhile and the fire...."

"It didn't die, Father. We both know that fire plays tricks with us. Some fires start burning before you realize it — and sometimes fires rekindle themselves when you think they're out."

Father Lawrence nodded his head but he did not say anything. Sophia knew she had only distracted him a little with her clever comment, and told herself to be still.

"Whenever that fire has gone, I've felt as if I'd lost someone dear, someone who was the better part of me. But is it wise, Sophia, to trust something that goes away for years like this inner fire does? Can something so unsteady, so uncertain, be divine? Right now, the fire is back, but I see how much my ambition is mixed up with it. This can't be the same fire Christ felt.... Mine seems more to do with wanting reassurance and gratification for myself. I wonder if I have ever really and truly loved...." His voice trailed off and he fell silent.

Sophia had the impulse to tell him that he was being too hard on himself, but it sounded trite; besides, she would be needlessly repeating herself. She restrained the urge and once more told herself to be still.

"I want to feel the fire Christ felt, Sophia. I want to cast His fire on the earth."

"Maybe you are, Father. It's just that fire does such contrary things, because that is its nature. It warms and gives light *and* it devours and consumes. Fire will do this until the world becomes something else."

"Until it becomes something else," Father Lawrence repeated.

Sophia sensed he was feeling more hopeful, and was pleased that perhaps her words had helped him a little.

"You brush away my torturous thoughts as if they were only flies!"

"*Other* people's thoughts, Father...my own are harder to get rid of."

Father Lawrence was silent. Sophia felt he was picking up that she had something to tell him. He was leaving it entirely up to her whether and when she said more.

"I had a dream tonight."

She felt tears coming. Her throat tightened as she attempted to hold them back.

"An important dream?"

Sophia nodded, and dabbed at her eyes with the end of her shawl. She felt silly. She opened her mouth to speak, but nothing came out. Father Lawrence took a small step forward and looked up at the sky. Now that she was behind him and he was not looking at her, it was easier. She told him her dream, about what the woman had said to her, sobbing when she got to the part about having a child. After she finished the priest turned around.

"So, you don't know who the woman was...the one who told you about the child?"

"She gave no name and I didn't think to ask her for one."

"Do you believe her?"

"How can *I* have a child, Father?"

"Maybe she didn't mean it literally. There are many ways to give life."

"Such as?"

"Sometimes I have had the strong impression that there is a

truer, more inspired version of myself trying to be born. Perhaps the woman in your dream meant something like that."

"I don't know, Father."

"You'll probably have some idea about what the dream meant before too long."

As they stood quietly together, the moon began its descent.

"I'm honored you shared your dream with me, Sophia. When you were speaking I felt alive and as if something beautiful had touched me. You've kept your nose to the grindstone and I've always appreciated and relied upon your good sense, but I also know that there's another side to you. I believe you've seen and experienced a great deal."

"A person can experience too much, Father."

"What do you mean?"

Sophia patted his arm, "What happens when the cup is full, but the pouring doesn't stop?" She rocked a little on her feet.

"Are you getting tired? Let *me* look for your goats."

"You stay put or get some sleep. I'll find them soon. You'll only scare them off."

The priest knelt on the ground in front of her and bowed his head.

"What are you doing, Father?"

"You've been my confessor and my good friend again tonight. Please, put your hands on my head and bless me."

"What?"

"You don't have to say anything. Just put your hands on my head."

Soon after leaving Father Lawrence, Sophia heard the desperate bleating of her goats. She walked as quickly as she could, fearing the next bleats would be their last. She found Malena and Maxine with their heads caught between narrowly spaced fence posts. When she felt around the ground, she could tell that the vegetation within reach had been reduced to nubs. She talked softly to them and ran her hands along their trembling flanks, trying to quiet them before pulling them free. A man came out of the house holding an ax, his wife behind him.

"Sophia, this is the third time this summer! I will clobber those two over their ugly heads if they come near my garden again."

"Adam. Good evening. I would clobber them myself if I didn't need them. The devil's in them, I've always believed."

"Then get Father Lawrence to cast the devils out, or get a stronger pen."

"A pen would be better. Could you help build one?"

When Sophia returned home with her goats, she tethered them to their post with the rope Adam had given her. Afterwards, she went into her house, kicked off her shoes, hung up her shawl and skirt, and went to bed. She thought, tired as she was, that sleep would not be a problem, but it was.

When the sun rose, she got up with it despite her lack of rest, and started her usual round of chores. As she swept the floor, she caught herself humming and noticed that the broom was moving across the floor with a new lightness and vigor. She paused and searched for an appropriate word. *Excited, that's what I am. Like a child…like a woman in love…like an idiot… I don't feel old at all…. Is this mere foolishness? Am I 'touched,' as some of the villagers would say… or….I don't have to decide. I don't have to think.*

She shifted her weight to the balls of her feet and went gliding across the floor, until she remembered how old and heavy she was, and became flat-footed again. When the floor was swept clean, she took a chair outside and sat down, closing her eyes so she could remember things better. She remembered Jeremiah's story and her conversation with him, and wondered at how much courage it took to completely cast oneself into experience like he did. And he got others to do so too— not only the children, but fairly sensible adults like herself. She remembered Father Lawrence kneeling for her blessing, recalled how awkward and embarrassed she had felt until she had actually put her hands on his head and sensed the surprising heat pour through her gnarled hands, and heard herself say — as if another was speaking — "My friend, She is purifying the fire that warms the earth and the hearts of men. Your suffering is part of Her labor."

Chapter Three

Sophia was returning from a visit with Angela. Since her eventful night, she had been drawn to her company, discovering she could tolerate Angela's quirks of character and, more surprising, Angela could tolerate hers. She had also found out that she rather enjoyed being around a woman very different from herself. As she walked home, thinking of their unlikely relationship, she kept an eye on the dark, heavy clouds rolling in from the west. When the wind started gusting, she picked up her pace.

The storm struck when most of the villagers were sitting down to eat. They had prepared: animals were already in their shelters, windows were shuttered and barricaded, and any object that could be damaged was brought inside. Before the villagers had finished their dinners, there was the sound of thatch and shingles blowing off roofs and the clattering of a few forgotten buckets and pots across the stone paths. Then the temperature dropped precipitously, forcing the villagers to put their children to bed early; but the moaning and shrieking they heard outside kept most of the young ones from sleeping.

Just when the villagers thought that the wind was dying down, it spun itself into a howling fury. A few pale faces appeared at barely cracked doors. Neighbor yelled to neighbor, proffering help or asking for it, but soon even the loudest shouts were drowned out. Lanterns and candles were extinguished as the wind forced its way into every tiny crack. Mothers hugged their small children tightly to their breasts, murmuring unheeded reassurances, while fathers kept older ones from rushing into danger.

Sophia could not remember a storm like it, and though venturing outside was the last thing she wanted to do, she was worried about her goats. They had a small new shed and pen thanks to Adam, but she doubted even it was sturdy enough. She was hoping her nearest neighbor, the good-natured farmer who lived a quarter of a mile away, had room in his barn for them. Setting down her lantern, she untied the goats' tethers and wrapped them around her hands. She was prepared for them to balk, but she had underestimated the strength terror would give them. They dragged her through the dirt and hay until she released their tethers. Sitting up, she felt stupid and bruised, but after checking herself, she knew she had not broken anything. *Thank God extra flesh pads the bones.* She was in one piece, but her goats were gone. How far and where, she had no idea. As soon as the storm let up, she would have to go look for them.

She was still sitting in the hay when the air tingled around her. Lightning struck; its ghostly light filling up the shed was followed immediately by a clack and crash that reverberated through her whole body. Stunned and deafened, Sophia fixed her gaze on the lantern and its light. They were rapidly retreating reminders of a world now very distant. The world was falling away and in that fall, unraveling, its threads splitting into tinier and tinier fragments until they were nearly nothing and too weightless to hold together. There was no pattern to anything any longer, and no way to locate herself in space and time.

And then Sophia had a distinct impression of hands. The hands were not made of skin and bone. They seemed to be made of nothing. She recognized them as weaver's hands and they set to work. Gathering up the multitude of tiny threads, they wove everything together again. Order and pattern returned. Sophia remembered where she was, who she was, and knew what needed to be done next....

At a lower elevation than the village, in a wide valley dotted with small farms and oak trees, a man dragged a four-year-old girl across a field. He had abandoned his wagon when lightning struck a tree, spooking the horse. The man held the girl tightly by the hand, his uncut, ragged nails digging into her flesh. The wind was strong enough to have blown her across the grass if he had not held on. When she stumbled on a large branch and cried out, the man jerked her arm before her knees touched the ground. She yelled in terror, her shoulder throbbing with pain. When a cold rain began pelting them, the man broke into a run. He headed toward a large barn, snatching up the girl so that her legs could wrap around his waist. His sharp-angled and sunken face was next to hers. The jostling up and down on his bony hip and his awful smell made her sick. She gagged and would have vomited if she had had any food in her stomach.

The barn was rank with molding hay and small animal droppings. Bats flitted in the corners and she heard someone whimper. The man dropped her down into the hay.

"Who's there? Speak up!"

When he stopped shouting, silence descended on the barn as

if all its inhabitants were afraid to rouse that voice again. Then lightning struck, its light injecting the surrounding space like pale yellow venom, paralyzing every insect, bird, beast, and human moving within it. Every creature was momentarily transfixed, pinned mercilessly in its separate place until the thunder slithered away. The girl had wanted to close her eyes; she had not wanted to see like that, but she had been transfixed too.

The man left her. In a short while she saw a lantern swinging, moving toward the piteous sound that came from the far corner. She followed the light until it shone on a boy, only slightly older than herself. He crouched near a pile of hay, holding a loaf of bread. Complete darkness fell again as the man blocked the lantern and the boy from view. When the light shone once more, she saw that the man had taken the boy's bread. He started walking back toward her, the lantern swaying in his hands, casting parts of his face in shadow. He looked like a goblin.

As he approached, the girl became aware that she was watching him and was shrinking away from him. It was as if she were no longer one, but two. A part of her did something and another part watched. She saw how the part that just watched had been around for a very long time. The girl felt as if she had just woken up — even though she knew she had been awake before — and this amazed her.

The man broke off a piece of bread and threw it in her lap. She licked her lower lip, but glancing back in the direction of the boy, she hesitated in picking it up. It did not feel right to take and eat his bread. "Eat," the man yelled at her.

She missed her mouth the first time. When the man snickered, she flinched. She was too scared to eat, and her mouth was so dry. She started crying. The man broke off a piece of bread in his hand, knelt down in front of her and placed it so gently in her mouth that it surprised her. Still, she did not trust him. After feeding her several morsels in this fashion, he abruptly stood up.

"That's enough. Stop crying. You're spoiled, like your mother was. Nothing — no one —was ever good enough for her."

The girl could not understand what he said, but nodded her head because she knew he expected it and that he was angry. But there was no pleasing him. He suddenly turned his back to her and started moving away. She got up and ran toward him, screaming, but froze again when he raised a grimy fist and started coming toward her.

"Shut your mouth! I'm showing you how it feels when you're ignored, when other people go about their business as if you didn't exist, as if you were nothing more than a hole in the ground. Remember it. You'll thank me some day!"

She looked at him, silent. He lowered his arm, turned around, strode out into the rain, and never looked back. She followed him, but stopped before leaving the barn. The man was running across the field, his long hair and shirt whipping in the wind. Parting the heavy curtain of rain, he disappeared behind it. She turned around and peered into the barn. It was very dark, and hearing nothing from the boy, she ran out.

Icy rain slapped her face, neck, and back. She stretched out her hands, wanting something to hold on to. Rain stung her eyes. She ran until she stumbled and fell at the base of a large, twisting oak, gashing her arm. She dug her way within a slight indentation between two large rocks covered with lichen, wrapped her hand tightly around a branch, and brought it close to her face. It smelled good. Within a few moments she drifted off to sleep.

Chapter Four

Someone was humming as the girl woke up. Opening her eyes, she saw two wrinkled cheeks. An old woman was smiling at her. She was sitting in a chair near the bed and was holding the girl's hand. The old woman's fingers were not the long, smooth ones of her mother's. They were crooked, round, and dry, but they held her hand carefully – not too tight, and not too loose, either.

She looked around the small room. The sun was shining through an unshuttered window. The walls were bare except for a few hooks with clothes on them. There was not much to see. But the blanket that covered her was beautiful, and there was a nice-looking rug on the floor. It smelled funny in the room, but a breeze was coming through the half-opened window, and it smelled like the garden at home. A bird was pecking on the window's narrow ledge.

"That's Hilda and she's very hungry. I don't think she ate much during the storm and she's making up for lost time. The last couple of days she's been singing for me after she eats. She sings very well, much better than I do. My name is Sophia."

The girl stared at her.

"Hilda and I are both glad you're awake. And you don't have to worry. We're taking care of you until we find your family. Are you hungry? Would you like some soup?"

When the old woman released her hand, the girl clutched at the old woman's. "Well, maybe we both need a little more rest."

When the old woman pulled back the covers and eased herself back into bed, the girl moved over for her, and when the old woman reached out an arm, she snuggled next to her. She could hear the straw shifting underneath her.

"What's your name?"

Fitting herself into the new combination of softness and angularity the girl promptly fell asleep without answering the woman who had called herself Sophia. When the old woman's loud snoring woke her up a few hours later, she sat up and turned toward the window, looking for Hilda. A man was looking in, a tall man with a beard and a black robe. He smiled and waved at her. Though he did not look like the man in the barn, she scooted under the covers, waking up Sophia.

"I'm sorry. I didn't mean to disturb you," he said. "I came to see how you two were doing."

Sophia sat up with some effort. "Are you in the habit of depriving people of their sleep as a penance, Father Lawrence?"

He laughed. "The tongue and the wit are sharp. The patient must be recovering. I was worried about you, little mother. You wore yourself completely out, but insisted on caring for the child yourself."

"I'm still worn out. What are you going to do about it? Worry never put food in the stomach. You could make us some soup. We're very hungry."

Father Lawrence held up a small sack. "I've brought some things for it, and I have something sweet for the child."

The priest drew back his head. A moment later banging and clanging could be heard in the other room.

Sophia moved her hair away from her face. "Child, that is Father Lawrence, a good friend and a holy priest, but he will be the ruin of my poor dishes if we don't watch him. Can you get up?"

She nodded, but waited for Sophia to get out first. Sophia dressed and layered her in borrowed clothes of various sizes. In a few moments, they were in the kitchen. Sophia sat in a chair next to a small table and patted her lap. Though the girl hesitated, she accepted Sophia's invitation. She appeared to enjoy her perch, and from there kept a wary eye on Father Lawrence. When the simple meal of soup and bread was ready, the priest said a prayer and they began eating. Sophia was going to spoon-feed the girl, but she took the utensil from her and dipped it in her bowl.

"Do you know her name?"

"I've asked, but she hasn't said a word."

"She looks better than she did three days ago. Your unrepentant goats had a divine purpose, Sophia. Who would have guessed!"

"Divine purpose! Their divine purpose was nearly the death of me! But I can't blame them. It was stupid of me to go so far."

"You walked nearly twelve miles, Sophia!"

"Something got into me...maybe it *was* that divine purpose you're always mentioning. When I got to that oak there, they were grazing as if nothing had happened...and then I saw that small arm poking through the leaves. I think I said, 'Good morning,' something like that...and this little girl stands up. She looks at me and reaches out and pets Maxine, and Maxine doesn't move. Maxine's never let anyone touch her like that before."

"I was worried about you, Sophia. I wasn't ready to lose you. The girl is fortunate. You were fortunate."

"I wish the good fortune had been spread about. I heard Agnes and William lost their two youngest. Is there anything I can do?"

"You need rest. I've sent a letter to Agnes's sister to let her know. I'm hoping she'll come soon…they were hit hardest. Few families were completely spared."

"It was the worst storm I've ever lived through."

"Everyone's saying that. Father Joseph sent word that in his parish an old farmer — along with his granddaughter — was lost. For a while everyone thought the farmer's grandson had also drowned, but the boy was found later hiding in an old barn not far from where you found the girl."

"He's all right?"

"I haven't heard otherwise. And it looks like Jacob, Helen's husband, has gone for good. Two days before the storm he took his things and left."

"That man's been coming and going for years. There's no news there."

"It's different this time. Helen believes he's not coming back. It will be harder for her. She says she has no regrets. It's her son, Aaron, she worries about. He's taking it hard. She's asked me to talk to him."

"How old is Aaron now?"

"Nearly eleven. Helen's told me his father has crushed the boy's heart many times by making promises he never kept."

"Hearts mend."

Father Lawrence looked closely at Sophia. "*You* seem to be on the mend. I would even say you look better than ever."

"I *do* feel well, considering. Do you think she's from around here? I've never seen her before."

"I haven't either, but maybe someone in the village has, or someone from Father Joseph's parish where she was found. I'll make more inquiries. Maybe that boy who was found in the barn knows something"

"How are *you* holding up, Father?"

"Fine. I'm feeling like I'm needed. Saving lost sheep agrees with me." He gave a wry smile. "There's no time to torment myself."

Sophia coughed, violently. The girl slipped off her lap.

"You may look and feel well enough, but that's a nasty cough. You need to see a healer. And those dizzy spells you've been having are starting to worry me…"

"What can a healer do for me that I can't do for myself? It's not that serious. Don't worry, Father…but I *did* frighten the child."

Sophia gently motioned for the girl to come close to her. When she did, Sophia stroked her hair. "It's all right. Don't be scared."

Father Lawrence brought out a sweet biscuit and held it out to the girl, who took it slowly, eyeing him all the while.

"She trusts you, but not me yet. I wonder how she's been treated. Who would leave a child alone like that? What happened to her parents?"

"There were cuts and bruises on her arms that needed bandaging, but no broken bones. Her hair is thick and beautiful, as you can see — I love the red and gold together — and her skin and teeth are fine. She has eaten well enough in the past, though she is a bit scrawny now. If I had to guess, I'd say she's been loved and cared for until recently."

"She's a riddle, then, and one we may not be able to solve." Father Lawrence got up and knelt down by the girl's side. She grabbed at Sophia's skirt. "What's your name, little one?"

The girl stared at him, silent. Father Lawrence looked at Sophia.

"When she decides to, she'll talk. Forcing things will only make it more difficult for her."

Father Lawrence stood up slowly. "You're probably right. The boy they found in the barn said that he had seen a mean man who took his bread. He was with a girl with red hair. He didn't recognize either of them. I will talk to the boy myself, then wind my way further down the valley and see if anyone knows who she is."

Sophia bent her head and placed her cheek next to the girl's. When she raised her head, her eyes were wet.

"It *was* about a child."

"Your dream?"

"You remembered."

"How could I forget a dream like that? And I remember I said it *couldn't* literally be about a child. Giving counsel to others is uncertain business."

Sophia laughed. "But you did say my dream was about new life, and you were right about that. The new life is in here, Father." Sophia placed her hand over her heart and then moved it in a large circle over her body. "My whole body feels alive. Nothing feels the same inside, not even my bones. I've heard other women, the ones who are pregnant...but of course it isn't the same..."

"Be careful, Sophia. I say this as a friend. We may find the child's parents soon. Try not to get too attached; it will make it harder on you. Let me bless you both before I leave."

Weeks went by. Father Lawrence visited villages as far as three days distant, but learned no more about the girl. After speaking with the boy found in the barn, he believed the girl had been there, but who the man was and his relation to the girl remained a mystery. Father Joseph, who had some authority because he was older and ministered to the largest parish in the area, recommended placing the girl in the home of a good family.

"There's a couple in my parish who want children, but haven't been able to have any of their own. They would take good care of her."

"Sophia could raise her."

"Sophia? She's too old. You know that."

Father Lawrence took a deep breath. "Father, you've been acquainted with Sophia for many years and I know you have the girl's best interests at heart, but I don't think you fully understand the situation. You haven't seen Sophia and the girl together. The girl has made remarkable improvements living with her, and there seems to be a strong bond between them already. The girl trusts her."

"I heard the girl was mute after she was found. Is she speaking yet?

"No," Father Lawrence said, hoping that Father Joseph would not interpret that fact in a way unfavorable to Sophia.

"I don't doubt what you say, Lawrence, but what good will that bond be if Sophia dies in a few years' time?" When Father Lawrence opened his mouth to respond, Father Joseph waved the comment away. "This may sound harsh, but I'm not sure about Sophia's ability to raise a child properly...a child who has already had more than her share of troubles. When did Sophia last set foot inside the church? And I suppose she is still living in that little cottage, the one removed from the rest of the village. I know you respect Sophia, Lawrence, and I've heard how she cares for the sick, but she has a solitary nature and I have had questions about that. It may be a sign of some instability or of some lack of balance in her character."

"Sophia is the most reliable and steady person I've ever known, and if you saw the two of them together, you would realize that she..."

"I don't have to see them together. The girl needs companions. She needs to grow up around people. For as long as I've known her, Sophia has always preferred her own company, with the rare exceptions of you, Father, and that beggar..."

"Jeremiah."

"But you are the exceptions. Such habits don't change overnight...No. I will ask that couple, and if they decide not to take her, I will find another family. You should ask around your parish, Lawrence. We should consider Sophia only if no one else wants the girl. I'm sure by early spring we'll find her a family."

Despite Father Joseph's prediction, spring came and no one had offered to take the girl. Families were still tightening their belts because of the storm. The girl was too small to be of help, and meant another mouth to feed. Fear also kept potential parents away. Some believed that Sophia was at least a dabbler in the magic arts and that she had probably already exerted an unholy influence on the girl. And then there was the girl herself. Where did *she* come from? What did her silence mean? Would she *ever* speak?

Some women came and observed the child and were struck by how fiercely she clung to Sophia. The childless couple from Father Joseph's parish came twice, but after the girl ran off both times and hid, they gave up. Sophia was pleased, and was reassured by Father Lawrence that her pleasure was just and natural, and not a selfish indulgence.

While the search was going on, Sophia had another significant dream. She and a young girl were running in a field profuse with flowers of various shapes and hues. The girl plopped down on her stomach in the grass, raised her forearms, and held her face in her hands. Sophia, who was a young but mature woman in the dream, did the same. They were facing each other and gazing into each other's eyes. As Sophia was looking, she realized that where she began and ended and where the little girl began and ended was no longer clear. She was both herself *and* the child, and the child was herself and Sophia. It gave her such joy – this play of identities that existed between them. And she knew that her older self had endured and learned much so that the younger could begin living from a place of greater openness.

The next day Sophia took the girl into the forest with her while she collected leaves for medicinal purposes. Although the dream had cast her into a sort of trance, she kept a watchful eye on the girl. When a red-tailed hawk swooped close to their heads and the girl ducked, she felt the child's terror as if it were her own.

"Don't be scared, little one. It's a day for good news. The hawk was only coming to tell us that."

That evening, when the candles were lit and supper finished, Father Lawrence came by with more sweet biscuits in his pocket. He handed one to the girl. She took it, keeping her distance, and without looking up at his face.

"I spoke to Father Joseph today, Sophia. Although he has his doubts — which I don't share — he decided you should keep the girl. He says she should be baptized in case her parents didn't see to it. Now you are her mother — officially."

"Her mother...I like the sound of that, Father. She'll need a name and godparents. I would ask Angela, but she's ill again. What about Catherine and Simon? They're good people...the best. What name would be good?"

"You don't have to decide everything tonight."

Sophia took the priest's hand and kissed it, something she had never done before. "I never thought I would have a child." She released his hand and looked up at him. His eyes were glistening.

"You were meant to be together, Sophia. I sensed that early on when I saw you two lying together in your bed."

"But what if Father Joseph is right? *Am* I being selfish? I am not a young woman, though I don't feel as old as before.... But what if I die in a few years, or a few months? No child should be orphaned — and she would be orphaned twice. And what if I became ill? What kind of life would she have? I would not want her spending it looking after me."

"How can anyone know the future? You could be 40 years younger, Sophia, and die suddenly or get sick. Nothing is certain. I believe you're God's gift to this young girl and this girl is God's gift to you. I don't know for how long. Remember your dream? You were supposed to catch the star and then let it go."

"Those words might effortlessly roll off the tongue, Father, but the doing of them will not be so easy."

After Father Lawrence left, Sophia put the girl to bed then plopped down in her chair. She heard the child cry out in her sleep, and got up and went to her. Placing a calloused hand softly on the girl's forehead, she closed her own eyes. The girl quieted. As Sophia stood there, she thought about her dream and what Father Lawrence had said about letting go, and then she had an intimation that made her mouth fall open. She sensed how much would pass back and forth between herself and her child, and she knew that even death would not be able to stop their giving to each other.

Chapter Five

Sophia was enjoying a quiet breakfast with her adopted child when she heard several quick raps on the door. She knew who it was even before she opened it. It was not unusual for Jeremiah to show up during a meal, and he was always welcome; however, on this morning, preferring time alone with the child, Sophia looked him up and down a couple of times. Jeremiah was not intimidated. He peered around Sophia until he caught sight of the girl.

"It rained buckets last night, but what a beautiful morning for a baptism it's turned out to be!" Jeremiah waved his fingers at the girl, who giggled and waved back.

"Want breakfast? There's only..."

"Yes, thank you. I'm famished. Rain makes me hungry and I don't think I ate yesterday... I don't remember, anyway."

Sophia mumbled under her breath and placed another bowl on the table. She put more wood on the stove, added some water to the gruel, and stirred.

"Have you come up with a name for the girl, or am I not supposed to ask?"

Sophia said nothing.

"Ah, it is a secret then. Has she told you, little one?"

Although the girl had never said a word, Sophia looked at her and put her finger on her lips. The girl imitated her with such seriousness that both Sophia and Jeremiah burst out laughing.

"So for a few more hours the name remains a mystery. One mystery among so many others. I want you to know, little one, that speculation about where you came from is rampant. I have my own ideas..."

Sophia quickly spun around. "I wish people would find something better to do — and that includes you." She shook her finger at him. "She doesn't need a lot of wild rumors. People should hold their tongues."

"People are not angels, Sophia. They need their stories just like they need bread."

"Well, children can get hurt by them."

"And you can't stop that no matter how hard you try. But you can tell her stories of your own..."

Sophia brushed back a stray hair. "I'm out of practice. Come to think of it, I was never very good at storytelling."

"Father Lawrence and myself — we can tell her stories. You will, too. You'll see."

"I haven't told her a story yet. Oh..."

"What is it, Sophia?"

"I *did* tell her a story. We were in the forest and a hawk flew close to our heads. I could tell she was frightened and I told her that the hawk was coming to give us good news. I had forgotten that." Sophia smiled. "It was a very *short* story."

"It was a good one, though, and you told it naturally...because you love her."

With a full belly, Jeremiah was making his way down the narrow path to the village when he met up with Angela. She was carefully carrying a small dress.

"Good day, Jeremiah. I suppose you'll be there at the baptism."

"Sophia wouldn't let me miss it. Did you make that dress?"

When Jeremiah stretched out his hand to touch it, Angela turned aside, putting the garment out of reach. "It's her baptismal gown. Yes, I made it."

Jeremiah looked down at his hands, wondering if they were still dirty despite washing himself carefully before breakfast.

"I'm not letting *anyone* touch it."

"Well, it seems quite suitable. Are you feeling better?"

"Yes, thank you. Making this was good medicine. It was Catherine's idea, you know. Sophia doesn't bother her mind with such things."

"Catherine's a good woman. And Simon is a good man. Sophia made an excellent choice in godparents."

"Some people are saying they are too old, but they aren't *that* old. And they're happily married. How often do you see that? And those three children of theirs…hard-working, every single one of them."

"They've always been kind to me."

"You're easy to be kind to, Jeremiah. You are a good person too."

Jeremiah's ears reddened. "Well, good day to you," he responded abruptly and started walking down the path. Angela wondered if she had unintentionally insulted him.

By midmorning, a small procession was winding its way under

the trees across the large meadow to the church. Several men took turns holding the girl. This was Angela's idea; she did not want the gown sullied. Sophia did not like all the fuss over a dress and told Angela the girl was not fond of strangers, but Angela would not listen and told Sophia to coax the girl into being carried. Angela gave detailed instructions to the men about how to hold the girl without crushing her gown. For her part, the girl would let herself be carried only if Sophia was there to hold her hand.

Angela wastes a great deal of energy on trifles. It was an uncharitable thought, Sophia knew; at least she had not said it out loud.

Father Lawrence was standing at the church door with Catherine and Simon. Most of the villagers had turned out and were already inside. There was rarely such lavish attention paid to a baptism, but word had gotten out that the godparents would be putting on a quite a feast afterward. It was considered rude to appear at the one and not the other.

The frightened girl was set down next to her godparents. Sophia kept one of her child's hands in hers, and Catherine took the other. Simon and Father Lawrence went ahead of them into the church. Jeremiah held back, going in only after everyone else had.

The church was packed and warm. People murmured and shifted about until Father Lawrence raised his voice and greeted them. He began praying. Sophia looked for Jeremiah and saw him standing by the door. His eyes were closed and she knew that he would keep them that way so he could hear Father Lawrence better. He admired the priest's voice — more than admired — he was envious. She knew it was difficult for him to admit that, and a source of shame. When he was his more open-hearted self, Jeremiah would tell her it was miraculous how Father Lawrence said the same prayers and told the same stories year after year and still managed to make them sound as if they were being said and told for the first time. She remembered how he had compared the priest's voice to a bee and words to flowers. "He has a voice that can collect the golden powder that lies on every word," Jeremiah had told her.

"And what will the child be called?" Father Lawrence asked, turning to Catherine and Simon.

"Sophia should tell you," Catherine whispered.

Father Lawrence bent down and Sophia spoke in his ear. The villagers watched the priest, hoping to see a reaction, but his face gave nothing away.

"Despite many efforts, we've never found this child's parents, and so we've never discovered her name. Sophia found her after the storm, as you all know, and she has taken good care of this young girl for many months. She is now the girl's mother and after careful consideration she has chosen a name for her. It expresses what the child has given her and what she hopes for her."

The church was completely quiet. Father Lawrence stood there reflecting, for what seemed a long time.

"She will be called Lucia. *Lucia*! Such a beautiful name! It means light. On Easter we sing, 'Christ, our light.' But Christ also said *we* were meant to be a light. 'You are the light of the world,' He told us. And He also said, 'Let your light shine before men.'

"Now Christ was saying this to his disciples, who we know were imperfect men. They were ambitious in a worldly way, they quarreled, they doubted, and they did not understand how Christ felt things — but still Christ was telling *them* to let their light shine before others so that God could be praised. Christ could see the light in them despite their failings. He could see what they couldn't. There is light in all of us, Divine light. We don't have to work to put it there; it is there already. What we need is the courage and the faith to bring forth our light into this world. I say faith, because we must first believe that the light is indeed in us.

"Lucia came to us like a light during a dark time. People we knew and loved died, crops were ruined, animals were never found, and homes were destroyed. Sophia thought she had lost her two goats. Now, I know many of you would say, 'Good riddance,' but you know she needs them…. Sophia has lived for nearly 40 years among us with no husband or child or any relation. Then this child appears and Sophia sees herself differently because of her. She sees herself as a woman who is now a mother, a woman capable of caring for another with the fullness of a mother's love. She sees herself as someone who has introduced a child to an entire village, and in doing so has a new appreciation for the place and people among whom she has lived for so long. For her, then, this girl was a light showing her something new. And for us too, she has been a light. We have seen how a life can be transformed. Now let us all help this child who has brought us joy in a time of grief by letting her see the light that is in each one of us."

The villagers watched Sophia smile and nod her head, and saw how Catherine and Simon stood near her dabbing at their tears. They were won over and found themselves wanting to agree with everything the priest had just said.

Father Lawrence continued with the ritual. Using holy oil, he made the sign of the cross on the girl's forehead, lips, hands, and feet. A wooden box was placed neared the baptismal font. Simon helped Lucia stand on it; then he and Catherine stood by her as Father Lawrence poured water from a bowl over Lucia's bowed head. Catherine dried her hair immediately; Angela hurried over and straightened Lucia's dress. When the girl pushed Angela's hand away, those who saw it laughed.

A hymn was sung and people left the church, heading quickly for the home of Catherine and Simon. Upon their arrival, they were surprised to hear several musicians already playing. Food and drink were plentiful and were arranged to entice the appetite.

Sophia, Lucia, Catherine, Simon, and Jeremiah ate together. Afterward, Sophia encouraged Lucia to wander about while she kept an eye on her. She watched as a feeble-minded young man approached Lucia and showed her a magic trick. Lucia looked intrigued. However, after being shown the same trick three times, Lucia left him and returned to Sophia and the others whom she knew around the table. Soon a bevy of children gathered around Jeremiah, pleading for a story. Jeremiah glanced and winked at Lucia, then stood up from the table and led the children to a place where a small makeshift stage had been set up. Lucia followed them. Jeremiah climbed the two steps up to the stage and waited for the children to sit down.

"A story you want . . . um . . .well, today I have a special story, a story about Lucia and her mother Sophia."

Several children pointed at Lucia and giggled. "He has a story about you."

"Have any of you seen a falling star?"

All of the children nodded, even those who didn't quite remember seeing one.

"Good, now I will tell you a big secret..."

A hush fell over the children.

"When a star falls from the sky—" Jeremiah, pretending his raised hand was a sparkling star, made a large, descending arc,

"—it means that a soul is coming into this world. I saw such a star just before Sophia found Lucia..."

A young boy, standing in the back, interrupted. "But she was already here. Was there a shooting star just before she was *really* born?"

"You're Aaron — Helen's boy — aren't you?"

"Yes, I am."

Sophia noticed that Father Lawrence was also observing the group of children.

"Well, Aaron, you're right: when Sophia found Lucia she was about four years old, but no one in this village had seen her before. So I think we can say she was born to *us* the day Sophia brought her home. But now I'm jumping ahead . . ."

Aaron had crossed his arms over his chest. "But she was *really* born before..."

Sophia let out a huge laugh as Jeremiah's face mottled with various shades of purple.

"It doesn't matter when she was really born...if you would give me a moment...I'm trying to show how important it is to pay attention to what's around you because everything has meaning. So let me ask you, young man: why do you think I saw a shooting star that night?"

The boy looked surprised by the question. "Weren't you looking up?"

Sophia laughed so hard she feared wetting herself.

Father Lawrence called out, "Aaron, could you come over here, please. I need you to do something for me." Father Lawrence waved at Jeremiah as Aaron started walking toward him. Jeremiah dramatically moved his lips in a silent *thank you*.

With Aaron gone, Jeremiah continued making his point about

seeing things as signs filled with meaning. Sophia settled back in her seat and watched Lucia. She knew her daughter was not capable of understanding what Jeremiah was saying; however, she appeared entranced by his gestures and by the sound of his voice. Jeremiah would often look toward her and smile or wink, and Lucia's face would beam. Sophia, delighted by what she observed, let her gaze drift over to Father Lawrence. He was kneeling on the ground facing Aaron, and they were talking. Later, when Jeremiah had left the stage and was sitting alone at a far table, she watched Aaron approach him. She was too far away to hear what they said to each other, but she could see how the boy handed Jeremiah some cheese wrapped in cloth and then backed away. She was wondering what Father Lawrence had said to Aaron, when Lucia came up and leaned against her.

"Are you tired?"

In answer Lucia rested her head against Sophia's shoulder, and Sophia decided it was time to go home. She thanked Catherine and Simon, said her goodbyes, and with Lucia's hand in hers, started back. The sun was still up, but it was cool in the shadow of the trees. Sophia took the path through the meadow, the one that paralleled the river. When she came to some large, flat stones, she sat down on one of them and signaled Lucia to sit on another close by.

"I need to sit for a while. It's been a full day…. Being near running water is like taking a good rest. Do you like it here? It's not too cold?"

Lucia shook her head, then let out a sigh. Sophia thought she might say something, and waited patiently for her to do so, but her daughter kept silent.

"I want to tell you a story, Lucia. I'm not a good storyteller like Jeremiah, but I'm going to try. I know you won't understand it today, and that's all right. I'm practicing. I'll try telling it to you again, I promise. It was true what Jeremiah said. We both saw a falling star a few months before I found you. That same night I also had a dream about a falling star. It was very beautiful — the way it flew through the sky. In my dream a woman spoke to me and told me I would have a child. I don't know who she was, I couldn't tell you her name, but I think I might have seen her many years ago. Ah, how wonderful that was! As I'm talking to you, Lucia, I'm remembering what happened. Someday, I will try and tell you about it.

"The night before I found you, we had a very bad storm, and Malena and Maxine ran away like they always do and I had to go looking for them. I walked a long way. . . many miles. And when I got to the tree, I finally saw them. I also saw a hand coming out of a pile of leaves and branches. It was your hand. When I got closer, you heard me and stood up and started petting Maxine. The sun was shining on you and you were so lovely. I just stood there for awhile, looking at you, and I knew you were Her child. You were the daughter of the Woman who had spoken to me. I knew She wanted me to care for you for the rest of my days. I saw how you shone on the sun as much as it was shining on you. You shone on everything around you...on me too... and it seemed to me that the whole world was welcoming you. The whole world was Her loving you. I think that for a moment I saw you with the special eyes we all have but hardly ever use. And the way you looked at me...I believe you saw me like that, too – with those special eyes. That is why I felt your name had to be Lucia because 'Lucia' means light. Oh, Lucia, I felt as if I had died and had gone to heaven. But I was still here on this earth, with Malena and Maxine and you. I took you to my house and the Woman continues to teach me how to care for you. And I'm so happy, now.

"So that's the story of how I found you and took you home. I introduced you to the village, to Jeremiah and Father Lawrence, Catherine and Simon, and many others. And you gave me such a precious gift in return. Once, many years ago, I saw how seeing and loving go together, how you cannot separate them, and you let me experience that again."

Sophia drew Lucia close and kissed her.

After the baptism, Jeremiah disappeared. When after several weeks Sophia still had not seen him, she started worrying. He had disappeared before, but seldom for so long. She was thinking about expressing her concern to Father Lawrence when she spotted him sitting on a milking stool, lost in thought. She and Lucia had come to buy food at the weekly market. Lucia had also noticed Jeremiah, and ran toward him. She tugged at his ragged shirt, pulling him out of his reverie. Jeremiah stood up immediately and bowed.

"Lucia, the delight of my eyes, the joy of my heart..."

"You are looking a bit underfed," Sophia said, coming up behind Lucia and observing how his shoulder bones poked at his shirt.

"There is only one cure for that, Sophia."

"I'm willing to administer it, but I want some news in return."

"She strikes a hard bargain, Lucia. But given my desperate circumstances, how can I refuse?"

Jeremiah walked home with them, Lucia holding his hand the whole way. He told her stories until the food was put on the table. Sophia saw how it was an effort for him not to look at it too intently.

"Go ahead and eat.... There's no meat on your bones. I do have questions for you, but I'll claim my half of the bargain later."

They ate in silence. Sophia noticed how Lucia's mouth fell open when she realized how quickly Jeremiah had consumed three bowls of soup. She looked at her mother. Sophia gave a little nod.

"Thank you, Sophia." Jeremiah was about to leave the table when Sophia cleared her throat. "Oh, I almost forgot. What was it you wanted to know, Sophia?"

"I wanted to know about that boy, Aaron. I noticed Father Lawrence spoke to him after the baptism and then he came up to you. What did Aaron say? And what did you say to him?"

"It's been a long time since you were so curious about the goings-on of young boys."

"I'm curious only because Father Lawrence seems to be looking out for him. So tell me, what did he say?"

"I know he sent Aaron over to apologize. When the boy gave me the cheese, I asked him if it was because Father Lawrence suggested it and he said, 'Sir, he told me to say I was sorry, but the cheese was *my* idea.'"

Sophia laughed. "So precocious! If Father Lawrence has decided to keep an eye on him, he'll have his hands full. He must sense something special in that boy. You were a boy like that, Jeremiah...full of strength, intelligence...passion. That's why I was drawn to you."

He reddened, as she knew he would.

"I knew you were paying attention to me, Sophia. It meant a great deal to me."

"I didn't pay attention enough. When you were going through your hardest times, I was thinking only of my own troubles."

"I remember how you looked at me; how you greeted me when others pretended they didn't see me. And you understood me...I knew you did. For the first time, I didn't feel completely alone in this world..."

"I'm glad I did something for you, my friend. I wish I'd done more."

"It was enough, Sophia. More than you know."

Years passed. Lucia grew up healthy and strong, but she never spoke. Catherine and Simon paid for a physician to examine her and he could not determine a cause. Healers offered various remedies, and though Sophia was skeptical, she tried them all, unsuccessfully. Father Lawrence told Sophia that she had probably been right all along: Lucia would speak when she was ready and not before.

Muteness did not keep Lucia from being a very active child. She climbed trees, searched for treasure, and pretended to be various legendary heroes, apparently preferring ones who wielded a sword. She mimicked the mannerisms of the few more pompous villagers to amuse Sophia and Angela, and once created an entire village out of sticks and odd pieces of cloth. A few children made the trek from the village to come and play with her and Sophia took her frequently to the village, but Lucia often appeared uncomfortable around other children and sometimes not even interested in them. Sophia wanted to attribute Lucia's lack of sociability to muteness. However, when she honestly assessed her feelings, she realized she feared that Lucia was too enthralled to and entertained by her own vivid imagination.

Catherine tried teaching Lucia lace work. That lasted only two weeks. Lucia would easily become frustrated and throw down whatever she was working on. Simon was much more successful at teaching her to read and write using pictures and pointing to make sure she understood. She took to reading and writing like a duck to water.

When others tried to communicate with Lucia through dramatic gesture — forgetting her hearing was unimpaired —Lucia would giggle uncontrollably. While generally well-behaved, she had bouts of wildness and there were times when she went looking for adventure. She did have her share of fears. The dark frightened her, as did spiders, and she became terrified whenever she saw lightning or heard thunder; even Sophia could not quiet her agitation then. Only Jeremiah's poetry and stories had a soothing effect. He began appearing whenever a storm threatened.

Lucia enjoyed Father Lawrence's many visits. She would prepare a new magic trick for him or come up with a game to entertain him whenever he stopped by. He always rewarded her with something sweet or said something nice about her. Her favorite activity of all, though, was listening to Jeremiah with the sun on her back and the smell of the grass wafting into her nostrils. She would sit with him for hours on the same large, flat stone near the river where she and Sophia had stopped on the way home from the baptism. For years, as he recited his verses or told his stories, she could not understand him. She did, however, appreciate the musical quality of Jeremiah's voice. What joy she felt when a word did eventually share its secrets with her allowing her to see new, fascinating, and exquisite facets of the world around her! Words acted like yeast and made her thoughts and feelings

swell and rise until they filled her heart and her heart could practically taste them. She wanted such discoveries and sensations to
go on forever.

Before he began speaking to her, Jeremiah would fold his tattered coat for her to sit on, and once brought her a misshapen
hat he had woven crudely out of straw. As she grew older, she
would look quizzically at him if she heard a lapse in his rhythm,
or a poor choice of a word or phrase. Jeremiah called her his
favorite critic.

On the whole, the village had recovered from the storm and
had enjoyed several peaceful years. Sophia and Angela's friendship deepened, despite the fact that they sometimes rubbed each
other the wrong way, and they began caring for one another during their various illnesses. The lovers, David and Anna, quarreled,
broke up, came back together and eventually married. Father
Joseph fell and hurt his hip — it never got better — and Father
Lawrence had to take on some of his duties. Sophia would remind him not to overdo things, that he was only human. Jeremiah
remained Jeremiah, but he disappeared less often and would re-
appear more quickly. Sophia knew Lucia had a great deal to do
with this. Catherine and Simon, Lucia's devoted godparents, enjoyed the occasional visits of their grandchildren.

The village soon forgot how Lucia had been found, and for
her part, Lucia could not remember living anywhere else. She was
part of the tapestry that was the village; a unique, colorful thread,
one that was artfully woven together with all the others.

Chapter Six

Sophia wanted to look for herbs and mushrooms, and was taking Lucia into the forest with her. The ground was soft and springy after a brief end of winter rain, and the trees held out perfumed arms to the sun. They would walk a little way, and then Sophia would stop and invite Lucia to smell the air or identify the animal or bird she heard scurrying in the bushes. At one point, Lucia fell behind, looking for the source of a peculiar scratching sound. Noticing that Sophia had walked considerably ahead, she ran to catch up. She stopped herself while still a short distance from her mother. She had never noticed before how Sophia tilted to one side even though she was using her staff; or how frail and very small she had become. When Sophia began coughing violently —as if she was trying to expel some growling beast inside her chest — Lucia's knees buckled and her own chest felt empty.

Sophia stopped and turned around. Lucia had only to look at her to know that her mother was rightly guessing her feelings. Sophia opened up her arms and Lucia ran into them and buried her face in Sophia's cloak. Sophia gently patted the back of her head.

"I want you to listen to me."

Lucia pulled back but kept her head down. She thought her mother might tell her that her cough was nothing and that she was fine, but that is not what Sophia said.

"Look up at the trees, Lucia. Most of them started from tiny seeds — like you — and now they are so big and strong. That's because many things helped them grow. It's the same with you, and way deep down you know that. If a seed could talk, it would ask why it was being dropped in the ground and buried. Or maybe it would ask why the water was softening it until it no longer recognized itself, or why the heat struck it when it dared to raise its head. But if these things didn't happen, it would never do all the growing it was meant to do. You are meant to become something so beautiful, so big. And everything will help you do that. Everything, Lucia, will help you grow. Not just what you like and makes you happy, but what you don't like and what makes you sad. "

Lucia wiped her nose with the back of her hand.

"Come on now — we have work to do."

After Sophia kissed her head, Lucia put her arm around her mother's. They had walked into a quiet, denser part of the forest when her mother stooped down, leaned on her staff, and pointed out the silver-green leaves of a bush.

"Cut those, Lucia…very good for coughs and aches."

Lucia slid her knife out of its sheath and began cutting, passing the leaves to Sophia who placed them in a pouch tied around her waist. They had been working only a short while when Lucia heard voices. She looked at her mother and could tell that she had heard the voices too. Sophia nodded and sat heavily on a nearby stump.

"I'll sit here. It sounds like some children have come to play. Join them if you wish. I'll rest for a while."

Lucia got down on all fours and crawled toward a break in the undergrowth. Several children burst into a small clearing with a great racket. Lucia gave a start and turned to look at her mother. Sophia was sitting very still and was watching her. Lucia moved further away from her mother and maneuvered herself until she could see the children while remaining out of sight. Most of them were boys and they were arguing and pushing each other while deciding which game to play.

"The freezing game…the freezing game," the bigger boys shouted. It seemed that some sort of agreement was reached. Lucia watched as Sebastian, the tailor's son, had his eyes blindfolded and was spun around and around by one of the boys until he could barely stay on his feet. When the spinner let go of Sebastian, Sebastian started counting and the other children took off running. Two of them came crashing through the brush not far from Lucia. She heard vehement cursing and knew they had run into nettles or sharp branches. When Sebastian got to ten, he yanked off the blindfold.

"Freeze, Stephen! I see you," Sebastian screamed, triumphant.

Lucia followed the line of his finger. She saw Stephen trapped by an impenetrable mix of brush and vine and a little to his left, a pair of dark eyes looking at her from behind another bush. Stephen had frozen in place like a statue; his arms were up to beat back the brush and protect his face, but they were no longer moving. The other children came out of hiding and began yelling at him, calling him slow, fat, and stupid until Sebastian came up and touched him and Stephen could finally unfreeze. The other children quieted down and moved back to the small clearing. It was Stephen's turn to be blindfolded.

The children played their game for nearly half an hour before wandering off. As soon as they had gone, the young man who owned the pair of eyes stood up from behind the bush and sprinted toward Lucia with a book in his hand. Lucia stood up quickly, her eyes fixed on him. She recognized him and was startled by how fast he moved.

"Hello, Lucia. Is your mother with you? Oh...I see her over there."

He strode toward Sophia while Lucia skipped at his side trying to keep up. Her mother was sitting with both hands flat on her knees and her head slumped between her shoulders. When she got closer to Sophia, her mother looked up. Lucia knew something was wrong. Her mother looked as if she was confused, as if she did not know where she was. Lucia ran to her and put her hand over one of her mother's and kissed her on the cheek. Sophia slowly turned her head toward her. Her eyes were dazed. Lucia kissed her again.

The young man behind Lucia was nearly shouting, "What is it, Sophia? Are you ill?"

Sophia held up a hand. "My head," she said gasping, "every once in while something flutters about inside of it. I think there is a bird that lives in there and sometimes it wants out of its cage. It's quieting down now." Sophia took a few deep breaths.

"Are you sure? Should I get help?"

Sophia shook her head. "I'm fine. I was watching the young people play. I felt sad watching them. I was remembering my own childhood and how brutal and shaming children's games can be, and then I had a dizzy spell." Sophia rubbed her temples. "I'm fine, Lucia. Don't worry. What are you doing here, Aaron?"

Aaron showed her his book.

"You must have read all of Father Lawrence's books by now."

"There are three I haven't."

"Well, I'm sure you'll get to them. My daughter also likes to read, though she is only eight…almost nine."

Aaron glanced down at the young girl. She was at his side looking up at him. Aaron stood up straighter and threw his shoulders back.

"I never liked those types of games they were playing."

"Neither did I," Sophia said, "but I remember how disappointed I was when the other children excluded me. Being left out was much worse. How is your mother?"

"She's having bad headaches. That's why I wanted to speak with you."

"They wear a person down…I know. Well, I have something that may help. I'll have Lucia take it to her tomorrow."

"Thank you for your kindness."

Sophia looked at him. He was an earnest, handsome boy whose feelings were easy to read. She liked that, and the open way his gaze met hers. He wanted to leave — she felt his restlessness — but he did not.

"How old are you?"

"Almost sixteen."

"Well your mother must be proud of you." Sophia, in trying to get up from the stump, dropped her staff. Lucia rushed to pick it up just as Aaron was also bending down to retrieve it. His head banged into hers and she ended up sitting on the ground, dazed.

She rubbed her head and started laughing when she saw Aaron rubbing his, too.

"I'm sorry, Lucia. I didn't see you. Are you hurt?"

Lucia shook her head. When Aaron held out his hand to help her up, she took it and let him pull her up.

"She's got a hard head, Aaron. She'll be fine."

"Does she ever talk to you in private?"

Sophia saw Lucia's mouth twitch and watched her eyes fill with tears.

"No she doesn't. But she finds ways to tell me things all the time. I know there is a great deal inside of my Lucia...a great deal."

Aaron looked at the young girl as if he expected to see what Sophia saw. He caught himself doing this, shrugged his shoulders and looked away, but then glanced at her again.

That evening, when Lucia was putting away the dishes, Sophia looked up from her mending. "Were you upset when Aaron asked if you ever talked?"

Lucia nodded, yes.

"Did you want to say something then?"

She nodded again and started to cry.

"Come here." Sophia put her mending down. Lucia sat down next to her and Sophia put her hand over hers. "You'll talk someday. Jeremiah says the same thing. I see how you're moving your lips and your throat. Even though nothing is coming out, I know you're practicing."

The next morning, Lucia wrote down Sophia's directions for a tea and put it in a pouch with several different types of dried, crushed leaves and herbs Sophia had picked out. In the afternoon she took it to Helen, Aaron's mother. Helen was very grateful and while she rummaged in her kitchen searching for something to give to her to eat, Lucia looked around for Aaron.

"Aaron told me that he ran into you and Sophia. He went to look for work this morning. There are not enough good paying jobs around here anymore, so he had to go see if some of the larger farms down the hill could use him. He is a strong, capable young man. He will find something. Hopefully I will at least see him on Sundays and feast days. I miss him already and it's been only a few hours!"

Lucia remembered how Aaron had helped her up. She remembered the hardness of his head, the feel of his hand, how tall he was, how quickly he moved, and how he made her laugh. She felt a sudden, deep ache in her chest and wished he had not gone.

Chapter Seven

On the eighth anniversary of Lucia's baptism, Father Lawrence stopped by in the morning to visit. Although not fully recovered from a recent illness, Sophia got out of bed to cook for him despite his protests. After they had eaten together, she asked Lucia to deliver pouches with various remedies to people who were ill. Lucia shook her head no. She had been left out of too many recent conversations between the priest and her mother and did not want to miss another.

Sophia insisted. "Father Lawrence and I have to talk for a while. You go on."

Lucia stamped her foot and didn't budge.

"Go find Jeremiah, then. You can deliver the pouches tomorrow. Be back before dark."

Lucia got up and slammed the door as she ran out of the house. After spending several hours unsuccessfully looking for Jeremiah and nearly giving up, she spied him sitting on the ground, his head resting on a fallen tree. His eyes were closed and he seemed far away. She hesitated before she went up to him, and did so only when he squirmed, trying to get more comfortable. When she sat down next to him, he stirred as if he knew she was near and opened his eyes, but he kept staring straight ahead and did not turn toward her or say anything. Tugging gently at his sleeve, she finally got his attention. He seemed sad and exhausted, and for the first time she sensed he was a very lonely man.

"I don't feel like talking, Lucia, even to you. Today all words seem empty. I feel empty."

Lucia shook her head, refusing his refusal, and pointed to her ear.

Jeremiah closed his eyes again and let his head fall back. "This isn't a good day, Lucia. I'm sorry."

She was stunned. Jeremiah had never rebuffed her like this before. She stood up and walked away as noiselessly as she could. When she had put some distance between herself and Jeremiah, she started stomping her feet and swinging her arms. She strode into a pile of twigs and leaves and kicked them furiously into the air. After several such kicks, she noticed the crackling sound when they flew off her foot. She liked it. She picked up a couple of sticks and rubbed them against each other, holding them close to her ear; then she used the sticks to hit against a tree and then a stone. She liked all the various sounds and the fact that she could make them. Picking up a slender leaf, she held it up by her mouth and tried to blow through it as she had seen some boys do. She could make only a small squeak. Harder and harder she blew until the leaf fell away and there was the naked sound of her own outgoing breath. She blew out loudly several more times and then shouted, trying to send her voice to the tops of the trees. She tried singing — wordlessly — experimenting with different notes. *She* was making these wonderful sounds.

Sitting down in the dirt with her back against a tree, she took a stick and wrote "No" on the ground. And then she said it so quietly that at first she had to imagine she had heard herself, then louder and louder, "No! No! No!" Then she tried, "Yes! Yes! Yes!" Hours went by as she tried out different words. She kept her eyes closed because by doing so she could feel how she was feeding and growing herself as she spoke each word. She lost track of time. When she started shivering, she opened her eyes, surprised that it was nearly dark, and ran home.

As she opened the door, she was surprised to see that Father Lawrence was still there. Sophia was at the stove and nodded when she came in, and the priest gave her a cheery welcome. Lucia knew he was trying to make up for Sophia's silence and their earlier dismissal of her. She felt grown-up because she had figured this out and because she could sense the heaviness in the air, as if serious things had been discussed or would be soon.

After dinner, Father Lawrence did the dishes and then the three of them drew their chairs close to the warm hearth. They stared at the fire and no one spoke for a long time. Lucia feared that they had already said all that they were going to say. She looked intently at Sophia, and then at Father Lawrence.

"This may be a good time, Sophia."

"How should I start?"

"Why don't you start at the beginning and decide what to tell as you go on."

Lucia was suddenly alert, curious. Sophia and Father Lawrence appeared so solemn. Sophia turned toward her. "You don't know about your birth parents and I decided that I don't want you growing up not knowing anything about me. I would have told you about myself earlier — I know you wanted me to — but some horrible things have happened to me and I didn't want to make you sad by telling you about them."

Father Lawrence moved slightly in his chair. Lucia noticed his eyes were wet. She suddenly felt a little afraid.

"Lucia, do you still want to hear my story, knowing it might frighten you or make you sad?"

Lucia nodded her head up and down several times. Sophia began coughing and Lucia sprang up to get her a cup of water. Sophia took it from her gratefully and drank the water without hurry.

"It tastes so good. It reminds me of the water I had as a child. It came from a spring, hidden in a grotto. That grotto was very special to my parents…but I should start from the beginning…

"My father was a scribe. He was employed by adventurers and businessmen who wanted to record their travels, draw up documents, or write letters. He traveled a great deal and eventually came to the town where my mother lived. He knocked on her door one day when she was barely nineteen, with an armful of clothes that needed mending. My mother made her living as a seamstress. She used to tell me that from the first moment she saw my father, she knew he was the only man for her. When she found out he was a scribe, she told him that if he taught her how to write her name, she wouldn't charge him for the mending.

"My father happily agreed. When he returned, he brought paper and his writing tools. My mother said he wrote her name, 'Clara,' very elegantly. She was surprised by his skill. I think my father was attracted by her simplicity and directness as well as her beauty…my mother was very lovely…and soon he realized he was in love with her. But my father was already married. After his wife had given birth, she had become melancholic. She couldn't care for their son, her husband, or her home. Although they had very little money at the time, my father had to hire a nursemaid.

"When his son died, he hired another person to help care for his wife and home. He constantly worried about his wife, for she seldom left the house and would sometimes lock herself in their bedroom for days at a time and would hardly eat. My father thought about leaving her many times, but he couldn't, for she had no other family to speak of. My father shared all of this with my mother. She told me that from the beginning he never kept anything from her, and that she wept so much when she heard about his situation that he took her in his arms to comfort *her*. One thing led to another, and they became lovers. They met in the grotto at night whenever they could, but they both understood that my father would have to go back to his wife. And he did. My mother told me she knew she had conceived me during their first time together.

"My father came back six times. I remember seeing him only twice. My mother got letters from him frequently and they always included money. We would go to the house of an old man who had many books. My mother would pay him and he would read the letters my father sent. She would tell him what to write back. She never learned to read or write, but would always sign her name. And although she couldn't read them, she kept all of my father's letters. I would usually go with her to the old man's house. Before the old man read, my mother would make me stand where she thought I could not hear. But I heard enough to understand that my father was very sorry he could not be with us. She always let me listen to the parts where he mentioned me.

"Because my mother had a child and no husband, she was looked down upon by everyone in the town. I was too. My mother used to carry me in her arms to the market. One day, several women began insulting her to her face. When she tried to get away from them, she stumbled and fell on top of me. My right leg was hurt and never got better. It was always a little shorter than the left, and gave me trouble.

"When I was very young, I thought my mother was a kind and tender-hearted person. But as I got to be your age, Lucia, I thought she was too much of a dreamer and was often angry with her for not knowing how to make our lives easier. She worked very hard, but we were always poor. And she often said I was beautiful, when I knew I was too short and plain to be called that. When I was about ten, I stopped believing many things she said, including what she said about my father loving us.

"When she started to have stomach pains, she sent me on my own to the old man. She told me I was to ask him to write to my father about her illness. I didn't think anything would come of her sending that letter, and I remember thinking that my mother didn't know how things worked in this world or what people were really like.

"But one day my father arrived at our door and I watched how he took my mother's hands and how they kissed. And he kissed me too. I knew immediately that I had been wrong about him and about my mother. He stayed in our house day and night and hardly slept. He slipped out only once, for about an hour, and returned with a bucket of water. He dipped a cup in it and gave it to my mother to drink. She was so weak he had to hold the cup to her lips.

"'You know where I got this water from, don't you?'" he asked her.

"My mother smiled at him. He turned toward me and explained that he had gotten the water at the spring in the grotto, the place where he and my mother would meet. And then my father told us that while he was fetching the water, it seemed that the whole world and all its activity and all its suffering were like words we couldn't translate yet. We heard things and we saw things, we even did things, but we didn't know their meaning. It was as if we couldn't read the book of the world.

"There were tears in my mother's eyes. I remember she reached for his hand. And then my mother rallied her strength and tried to speak. She mouthed something I couldn't hear. My father bent down and put his ear close to her lips and he held her head in his hands for a long while. When he raised his head again, my mother was gone. He grabbed me and held me close and said that my mother told him that love had taught her how to read the book of the world.

"Afterward, my father was going to take me home with him, when an aunt of mine came forward. She convinced my father she could do a better job of raising me because he had a wife to care for, and work that took him far from home. She told my father I would end up spending my days with a strange woman possessed by the spirit of melancholy. My father cried when he said goodbye and gave me a blessing.... He was so tender and thought he was doing what was best for me." Sophia's voice quavered. "I had been ashamed of my parents, but after that I was ashamed of myself for being so blind and stupid. And I was ashamed of the people in my town who had thought so poorly of my parents.

"So I went to live with my aunt, who immediately gave me the task of watching her children and cleaning the house. She said she was keeping me busy to help me forget my sorrow. I asked if I could learn to read and write, and suggested that if I learned, I could help her children with their letters, but she ignored me. My mother had taught me how to sew and I learned to weave from a woman who lived close by. People admired my work and my aunt encouraged me, but I had to turn over all the money I made to her. I discovered later that my aunt had burnt the letters and kept the money that my father continued to send me until he died a few years later. She had also burned all the letters my father had sent my mother over the years; she said she didn't like clutter around her house. My mother had kept them all in a box and had given the box to me. I was so angry about this that I refused to speak to my aunt for over a year. I know something about not speaking....

"When I was sixteen, the weaver's husband died and she invited me to live with her. She knew my situation. I gratefully accepted her offer and we lived together as friends for several years. My aunt never spoke to me again and pretended she didn't see me when we ran into each other at the market. It never bothered me. I was glad to be rid of her. I thought I was content with things until I went to a cobbler named John to have some new shoes made.

"'Are you the young woman who makes those beautiful rugs everyone is talking about?' he asked me.

"'Maybe,'" I said.

"'Well, I make shoes, good shoes. I notice you walk with a limp. I would wager that one leg of yours is a little shorter than the other. I can make you a pair of shoes that would make that limp less noticeable.'

"I said, 'I can hardly pay for a regular pair of shoes. I'm certain I couldn't afford your special shoes.'

"John suggested that we barter. He said, 'Sophia, make a rug for me. I will provide the wool and dye and whatever else you need. For my part, I will make you a special pair of shoes.'

"I broke down in tears in front of him and wasn't embarrassed. I wove the rug and he made the shoes. He asked me to come by at various times to try them on and asked to come over to see the progress of his rug. By the time the shoes and the rug were finished, we knew we were in love.

"Time seemed to fly by. I thought about John constantly and we talked about getting married. I told him that the priest would not marry us because I was a bastard...my aunt had made sure that everyone knew. But John wanted us to marry in the church and saw no Christian reason why we should be refused. But we were. John was angry about this and decided to complain to the bishop. When he began his trip, I walked with him...over his objections. After several miles I turned to go home, laughing when John expressed concern and said it wasn't safe. I've always been stubborn and unwilling to take orders, and I was in love."

Sophia started to weep. Lucia got down off her chair and sat on the ground near Sophia's legs, laying her head on Sophia's knee. She thought Father Lawrence would say something, but he didn't. He sat quietly waiting.

Sophia stroked Lucia's hair.

"This is the saddest part, Lucia. Remember this happened a long time ago and I lived through it. I hope it will teach you to be aware and watch out for yourself. Women especially, have to take care.... About an hour after I said goodbye to John, I left the road and found a place to have lunch. I was about to start walking again when four men approached me. I was nervous, but managed to calm myself down. They asked if I had any lunch left and one of them said, 'We're very hungry.' His laugh was coarse and very disturbing. My knees went weak. I had some bread left, but I said, 'No, I'm sorry. There's nothing left.' I stood and walked toward the road. The tallest one jumped in front of me while another man grabbed my basket."

Father Lawrence was weeping. Lucia stared at him and realized her own eyes were tearing up.

"Should I stop, Lucia?" Sophia asked.

Lucia shook her head no.

"All right then," Sophia took another drink of water. "The taller man wrestled me to the ground. I clawed at him while he was pressing down on me. I remember the scratches I made on his face, the blood. The other men started to make fun of him. His eyes went blank as if his soul had left his body. I remember that so clearly. Then he spat on me. When I raised my hand to wipe off his spittle, he grabbed my hand, separated out my thumb and twisted it and pulled it back until I felt something give. I remember crying out, then — mercifully — I passed out. When I came to, it was dark and very quiet. I had no fear, only a sense that my body was far away and could not move. I felt I had to get off the ground and willed myself to sit up. I accomplished this, but fainted again straight away. I did not wake up until I found myself in a bed in the home of a healer. When she saw me open my eyes, she sat on the bed and placed her hand on my forehead like mothers do when their child has a fever.

"'You'll survive, Sophia,' I remember her telling me.

"'Survive what?' I asked, though with how ruptured and bruised I felt — I knew.

"The healer held my head between her hands until I looked into her eyes. 'You've been violated, Sophia. You were badly torn up inside. Six of your fingers were broken. I set them as best I could. I hope that you will be able to use them, but you may have difficulty always getting them to do what you want.'

She continued stroking my forehead until I turned away from her and shut my eyes. Her pity was intolerable.

"As the days went by, everything seemed ruined. Everything was repulsive and ugly. I didn't want to eat. I didn't want to speak. I didn't want to hear anyone. I only wanted to sleep. I didn't even care about seeing John. He came anyway and would sit outside my room until I agreed to see him. He told me that some hunters had found me and carried me to the town. He said he had made each of them a pair of shoes to thank them for saving me. I would have died otherwise. I asked why they *didn't* let me die. By then the healer had told me that it was unlikely I would bear children. John didn't know that, because I refused to tell him.

"The healer said I was feeling sorry for myself and that was to be expected. But she also said that I had to start looking outside my own skin again at some point if I didn't want to lose everything. She scolded me for how I was treating John. I knew she had my welfare at heart, but I couldn't change. I couldn't see beyond my own misery. And the healer *was* right. I did lose everything. I lost John. I told him: 'We will never be the same, you and I. This thing will always be mixed up in everything that goes on between a husband and wife.' I was going to tell him then about not being able to have children, but it still hurt too much. John asked me why I was destroying everything. He said he could live with things being different as long as we had each other.

"I told him I didn't want his love anymore. It sounds so cruel now. It was cruel. I know I hurt him. I've never regretted anything more. He was such a good man and loved me so much. He told me he knew I had been badly hurt and that it would take time for me to heal. He said he would wait. I stayed in bed even after my strength was back. The healer threatened to turn me out for my own good. I still couldn't face John or my neighbors, so I stole away in the middle of the night. I didn't have a plan; I just left. I remember that night; there was a darkening of the moon. I'd been taught that when the moon grows dark in the course of a night, it meant danger and evil were abroad and that one should stay safely at home, but I laughed when I remembered that because I had nothing more to lose. I walked that night as if my feet had a will and a mind all their own.

"I walked for days, so many days that I lost count. Sometimes I had food and company. Sometimes I went hungry and saw no one. It made no difference to me. I came to this village. I came to this small cottage. I knocked on the door, and when there was no answer, I knocked harder. A passerby told me that the occupant had just died. 'She was buried in the church graveyard yesterday,' she told me. 'I'm sorry. Are you a relation?' I slumped down in exhaustion and hunger, burying my face in my hands. She said something like, 'Poor dear, her death grieves you so. Why don't you go inside and rest.'

"And so I found myself a little home, barely furnished and in sore need of a good cleaning, but perfectly suited to my needs. The same woman who had told me how the owner had died cared for me until my strength returned – her husband helped me, too. They are both dead now. I didn't tell them much about myself, but I listened to their stories about the old widow. I found out that she had lived in this cottage for over 30 years.

"In a few weeks they surprised me by bringing Father Philip, the parish priest at that time, to give me 'spiritual comfort.' Father Philip was an irritable, abrasive man, but very clever man. He looked at me in such a way that I knew he knew I was a fraud, and was not related at all to the dead woman. But he looked at my bandaged hands and realized some trouble had befallen me. He made a decision not to add to my sorrow. He only smiled, when my new neighbor observed what a pity it was that the old widow had received company only after she had passed on.

"I stayed away from the church and Father Phillip. He had been kind, but I wanted to keep to myself as much as I could. I tried, but several villagers became concerned about me. They assumed that my troubles had led me to despair. They tried to console and hearten me by telling me their own stories. At first I didn't really pay attention. I just smiled, nodded and thanked them. But when I started listening, I grew to love them. They had their faults and sometimes they could not see past their own noses, but I was no different and they were all carrying their own burdens as best they could...I decided I had to start carrying mine.

"I trained my fingers to weave again and eventually earned my living by making rugs. I also cooked and cleaned for the sick and when my fingers became crippled, I learned about healing plants. After many years, I found myself feeling somewhat at home. This was all before Father Lawrence came and before Jeremiah and I became friends.

"One morning...I had been in this village for about fifteen years...I remember sitting down because I was tired from cleaning. I was watching a wood louse scurrying under the door, when my attention was completely captivated by something that seemed to be passing by me above my head. The strange thing was I didn't see anything, nothing at all, but whatever it was had my full attention. I've often wondered how I could see *nothing* — but that's what happened.

"Then a word was given to me. But it didn't come with any

thoughts or pictures. The word was 'Woman.' I still couldn't see anything and I had no idea who this 'Woman' was or who had given me that word, but I loved Her utterly. I could have died thousands and thousands of times for Her and all that dying would have cost me nothing, absolutely nothing. My love for John couldn't compare. I can't express how happy I was. If the world felt what I felt then, it would be a different place.

"Over the years, I have thought about that love. It wasn't like ordinary love. Here, we see someone or something we admire and then we love them. Love comes after the seeing. But this love was different. It didn't come after seeing, it *was* the seeing. How can I explain the difference? Seeing and loving were one thing! I understood that time usually splits them up. Even if it is a matter of a very small amount of time, things get separated. But I was somewhere without time and I knew that loving and seeing were one thing and there is no word for it. And that experience was part of the mystery of the Woman, the one who had no name and whom I saw without seeing.

"I've never told anyone about this before today. I tried telling Father Phillip once, but it went badly. He thought I was trying to confess something. When I saw that, I knew he wouldn't believe that I could have such an experience. I also tried telling Father Joseph. I was scared, so I started by asking him if he knew anyone who had a vision. He looked at me as if I just told him I was considering murdering someone, and then he asked who was telling me they were seeing things! I found a way not to answer and began talking about practical matters, and he was very relieved.

"I don't know why I had this desire to talk to a priest. Occasionally I even went to church and listened carefully to what was being said. I listened to the prayers and hymns. But even after many years, I heard only a few things that could have been about that Woman I had seen. I remember hearing scripture read about a Woman called Wisdom. Wisdom was at the beginning of the world. She played everywhere on the earth and was the perfect image of God's goodness. And I remember hearing how She gives birth after much labor and pain and how She will descend one day out of heaven, like a bride prepared to meet Her husband. I heard the priests read these beautiful passages, but they never said anything about them, as if they were unimportant.

"For a while, I spent a great deal of time trying to figure it out, but after several years I knew it was something thinking couldn't solve. Sometimes I wonder what difference this all made. My life did not change. There was hard work with little to show for it, and many difficult and lonely hours. My memories would trouble me if I let them. Desire was a torment. Doing what needed doing seemed the only thing left. Over time, I've come to realize that my experience was not given to me to make me special or to make life easier, but to make me strong enough to live in this world without spending all my time wishing for another. And after I found you, Lucia, I believed that seeing Her had also prepared me to welcome you."

"I want to see her too," Lucia said firmly and clearly as she raised her head off Sophia's lap. "I want to see the Woman."

Father Lawrence and Sophia looked at each other and each saw their own wonder reflected in the other's face. Father Lawrence's jaw had dropped and Sophia was crying. Though she had been anticipating what had just happened for years, the reality was overwhelming. Her daughter had a lovely voice.

"I want you to see Her too," Sophia said, noticing how her daughter's eyes shone in the firelight. She put a hand on Lucia's head. Father Lawrence bent forward as if to speak, but decided he had nothing to say equal to the moment and leaned back in his chair, silent.

Lucia laid her head back down on Sophia's lap. The crackling of the fire was the only sound in the room for a long while.

"Thank you for speaking, Lucia. Father Lawrence and I are so happy you let us hear your voice tonight. You have such a beautiful voice. And I'm grateful that you listened so well to my long story."

"I've been practicing words."

"I know. But now I think it's time for you to go to bed – you seem tired. We will talk more tomorrow. Father Lawrence and I look forward to hearing everything you have to say."

"I do look forward," Father Lawrence said.

Lucia stood up and kissed Sophia on her cheek. She turned next toward the priest.

"Good night, Father."

"Good night, Lucia."

Still stunned, Sophia and Father Lawrence watched as Lucia made her way to the bedroom and closed the door behind her.

Father Lawrence stirred in his chair. "How shocking! After all this time she talked so naturally, as if it meant nothing at all!"

"I knew she would talk; so did Jeremiah."

"She spoke when she decided, when she wanted to, as you said she would. I wish I had said something, but I couldn't think of what to say."

"It was probably best we *didn't* make a big fuss."

"Do you think she'll keep talking?"

"I don't think anything will stop her now."

"I don't know what's more remarkable…Lucia speaking for

the first time after all these years, or you sharing everything you did."

"I'm glad I told you all of it. I hope that telling *her* everything wasn't a mistake."

"I don't think it was. Her first words…they came from her heart."

"Yes, they did. That pleased me, but what she said also made me afraid."

"Afraid? Why? It doesn't mean that she'll have to go through what you went through, Sophia."

"How do you know that, Father?"

Father Lawrence looked at the floor. "I *don't* know that, Sophia." He looked up again. "But what did the Woman say to you before — in that dream you had? Didn't She say that your pain was part of Her labor? Didn't you also say that my suffering was part of Her labor? Lucia's pain will also be part."

"That doesn't change the fact that I don't want to see her suffer."

"Of course, I feel the same."

They sat in the silence for a time.

"You know, Father, you've also passed over those passages in the bible about the Woman."

"I was wondering when you would get around to mentioning that! I know I'm guilty and I'm sorry for it. I didn't understand what scripture was saying. To be honest, I still don't; but I promise you I won't be ignoring those passages any longer, Sophia."

Chapter Eight

As Sophia had guessed, once Lucia started talking there was no stopping her. Her words, sparse and hesitant in the beginning, soon became a wild and tangled growth. She started talking as soon as she woke up in the morning and didn't stop until she fell asleep. Sophia told Father Lawrence that her daughter's countless musings, stories, questions, and observations were wearing her patience thin. The priest told her that Lucia was making up for lost time and predicted that her verbosity would soon moderate itself. However, months went by and Lucia's loquaciousness showed no sign of diminishing. Jeremiah, who was encouraging at first, began correcting her. Sometimes he would put a hand out to remind her to be quiet or would place a finger across his lips.

"Don't treat words so carelessly, and don't always speak as soon as you feel like it. Words need silence to grow and ripen. Listen to others and learn to listen to yourself when you speak."

Lucia knew he was right, but felt he was being too demanding. She complained to Sophia, assuming that her mother would intercede for her. Instead Sophia said, "Jeremiah believes that words are a gift from God."

"I do too."

"I know."

Lucia started to cry. "I'm afraid of talking when I'm around him. He's always telling me I'm talking too fast and too much."

"Are you?"

"I can't stop."

It took a great deal of effort for Sophia not to laugh. "Did I ever tell you what happened to Jeremiah when he was about your age?"

"No, what happened to him?"

"His father beat him whenever he caught him trying to learn to read and write, or when he saw him daydreaming. And when Jeremiah was only fifteen, he was kicked out of the house because he would never finish his work. Jeremiah would see something beautiful and he would forget everything else. And then poetry and stories started coming out of him. No one wanted to hear them at first, but nothing stopped him. Cold, hunger, ridicule, loneliness – he endured all of them because it was the price he had to pay to see beauty in this world and share it with others. He looks poor and ragged, Lucia, but Jeremiah is a king in the realm of words, a great lord and warrior. We are fortunate to know a man like that. You shouldn't expect he'll be easy to please. That is the price you must pay to have such a great teacher."

When they met again, Lucia approached Jeremiah with something like awe. For weeks, it was difficult for her to say anything in his presence. At first Jeremiah was delighted, thinking that she had taken his lessons to heart, but then the intensity of her attention began to embarrass him. Conflicting feelings about being admired caused him to become more self-conscious. He also realized that there was an imbalance, a fear in Lucia's silence. He missed their easy camaraderie. Wanting to right things, he started asking her more questions and invited her to help him find just the right word for a poem, or a sentence for a story. This worked. They began having conversations during which each would learn and say something new and unexpected. Time would fly as they tasted the joy of creating something together. Both changed as a result of this. Jeremiah discovered a new feeling — quiet contentment. Lucia learned how to pay more attention to others, and in a short while, had many friends.

As their relationship was righting itself, Angela became too ill to leave her bed. Sophia and Lucia helped her as much as they could. Sophia cooked, and massaged Angela's feet and hands until all touch became painful to her. Lucia cleaned her house and collected plants which her mother would then combine and use to make a tea. Sophia and Lucia would take turns holding Angela's head up so she could sip it. Father Lawrence and Jeremiah tended Angela's garden, while other villagers would bring by food and candles or cut and stack wood.

Lucia was both fascinated and repelled by the process of dying. She did not like going over to Angela's house, but once she was there she would stare at her while she slept or would sniff around trying to identify the strange odors that filled the room. Sophia would have to call her several times to get her attention. One morning, as Sophia was leaving for Angela's, she told her daughter to stay home.

"I think Angela needs quiet more than anything else now. You stay here and take care of things."

"But Mum…"

"I will send for you when it's time."

The next day, when Lucia was cleaning out the pen and washing the goats' udders, Jeremiah showed up, looking paler than usual.

"She's dead, isn't she?"

Jeremiah nodded. "Sophia asked me to fetch you."

"What was it like?"

"It was difficult. She couldn't breathe properly; but at the end, she was very peaceful and was ready to go; she wanted to go."

When they arrived at Angela's house, Lucia saw that several of the village women were outside milling about, waiting to clean and prepare the body. She and Jeremiah went inside. Father Lawrence was by the bedside and Sophia stood next to him. Her mother told Lucia that Father Lawrence had anointed Angela before she died and explained what that meant. She told her daughter that he had made the sign of the cross on her eyes, ears, nose, lips, hands, and feet with holy oil to purify her senses and open them to the true nature of things.

Lucia and Jeremiah stood on opposite sides of the bed. Angela's mouth was wide open, but it was not unappealing; it strangely added to the sweetness and serenity of her countenance. Lucia lost herself in the contemplation of it. Jeremiah whispered across the bed, "She's lovely, isn't she? Angela wasn't afraid of joy. That made her like an angel."

Angela's funeral was well-attended and marked by an exquisite blend of grief and joy. When Father Lawrence stood to give the sermon, Lucia was surprised by his tears and the quaver in his voice. She had not known how dear Angela had been to him. She wondered what he would feel if Sophia died, or if she herself died.

"When I was a young boy of seven, my mother died. But I refused to believe that she was gone. Even though I was there when she was laid in the ground and even though I threw dirt on her grave, I expected that I would see her again. I couldn't believe such a powerful presence, such a wonderful spirit, could ever leave this world. It would have been easier for me to believe that *I* was no longer in this world than for me to believe that so magnificent and real a person as my mother wasn't.

"Was this mere fantasy? Was I childishly denying what had happened? That is what I thought when I was a young man and looked back upon that time. But now, I think my sense of things was true. How can Angela be gone? Many of us believe that everything depends on the physical body. I did once. But then I began noticing that sometimes when I spoke to people who were standing right in front of me, they wouldn't be listening. It was as if they were miles away. I also observed how close I felt to my father even though I moved nearly a hundred miles away from him in order to study for the priesthood. Whenever I visited him, it felt we had never been parted. Being present to those we love depends less on our physical body, and more on our capacity to pay attention and appreciate them."

Father Lawrence's voice shook. He paused. Lucia saw him look quickly in Sophia's direction.

"Angela never thought any detail of life in the village insignificant, and she loved being in this world. She loved sewing and making beautiful things for people. She loved celebrations, her home, and the stars. How can she be gone? True, she is also occupied by another life, another world, just as I had gone away to study. But she is always near. And when we see each other again, it will be as if we had never really parted."

At the burial site, Father Lawrence said prayers, sprinkled the grave with holy water, and then invited the villagers to share their memories. Several women and children spoke about kindnesses Angela had shown them. Jeremiah said that Angela made his heart sing with the angels. Sophia spoke about her patience. Lucia desperately wanted to say something eloquent, but before she could organize her thoughts, the coffin was being lowered and the villagers were taking turns throwing dirt in the grave.

Afterwards, as Lucia and Sophia were walking home through the forest, Lucia suddenly stopped. Sophia, lost in her memories, kept walking. Startled by a loud cry coming from behind her, Sophia turned around.

"I don't want you to die! I don't want you to lie in the ground like Angela!" Lucia's hands were balled into fists. She was white and shaking. Sophia limped toward her, took Lucia's hand, and led her across the meadow. Sophia did not let go of her until they reached the river. They sat under a willow tree, where, at Sophia's suggestion, they took off their shoes and dug their toes in the grass. Lucia put her arm through her mother's and together they inhaled the calming fragrance of the river as they had often done.

"I don't want you to leave me, Mum."

"I know."

"Why did Angela have to die? Why did Father Lawrence's mother die? If you die, I will be all alone," Lucia sobbed.

"You're forgetting you have Father Lawrence and Jeremiah.

And there's Catherine and Simon. You wouldn't be alone. Many people care about you and love you very much. And remember what Father Lawrence said: I will still be with you even though you won't be able to see me anymore."

"But I want to see you. I'll be so lonely if I can't see you." Lucia grabbed Sophia tightly. When Sophia turned around to embrace her, she saw Jeremiah standing a little way off. She motioned to him with an inclination of her head.

"How are you two? I heard someone shouting."

"That was me," Lucia said, wiping her nose.

"Do you miss Angela?"

"I was thinking about Mum dying."

"You don't ever want to lose her. Is that it?"

Lucia struggled to speak. "She can't die."

"I don't want her to die, either. I know when she does I'll feel more alone in this world."

"You will?"

"Of course."

"What will you do?" Lucia asked.

"Hasn't anyone told you the big secret?"

"What big secret?"

Jeremiah sat on the ground at Lucia's feet. "The secret about desire, about its power if you name it and then release it. Are you sure no one has mentioned it?"

Lucia shook her head.

Jeremiah picked up a stick.

"This stick is desire. Some people hold their desires very close to them, but never give them a name." Jeremiah grabbed the stick tightly with both hands and held it to his chest. "We have to name our desires and then we have to release them. Releasing them is harder than naming them, but we need to learn to do that too." Jeremiah held the stick out in front of him. Gazing at it he said, "I want to be with Sophia, forever." He kissed the stick and then tossed it into the river and watched as it was carried downstream.

"The river is the stream of longing that runs through everything. Where is that stick going? Who knows? Maybe all the way to the sea, for the sea draws all the rivers to itself. If you name your desire and then release it into the stream of longing, what a great journey your desire will make!"

"I want Mum to stay with me forever, just like you do."

Jeremiah gave her a stick. "You know what to do."

Lucia looked at Sophia, who nodded encouragement. She took the stick. "I want to be with my mother forever." She kissed the stick, threw it with all her strength into the river, and then walked alongside the flowing water, keeping her eye on the stick. When Sophia called her back, she returned to find Jeremiah sitting near Sophia's feet.

"It didn't work," Lucia said. "I still feel sad, and I don't want Mum to go."

Jeremiah wrapped his arms around himself and looked up at Sophia. In that moment, Lucia knew how much he loved her mother. She could see it in the brightness of his eyes, the softness in his face, the stillness in his body. Jeremiah caught Lucia staring at him. He quickly stood up and ran off.

"Why did he leave without saying goodbye?"

"He was protecting his heart, Lucia. He knew he had uncovered it just then. Most people are not willing to do that, other than the very young and the very old. A person has to be very brave or trusting, or understand a great deal."

Lucia got down and put her hand in the river, feeling the water flowing through her fingers, tugging at her hand, making it feel alive. She wondered where the stick was and how long it would take before it got to the sea.

Chapter Nine

Lucia was at an age when she began caring about clothes and was bothered by the disparaging comments the other girls were starting to make about hers. "The other girls say that I am wearing things that are too small," she whined to Sophia. "Can you teach me how to weave so we can afford new clothes? Everyone thinks your rugs are so beautiful. People would pay a lot for them."

Sophia held out her hands. "See these. They don't do what I want anymore."

"You don't have to make the rugs; you just have to tell *me* how."

"It takes a great deal of patience and persistence to weave… and time. Can you sit for long stretches and do the same thing over and over again and pay attention when you're doing it, even though your body aches and you want to be outside?"

"I could learn….How *much* does your body hurt?"

"We would have to borrow a loom; I sold mine years ago. Then we would have to comb, spin, and dye the wool ourselves. There is no money to pay others to do it for us. One rug will take months."

"That long?"

"We could do it; but I want you to know that weaving is hard work. You could earn money in other ways. You're good with children. Why don't you offer to teach them to read and write like Simon has taught you, or I could show you more about plants and how to make remedies with them. If you want me to do this, we should start soon. Going into the forest is getting more difficult for me."

Lucia preferred the latter suggestion. And so they began spending more time together in the forest. Lucia already knew a little, having gone with her mother collecting in the forest before. Now, though, Sophia tried giving her daughter advanced instruction, showing her how to identify plants using all her senses, and testing her memory. "Sometimes the difference between a helpful and a harmful plant is very slight, Lucia. The details matter." Sophia shared with Lucia how the various plants affected mind and body differently. While Lucia was amazed at the power hidden in such innocuous-looking things, her wonder and astonishment did not help her remember much of what Sophia told her about them. It was frustrating for her and her mother. After a few weeks, Lucia began making up stories about particular plants. Sometimes the stories would help her identify them, but more often than not they were simply distractions. For a time, Sophia was entertained and did most of the finding and collecting herself; however, after listening to a long narrative involving a vengeful princess, poison, and a disloyal prince, Sophia had had enough.

"No more, Lucia! Your stories are amusing, but they won't put food on the table. They certainly won't get you the new clothes you want."

"But it's the only thing I like to do and the only thing I'm really good at!"

"That better not be true. Maybe you're spending too much time with Jeremiah. He's a wonderful storyteller and a poet; but look at him…he can hardly keep body and soul together. You're a woman; it would be even more difficult for you. I want you to be able to take care of yourself and not be forced to marry just so you can eat."

"No one will force me to marry and I'll take care of myself. And if you ever get sick, even if it's for a long time, I'll take care of you, Mum. You'll see."

In less than a year, Lucia found herself trying to live up to her brave words. Sophia rarely had the strength to leave the cottage, and many additional tasks fell on Lucia's young shoulders. She cleaned, cooked, and fetched water. She did whatever odd job she could find and had time for. Lucia took care of the goats, gathered leaves from the few plants she had learned to recognize, did laundry for the unmarried men, and taught several children how to read and write. Her new responsibilities made her quieter — more serious and less social.

"I never knew how many changes young people go through," Sophia told Father Lawrence. It was mid afternoon and Lucia was busy in the village.

"The old change, too…"

"You mean me, I suppose. Yes. It's true. And when the old change it's usually in a way that frightens the young. I don't want Lucia to be afraid; I want her to be happy. But I can't make that happen."

"She won't be a stranger to happiness; there's too much life in her. And I know you know this, but I'll say it anyway – if something should happen, I'll see to it she's taken care of."

"I know you will, as will her godparents. They are very fond of her."

"She's a vibrant and lovely girl. You've raised her well."

"We all have."

"You've raised me too, Sophia. Deny it all you want. I'm a better man and priest because of you. You are inside of me like my father is…."

Sophia was not the only one to mark the changes in Lucia — the villagers also noticed. A few young men shyly approached her because of the loveliness she had begun leaving in her wake. Lucia usually ignored them.

When Sophia observed this, she was curious about Lucia's impressions of the young men and asked her about them. Lucia told her bluntly, "They don't know anything and they act like children."

"And whom are you comparing them to?" Sophia asked.

Lucia blushed and refused to answer. She realized for the first time that she had been comparing all the young men she was acquainted with to Aaron. Even though she had seen him briefly — only three times in the last several months — and had said no more than a "Good morning" to him, he made a deep impression on her. Father Lawrence was always talking about him when he came to visit. It was clear he liked Aaron very much, and overhearing what he told Sophia about him was enough to encourage Lucia's own feelings of admiration. Aaron was providing for his mother, just as she was caring for Sophia, but he was also passionate about ideas. He talked about justice, truthfulness, and equality. He wanted the world to change and was confident that he would be part of that change. While most of the villagers were distrustful of those who held power – being generally suspicious of government – Aaron could be specific about why he did not trust them. He said the leaders were taking a wrong turn in building up the army and that this decision would soon bring people misery and not the prosperity they were promised. That Aaron was thinking about such things as the condition of the world and wanted to do something to make the world better was very appealing to Lucia — that and the fact that he was learning to ride horses.

Some nights as she lay in bed with Sophia, unable to sleep because of her mother's snoring, Lucia thought of boys — particularly Aaron. When she did, she felt she was leaving a quiet, protected pool and was being pulled into deeper waters where there were powerful currents and new, strange, and attractive objects. She sensed the complexity and turmoil she was moving into and was both troubled and drawn by it.

Next to her, Sophia was also dreaming — of streams sparkling in the sunshine and overhung with trees, dreaming of multi-colored fish that leapt effortlessly from the water. The fish arced high in the air then fell back into the blue-black abyss, weighted with surrender.

Chapter Ten

The days were growing shorter and the air cooler. The leaves, flirting with the approaching silence, pulled up the secret fire of the trees. On sunlit days, the sight of their leafy red and gold made the villagers beauty-drunk.

With the coming of autumn, Sophia was like a fully conscious leaf. Though her physical strength was ebbing, there were moments when she flushed with a wildly glorious presence. At those times it was difficult for her to pay attention to anything else or to speak. When they passed, she had the clear sense that her physical body would soon be dropped.

She told Jeremiah and Father Lawrence what she felt, but put off telling Lucia. Afterward, Jeremiah began stopping by nearly every day. He would place a chair against the wall facing the foot of Sophia's bed, and would simply sit by her, often saying nothing at all. Sometimes he would take Sophia's hand and hold it gently in his. Though physical contact between the two of them had been rare, this holding of hands seemed something natural to both of them.

Several days a week, Father Lawrence brought food and fixed a meal, or he would send someone else from the parish to do so.

Catherine, Lucia's godmother, helped Lucia bathe Sophia. Lucia felt comfortable around her godmother but began feeling awkward and shy around both the priest and Jeremiah for reasons she did not understand.

One afternoon when Lucia was out working, Father Lawrence came by, bringing a generous supply of potatoes, onions, turnips, cheese, honey, and some bread. He started a fire in the hearth, spread some honey over a piece of bread, and gave it to Sophia. She was sitting in a chair wrapped in a blanket, her cloak, and her tattered shawl. She never felt warm anymore. He sat across from her and watched her while she nibbled at the bread.

"Father Joseph died yesterday."

"Lucia told me. He was a good man."

Father Lawrence stretched out his legs and wondered how long his boots would remain serviceable. Quietly, he asked, "Are you afraid of death, Sophia?"

"Afraid? No. Not for myself…only for Lucia."

"I wonder if my mother sensed her death and what her feelings were. She died in her sleep, as you know." He drew his legs up. "I don't think I told you…after she died, I believed that if I fell asleep when it was dark, I would die too. I was so scared. My father talked to me about it, and afterward he kept a candle lit or made sure that the fire burned through the night. He did that for many months. One evening, despite my protests, he blew out all the candles and let the fire die down. I yelled for him to come to me, but he didn't, so I kept myself up for most of the night. Eventually I couldn't keep my eyes open any longer and fell asleep. When I opened my eyes, it was midday and the light was so bright I thought I had died; but it was not my mother who greeted me, it was my father. He had been sitting by my side for hours waiting for me to wake up. I remember he smiled and said, 'Welcome, to a new day, my son. You live!' He had never reproached me for my fear or weakness, but he did not want me to remain in their grip.

"Though my mother was gone – and I never got over that — I saw how wonderful my father was and how much he loved me. That love made it possible for me to go on living even though my heart felt like it was a huge hole. I think that was my first inkling of God, Sophia."

"Are there inklings that are not woven with pain and suffering, Father?"

"I don't know. Maybe…what about you, Sophia? What was your first inkling?"

"Seeing how my parents loved each other despite everything – that was mine."

"There is pain and suffering in your experience as well. And there is also love."

When Sophia started needing assistance to use the chamber pot, to sit up in bed, or move to a chair, Lucia stayed closer to home. She knew her mother was dying, without having to be told. She knew that Sophia had spoken about her death to Jeremiah and Father Lawrence and was angry with all of them for not saying anything to her; and, at the same time, she hoped they never would. She felt an urgent and pressing need to find out about her birth parents and seemed to have no choice about this. Even though she saw how it tired Sophia, and though she knew Sophia had already told her everything she knew, she had to ask her the same questions repeatedly. *Why did that man take me away from my parents? What do you think my parents were like? Will I ever find out who my parents were?*

Sophia patiently tried to answer Lucia's questions in an honest manner, but also in a way that would bring her some comfort. However, she could tell Lucia was disappointed with her responses, though they also seemed to be what her daughter had expected. For her part, Lucia tried to hide her feelings from Sophia, not wanting to upset her, but she knew the frustration she saw in her mother's face was the reflection of her own.

At a particularly painful time for Lucia, she said something to her mother she wished she could have taken back as soon as she said it. "I don't even know my real name. You called me 'Lucia,' but my real name is probably something different!"

"I know. But the Woman I saw, the Woman who spoke to me, She bears your name. She knows who you are. You are Her child before you were ever mine or before you were even your parents' child. You are *Her* child, Lucia. Isn't that what matters?"

Sometimes Lucia felt her mother was too resigned to being ill. She wanted Sophia to struggle more, to fight her way back to health. She told Sophia that special people – and she insisted Sophia was one of those special people – could make themselves better if they wanted to. When Sophia heard this, she snorted like she did when she thought something or someone was ridiculous. Lucia did not like it.

"Don't you believe it, Mum?"

"No, I don't."

"Maybe *She* can heal you then, Mum."

"You mean the Woman I saw, the one who spoke to me?"

"Who else?" Lucia asked. She sounded more irritated than she wanted to.

"Come closer, Lucia," Sophia said. Lucia bent over the bed

and put her face next to her mother's. Sophia gently stroked her cheek with the back of her finger. Lucia kept still, but felt herself resisting the gesture and its meaning.

"I am as She is," Sophia whispered, as if telling Lucia a great secret.

"What?"

Lucia wanted an explanation. Instead, her mother answered, "There is no lesser healing for me now."

Sophia looked into Lucia's eyes and Lucia looked into hers. Her mother was closer to her than ever, and yet so far away at the same time. Unable to endure feelings which in contradicting, intensified each other, Lucia straightened up and ran out of the room.

Chapter Eleven

Christmas was only a few weeks away, and since Sophia was having a remarkably good day, Lucia took the opportunity to pick up the new shawl she had had someone knit for her mother. Because part of the shawl's payment included some leaves for a tea that aided digestion, Lucia took her cutting knife and her medicinal pouch along with the lunch Sophia had made for her. As soon as she left the house she felt lighter; however, her sense of relief was soon accompanied by guilt and then worry.

It was cold and overcast and there was a strange lightness and stillness in the air which Lucia had learned to associate with snow. The deer track she followed into the forest was covered with decaying, nearly colorless leaves whose dark and intricate veins had nothing more to do. The leaves made no sound when she stepped on them. The evergreen trees were also silent and patiently waited to bear new burdens of snow, while the deciduous trees stood like a defeated but dignified army. Lucia knelt down by a low-lying shrub, took out her knife, and began cutting stems.

A snowflake landed on her sleeve – a tiny, perfect star. Lucia wanted to gaze upon it, but it melted so quickly. Something about this struck Lucia as unbearably sad. She rocked back on both her heels and began crying. Then dropping the knife, she held her arms out in front of her, hoping to catch another snowflake, but no more fell – not a single one.

By the time she paid for the shawl and was returning home, it was growing dark. She was near the church when she heard voices. They belonged to Father Lawrence and Paul, a farmer with five children and a sickly wife. She heard footsteps, and then collided with the solidly built farmer.

"Lucia! I'm sorry. I didn't see you there. Are you hurt?" Although her shoulder ached she told Paul she was fine.

Father Lawrence suddenly appeared. "Are you sure?"

"I'm sure."

Paul excused himself after apologizing again.

"You're out late, Lucia."

"Sophia was much better today, Father, and I had to pick up the shawl that I had made for her."

"A thoughtful gift....Could I come by a little later?"

"She would like that."

"How are *you* doing?"

Though it was dark, Lucia felt as if the priest could see her. "Fine. Thank you, Father."

"I'm glad to see you out. I know it's hard for the young to be around sickness, even if they love the one who is ill very much."

Lucia felt as if she had once more collided with something, and forced herself not to cry. She did not want anyone to know how precarious her emotional balance was, how easy it would be for her to fall into despair, and how she doubted she would ever get up again.

"See you in a little while then, Father," Lucia responded, not knowing what else to say.

When Lucia got home, she was exhausted. Sophia was sitting, waiting for her in the kitchen. Lucia kissed her on both cheeks.

"Why are you up, Mum? You go to bed. I'll make us supper."

"No. You go rest. I'll do it. What do you have there?"

"A surprise. Don't bother cooking. I'll be up in a little while and I'll make us something."

Lucia went into the bedroom, carefully placed the shawl under the bed on top of her pouch, took off her shoes, crawled under the covers, and fell into a deep sleep.

Something irritating woke her up, an acrid smell. Coughing violently, she opened her eyes. Father Lawrence was standing in the doorway. Was she dreaming? He appeared to be on fire. Light radiated from his face and his eyes were burning coals. Around his entire body was a brightness that hurt her to look at. She blinked and when she opened her eyes, he was bent over her. She felt him tucking the blanket firmly around her. He gathered her up in his arms, scooping her up as if she weighed nothing. She told herself that it could not be happening, but she knew it was. She could see how the smoke filled the bedroom and how the flames licked at the doorway.

"Mum! Mum! Where's Mum?" she cried, suddenly frantic.

"I have to get you out of here," the priest said as if commanding himself.

"Put me down."

"No."

Lucia fought him. The priest struggled to hold on to her. She felt him gather his strength.

"Sophia's dead. She's dead."

Lucia wrenched herself out of his arms, then crouched down and reached under the bed to get the shawl. She pulled it toward her and held it to her chest as if in rescuing the shawl she was saving her mother. As soon as she stood up, Father Lawrence wrapped the blankets around her again. He opened his mouth to say something, but began making gagging sounds. Hearing him, and seeing how his hands were red and swollen and how his nose and cheeks were blistering, Lucia was frightened into submission. He picked her up, swung her over the windowsill and yelled at her to roll away from the house, which she did. He climbed out after her, checking to see she was at a safe distance. Taking the shawl out of her hands, he quickly moistened it with newly fallen snow. He ran back to the front door. Lucia struggled out of the blanket. She saw Father Lawrence's back, dark against the flames, watched him wrap his head in the shawl. "Jesus Christ!" he shouted, and then he plunged back into the burning cottage.

"Mum, Mum," she whimpered, until she saw Father Lawrence carrying her out. An arm swung back and forth, offering no resistance. She knew Sophia was dead.

"Lucia, spread out the blanket." Lucia did as she was told. Father Lawrence laid her mother down as gently as he could. Some of her clothes and hair had been burnt away and she was covered with soot, but otherwise the fire had not touched her. She looked small, shrunken. Father Lawrence removed the shawl from his head and gave it to Lucia. Suddenly his face clenched, his eyes closed, his shoulders hunched forward and he grabbed his left arm. Lucia quickly took the measure of his pain, fathomed its intensity. She thought she heard thunder, and began screaming. A firm tug on her sleeve brought her back to her senses.

"Lucia! It's all right."

His voice was rasping; she could barely hear it, and he was breathing like a hunted, wounded animal. He tried to spit into his palm. It took several attempts — the great heat had sucked all moisture from his flesh.

When he succeeded in producing a little spit he mixed it with some snow. Bent over Sophia's body, he took the thumb and finger of one hand, placed them in his saliva, and made the sign of the cross on her eyes, lips, nose, hands, and feet. Lucia could not hear what he said, but she supposed he was anointing Sophia's body as he had Angela's. When he finished, he covered Sophia's body with the blanket and then sat back heavily on the ground, bringing his knees up. Cinders and pieces of smelly hair fell from his bowed head. Lucia scooted closer to him.

A group of young men, who had been drinking in the forest, came running when they saw the flames. They shouted as loud as they could for Sophia and Lucia, supposing the mother and daughter asleep inside. As they drew near the fire, they heard a male voice, cracked and barely audible, and saw what they had taken for a large stone – move. They walked in the direction of the voice — silent now so as to hear better — and keeping close together. And all the while the swirling snow fell upon their heads and shoulders, covering them like a soft and weightless mantle.

Chapter Twelve

Lucia entered the church between Catherine and Simon, keep-ing her head down. Her godparents led her to the front of the altar where a large, simple wooden box rested on a table. A tall, slender man was holding a torch so that its light fell into it. She tried to see his face, but the light's glare hid it from her. She noticed how the man rocked back and forth as if her staring at him made him nervous. He cleared his throat.

"I'm sorry about your mother, Lucia."

She knew that voice. Aaron. He was the man holding the torch. She was glad he was there and wanted to thank him for what he said, but her throat was squeezed shut and nothing came out. Catherine and Simon were looking at her mother's body. She knew she was expected to look too, and though she did not want to, she glanced down at Sophia's body. Sophia's face was grim – it had none of Angela's serenity – and the body was rigid and small-looking. Lucia knew that what she saw was not really her mother and it repulsed her. The only thing reminding her of how her mother had been was the green fir branch someone had placed between the stiff and gnarled hands. Lucia reached in and touched it, trying not to come in contact with anything else.

Catherine leaned into the box and kissed the forehead. When Simon bent over and kissed the lifeless hands, Lucia made a low whining sound, surprising herself. She was even more surprised to hear that sound echoed by Aaron. Her godparents appeared startled, too. Simon patted Aaron on the arm and then gently drew Lucia back. Someone handed Lucia and her godparents candles. Lucia could hear prayers being said and looked around the church. It had been a long time since she had been inside. She asked Catherine if she had seen Jeremiah, but she said she hadn't. A moment later her godmother tapped her on the arm. Father Lawrence was coming toward them. Lucia watched as Aaron thrust his torch at another young man, went up to the priest, and offered his arm. Lucia was shocked when she saw how Father Lawrence's dark hair was streaked with white. Bandages covered his hands and nearly half of his colorless face. He walked, stooped as if he were an old man, and looked as frail and preoccupied as Sophia had toward the end.

Aaron grabbed a stool and placed it near the priest, then helped him sit down. Lucia heard Father Lawrence thank Aaron and knew he said something else to him, but she could not hear what. Aaron beckoned her to come closer.

"Lucia," the priest said, "I had to see you. I'm going away in a few days. Besides the damage you can see, the doctor says there is a problem with my heart. I've been told to take a long rest and the bishop has ordered me to leave the parish for a while."

"How long? I thought you said you were all right."

"I don't know, Lucia. Another priest is taking my place. You will stay with your godparents. They are very good people and love you. They will care for you as if you were one of their own." He was quiet for a moment and then continued. "As you know,

Paul's wife is very ill and he needs help with his home and with the children. He's willing to pay what seems a fair wage." Father Lawrence paused. He looked exhausted.

"I'm so glad you weren't hurt. And I want you to know that your mother didn't suffer. I think she died very quickly when she was trying to light the stove. When I saw her lying on the floor, I knew there was nothing I could do for her. I'm afraid that there is not much more I can do for you either, Lucia, except bless you, if you would let me."

Lucia immediately knelt in front of Father Lawrence. He raised his bandaged hands over her head and whispered, "Accept the blessing, Lucia, of all the holy women who have helped us see how earth and heaven belong to each other. Accept the blessing of your mother, Sophia, and her mother, Clara. Accept the blessing of Christ's mother, of my mother, Elizabeth, of Angela, and of all the holy women. May you grow up to be like them: strong, loving, and wise; and may you see the Woman, Lucia, as Sophia did, and may you help Her in Her work. I give you this blessing with my whole heart." Father Lawrence smiled. "Someday you will bless others as I am blessing you now."

Lucia had never heard such a blessing. She felt strength and love pour into her and knew they were coming through the priest. Saying, "Thank you, Father," she rose. Aaron grabbed the priest as he struggled to rise from his seat. Lucia was moved and didn't know if it was because of Father Lawrence's condition, or because she had witnessed compassion once more in Aaron.

She was unable to speak to Father Lawrence again that night. Many villagers were waiting to say something to him, to touch him, to express their sorrow and regret. Some were wishing they had approached him earlier with this or that problem or difficulty. Some were thanking him for his kindness. A few wanted to know about the priest who was taking his place.

There were prayers and then a single voice sang a hymn. When people began leaving the church, Lucia did not want to move. When her godfather took her hand, she looked up at him.

"Please, I would like to stay awhile."

Simon nodded his consent, took his wife's arm and joined the rest of the villagers outside. After everyone had left, the church let out a huge sigh and settled into an unencumbered stillness. Lucia blew out her candle and noticed a light coming from the back of the church. Aaron was waiting for her — she knew that. She sat there unhurried, letting the soothing, undemanding silence enfold her. For a few moments she wondered why Sophia had not brought her to church more often. She did not ever want to leave. She heard Simon's voice, apologetic, asking her to come outside, and so she got up and headed to the door. By time she got there, Aaron was gone.

The sun appeared stuck and lifeless, captured within pale tendrils of wintry cloud. Looking around at the mourners, Lucia saw how their breath and the breath of the new priest, Father Ignatius, mingled and hung suspended in the cold air. Father Lawrence's replacement was a slender man of average height, who had an uninspiring voice and manner. As Father Ignatius voice droned on, Sophia's remains were lowered into the ground. The deeper into the earth the body was lowered, the lighter Lucia felt, until her body seemed more like air than anything of substance. When the villagers approached her to express their shared sorrow and sympathy, she startled, astonished by her own lingering visibility.

Catherine and Simon brought Lucia into their home, and

from the first day treated her as if she were their own daughter. She was given her own small room and never was in want of anything. Simon told her that he knew about the arrangements Father Lawrence had made.

"I have spoken to Paul, Lucia, and he understands you may need time before you take on responsibilities for his children."

Although Simon and Catherine were thoughtful and generous, Lucia rarely spoke to them, and they did not know what to say to her to draw her out. Catherine sensed Lucia's pain and often wanted to take her in her arms and comfort her; but when she approached Lucia, the girl would leave. Simon saw the hurt this caused his wife, and counseled her to be patient. He reminded her that Lucia had not spoken to Sophia for many years.

When Lucia went to work for Paul, she quickly sensed the gloom that had settled over his household. It was caused not only by the sickness of Paul's wife, but also by Paul's ongoing conflict with his eldest, a seventeen-year-old young man named Jude, who had a reputation for being an aimless sort, a liar and an indifferent farmer. Several villagers even suspected him of thievery, though there was never any proof of his wrongdoing. Jude, well aware of his notoriety, was always trying to turn the tables by accusing the villagers of spite and small-mindedness. Whenever he could, he tried to impress Lucia.

"I'm joining the army," he told her one day.

"Why would you do that?"

"So I can leave this stupid village. I don't want to farm all my life. There's no glory in it. Maybe girls are happy living in places like this, but it's no life for a man who wants opportunities and is smart enough to grab them when they come."

Lucia tried to hold herself in check, but was too provoked. "I'm not happy here either," she exclaimed tearfully.

"You women – that's what you do – you cry and complain, but you always stay where you are. I'm going somewhere. I'm going to *do* something."

Lucia stopped crying and looked Jude fiercely in the eye. "What if you get killed? What kind of life would you have then?"

"Better dead than stuck here, seeing and hearing only this day after day." Jude swept his arm before him as if to include the whole house, but the whole time he stared up the stairs toward the room where his mother lay dying. Lucia was repulsed by Jude's callous disregard of his own mother. However, she remembered how eager she had been to leave the house when Sophia was ill, and so understood his feelings.

The sadness and anger in Paul's house weighed heavily on Lucia. When she was with the younger children she tried to hide her emotions, but this effort, along with the increasing work, left her exhausted and dispirited. Catherine noticed Lucia's mood and made clucking, worried noises when she thought Lucia could not hear.

Lucia began stopping by the church on her way back from Paul's. It felt like home. No one bothered her or worried and fussed over her when she cried. The church was quiet and rarely occupied. Frequently, she curled up and slept deeply for an hour or two. Once she slept so long that Simon had to come looking for her.

While many of her friends and young acquaintances were bursting with dreams, Lucia felt as if she had already come to the end of a long and very difficult life.

Chapter Thirteen

One afternoon while Lucia was sitting in the church, she heard light footsteps behind her. A few moments later, feeling a tap on her shoulder, she turned to see who it was and saw Jeremiah nervously pulling at his beard.

"Sorry, Lucia, I did not mean to frighten you."

Jeremiah's hair was uncombed and his face was dirty. There were dark circles under his eyes and he seemed sunken into himself. Lucia wondered if he had spoken at all since Sophia died.

"I've missed you, Jeremiah. Where've you been?"

Jeremiah was evasive, telling her only that it had been very difficult for him to be in the village – that everything reminded him of Sophia's absence. He invited her to meet him at their usual spot – the one where they had talked together about words and poetry — and after she agreed he asked after her godparents and inquired whether they were treating her well. When she told him they were treating her very well, he gave her a tired smile. "When we meet, can we talk about Sophia?"

"Oh, yes," Lucia replied. "I've wanted to for so long."

In two days they met at the stone in the meadow after Lucia

had finished her work. Late spring flowers balanced on their supple stems, catching the sun's last rays.

Lucia began. "Did my mother ever tell you about her vision?"

"Which one are you talking about?" Jeremiah asked.

"She had more than one?"

"Your mother saw and experienced a great many things — more than most, I think."

"Well, I mean the one she had when she was still young...after she was hurt by those men...after she came to our village. Did you know she was hurt?"

"Yes. She told me. And I know she hurt a man who loved her. Now tell me what you remember, Lucia."

Lucia told him what she recalled about Sophia's vision of the Woman, grateful for the opportunity to speak of happier things.

"She never told you about it, Jeremiah?"

"No. It surprises me. We shared many things with each other. I think she knows she was remiss, and so she inspired you to tell me what you just did." He closed his eyes and his lips moved. Lucia wondered if he were talking to her mother or to himself.

"So Sophia told you that she saw something she couldn't describe, and that she only knew what she was seeing because she heard the word 'Woman?'"

"That's right."

"And she said she would have gladly died a thousand deaths for the Woman and wouldn't have considered it a sacrifice at all, and that seeing and loving happened together?"

"That's what she said."

Jeremiah sat in silence for a long while and Lucia did not disturb him. She watched the red-winged sun lower itself into the trees while a hawk sat on a bare tree branch, watching for prey. Jeremiah's face glowed and Lucia looked back at the sky, wondering if his face was reflecting the sun's light.

"Thank you for being patient. Few people are, you know. Sophia found it hard, but she got better at it after she found you." Jeremiah laughed, then grew serious again. "What you just shared with me was so beautiful! I want to give you a gift in return. Go gather some twigs and small branches and bring them back here."

Lucia slid off the rock and scoured the meadow's perimeter. When she had an armful, she walked back to the rock where Jeremiah was still seated. "Put them down." She dropped what she was carrying and he jumped to the ground. Grasping a small branch, he made a large circle in the dirt away from the pile. Then he went back to the pile and knelt down beside it.

"Pay attention, Lucia."

"I am."

Jeremiah picked up a twig and used it to touch several others. Sometimes he tried to burrow the stick in the pile until he made contact with a particular one buried under all the others. "This is how we usually use words. One word goes in search of others. Do you see that?"

Lucia nodded.

Jeremiah placed a stick just outside the circle he had drawn in the dirt. He then pointed to a spot on the ground a little distance away and asked Lucia to stretch out on the ground and face the stick. Lucia had a passing thought about getting her clothes dirty, but followed his request.

Jeremiah squatted down and slowly moved the stick away from the circle and toward her. "Imagine the stick is a word and the circle that it is coming from is nothingness. That is how words come to me sometimes, Lucia. And when they approach me like that, I know I don't know what a word really is. And I don't know what the nothingness really is, either."

"Is nothingness like darkness?" Lucia asked, looking up at him.

"A little like that, but very different too. Whatever it is, Lucia, it draws me so powerfully." Jeremiah took hold of the shirt around his chest and pulled it forward. "When I was younger, I thought the best part about being a poet and a storyteller was finding just the right word or phrase. But now what is so much more wonderful is the nothingness where words come from. It is so ravishing, so intriguing. I know what I'm seeing is not really nothing; but I can't tell you what it is, or how I know it's not really nothing, or why I can see it at all."

"Sophia saw nothing, just like you do."

"Ah," was all Jeremiah said.

Lucia raised herself into a sitting position. Jeremiah sat down across from her and closed his eyes. He did not say anything again for a long while.

"Jeremiah," Lucia said quietly.

"Yes, oh...I'm sorry. I drifted off....What did you say?"

"I said Sophia saw nothing, too, just like you do."

"Not exactly like me."

Jeremiah went behind the stone and returned with a flower with small white petals. He placed it in the center of the circle. "Now, come, stand in the circle and look at the flower." Lucia did as she was told. Crouching, Jeremiah reached in, picked up the flower, and lifted it up toward her. "What do you see, Lucia?"

"The flower. And how the flower is in the circle."

"Good. Now where are you?"

"I'm in the circle too." Lucia turned and looked at Jeremiah quizzically. "I'm standing in nothing?"

"Yes, very good."

"The flower is in the nothing, too," Lucia added. "Is the flower a word?"

Jeremiah nodded and sat down on the stone. Lucia joined him.

"Jeremiah, is this about Sophia's vision?"

"Sophia didn't have a vision. She had a revelation."

"Is that better than a vision?"

"Oh, yes!" Jeremiah, using a stick, pointed toward the circle. "When you see words come out of nothingness, it is a little like seeing the stars emerge magically from the darkness, or like watching a child emerge from an invisible womb. And as I told you earlier, this kind of seeing is a vision and a great gift. But Sophia didn't see words coming out of nothing. Sophia heard the nothingness express itself."

"What did it say? Oh, I know. It said it was a woman."

"No. Sophia didn't say *a* woman. She said she only heard 'Woman.'"

"How is that different?" Lucia asked.

"One woman was not meant, nor many women."

"What, then?" Lucia asked.

"I don't know," Jeremiah replied.

"Please tell me something, Jeremiah," Lucia begged.

"Give me a moment, then." Jeremiah walked off. Lucia sat on the stone and watched as Jeremiah walked into the bordering forest and blended into the trees. He seemed to be gone a long while. The first stars made their appearance. Lucia wondered if she should go home – she knew her godparents would be worrying about her. She was about to leave when Jeremiah emerged from the darkening woods. For a very brief moment, Lucia sensed that she was an open space for her friend, a space like the clearing in the meadow or the sky above their heads. She expected he would sit down next to her on the stone, but he stood and kept his distance. His feet kept moving – small steps across the earth – and he swayed.

"Is something wrong, Jeremiah?"

Jeremiah shook his head and made a visible effort to calm himself down. "I asked Sophia about that word 'Woman.' I think she answered me." His head dropped and he was silent.

"Jeremiah?"

"Yes. I apologize. I will try to express what I learned. There's a story. The story of the Garden of Eden. In the garden, Adam had the company of God and he lived among many interesting plants and animals, but the first man was still unbearably lonely. God felt Adam's loneliness as if it were His own. So once, while Adam was in a deep sleep, when his soul had left his body to return home to the spirit world, God took a bone, a rib from Adam's body, healed the wound His work had left, and then fashioned from that bone a new being. For the first time, God does something very carefully. Before, He made things by simply intending that things should be, but, in creating this new being, He exercises great care and compassion. God is acting like a woman here, like a She.

"When this new being was brought to him, Adam saw something we cannot imagine. Our mind and our senses have become so dull, so filled up with the worries and things of this world. But Adam's mind and senses were still keen and open. In the new being standing before him, Adam saw something of the inner essence of himself. And when he looked at her, Adam simultaneously contemplated the secret meaning of the body and the ingenuity of divine compassion.'"

"Oh, Jeremiah, that is so wonderful!"

"Yes, it is…. And Adam called this being 'Woman,' and his deep, unbearable loneliness vanished. By fashioning woman, the Divine learned how to partner with Itself. In healing Adam's loneliness, God first discovered and then healed His own.'"

Lucia suddenly understood something and rocked backward on the stone, stunned. "Eve is the Woman Sophia saw?"

"Yes. But Sophia did not see Eve alone. Sophia saw much more. Eve was only part of it. And remember, Sophia was first enraptured by something she could not talk about at all. There is something even above 'Woman,' something that could not be revealed. What *was* given to your mother in that word, 'Woman,' was a seed that contained everything, a way of understanding everything that will transfigure us with its beauty.

"And you need to remember something, Lucia. Adam called the Woman 'Eve' only after she had reached out to taste what was possible. The Woman was not content to be a mirror. In her innermost being she wanted to begin something new. And so she stretched out to the future even though she knew it meant separation and suffering. And Adam, immediately stirring with life, and seeing the greatness of what she did, called her 'Eve,' the Mother of all the living. Eve is the ever-present ancestress of all women, and she is the life and knowing of men.'"

Lucia began crying. She did not understand Jeremiah's words, but she knew they were true. She also knew they had everything to do with her. Jeremiah moved nearer, his hand hovering over her shoulder as if to touch her, but he stayed his hand and backed away again. Lucia felt agitation and knew it was his. As if to calm himself, Jeremiah quietly began to talk about words, as was their custom. And as he did, Lucia felt as if she was coming out of a trance.

"Words are gifts, Lucia, even if they come to us in ways that appear ordinary. They are the seeds of God's world, the seeds of heaven, and we need to try to listen to them and speak them carefully. Words are precious even to the highest angels."

"I love words and I want to write stories and poems. I want help people see what is beautiful, like you do."

"Whatever you wish," Jeremiah said.

"And can I share what I write with you?"

"Of course, whenever you want and whenever you find me."

Then Jeremiah did something Lucia felt he was moved to do almost despite himself. He approached her again and tenderly held her face in his hands and kissed the top of her head as her mother used to do. Then he bowed and handed her the white flower.

And so Lucia began writing whenever she could find time. Simon gave her ink, pen, and paper, and smoothed a little board she could carry around to write on. Catherine made her a satchel to carry it all in. At least once a week Lucia sought out Jeremiah. When the weather was suitable, they sat in the meadow. When the cold season set in, Catherine and Simon welcomed Jeremiah into their home. They provided Lucia and Jeremiah the uninterrupted privacy their creative endeavors seemed to require. When Jeremiah appeared at the door, he was always presentable, his hair washed and combed. And when he left, usually carrying extra food for later, he always bowed to Catherine and Simon and thanked them.

Lucia once asked Jeremiah, "Why don't you say anything about my poems or my stories? I don't know if you like them or not."

"I will let you know in good time. Beginnings need space and time. We have to let them be."

"Can I ask you another question — something more private?"

"Private? I don't know...."

"I've been wondering how you knew so much about Sophia's vision...I mean her revelation. How did you know all that?"

Jeremiah looked at Lucia without saying anything, but she felt gratitude and joy surge within her and knew it was not hers alone. "You've had a revelation, too. When? That night... when we were talking about Sophia?"

Jeremiah smiled and winked. "Some secrets must wait to be told...even to the best of friends."

Chapter Fourteen

One early Sunday morning in her fifteenth year and nearly two and a half years since Sophia's death, Lucia took up her writing satchel, wrapped herself in the shawl that had been meant for her mother, and went to her favorite place along the river. Rays from the sun were completing their long journeys and were gently tapping on the tiny windows of dew making their temporary appearance on the plants. The cool edge of the air was already softening. Lucia sat on a spongy hummock by a willow tree that fell over the stream like a veil. A chorus of birdsong released itself through the leaves, simplifying to a few notes as the sun rose in the sky.

Carefully, she took out her pen, ink, paper, and writing board and sat there, looking at the blank page, waiting for something to come. Nothing did. She remembered Jeremiah had said this happened sometimes, but it was nothing to worry about since those times were reminders that words were gifts and not to be taken for granted. So she sat and sat some more, but nothing came. Lucia put down the writing board and watched the river.

She was empty and her emptiness was an ache without a cure. Sophia was dead. There had been no word from Father Lawrence, and even Jeremiah seemed to be avoiding any private moment with her. What was it Jeremiah had told her when Sophia was still alive? It was something about desire…he had said that people had to do something with desire. Lucia tried to recall what that was. She threw stones into the river until she remembered. Jeremiah had said that people had to name their desires. Well, what did she really want?

Lucia picked up her writing board, dipped the pen in the ink, and after listening to herself, wrote, "I want to have a great adventure." As soon as she wrote those words she felt as if her heart was leaping inside her chest, sparking a fire. What Jeremiah had said was true: desire made her strong and it could take her somewhere, somewhere wonderful. She could feel it.

She put the board down and stepped into the river, yelping when she felt its coldness spread up her legs. She took off the shawl she had intended for Sophia and held it out, looking downstream. Without thinking, just feeling as if she had to give some sign that she was ready, she placed the shawl on the water and sensed the current pulling at it. Lucia opened her hand and let it go. She watched it float on the water's surface, gathering fallen leaves and twigs and other branches until, twirling in slow circles, it disappeared around the bend.

After the time by the river, Lucia changed. She became light-hearted, so much so that she felt as if she was floating above the village, above the small gossip and the ordinariness of everything. Some days she caught herself imagining she was a princess disguised as a peasant. She would laugh at her own childishness, but she knew her laughter was not wholly sincere. Her new sense of herself even cast a spell on the villagers. They began feeling that her destiny was something greater than theirs. This made them feel less than her, and being respectful, they kept their distance. Lucia mistook their aloofness as proof of a lack of understanding and affection for her. This made her sad and lonely, hungry to be off to new places.

A year after his mother died and despite the fact that his father desperately needed him, Jude left the village to join the army. The villagers were appalled and called him a selfish and ungrateful son, a monster. No one understood why Lucia defended him, but she knew that she and Jude had something in common: ambition and a desire to live a larger life. Jude was willing to leave everything behind for it. He was willing to die for it. She wondered what she was prepared to sacrifice. Aaron wanted a larger life as well. He wanted to change the world. What would happen to him if he tried? Would he be hurt, even killed? And how much would be asked of her if she followed her desire like Jude and Aaron did? She knew that a real adventure had to cost something. She remembered how Jeremiah had said that Eve had become the Mother of all the Living because she reached out for what was not yet, though she knew it would cost her dear. Lucia did not feel especially brave or generous – she knew she was not either. She could only hope that the strength would come as it was needed.

Chapter Fifteen

Lucia would yawn and doze through Father Ignatius's sermons, but when he spoke of Christ's mother, Mary, she would sit up and listen carefully. Father Ignatius spoke of Mary as the new Eve and Lucia knew that Mary, Eve, and the Woman Sophia saw were related, but she could not see how. She wished Father Lawrence was around so that she could ask him, but he was not, nor did anyone know where he lived so she could write him.

One Sunday, Father Ignatius mentioned that Mary, Christ's virgin mother, had appeared to a young girl in the White Mountains in the far eastern part of the country. Lucia was intrigued, and when after the mass she overheard Suzanna, an elderly villager, introduce her sister, Sara, as someone who had recently made a pilgrimage to the White Mountain, she hung around and listened to everything. Sara had spent nearly two months at the shrine and apparently she knew things about the appearances that were not generally known. Lucia noticed that Suzanna seemed embarrassed when her sister shared this and began walking away before Sara could elaborate. Sara, apologizing to her disappointed audience, hurried after her. Lucia ran home and asked Catherine if she knew anything about the appearances.

"Only a little….Our Blessed Mother was supposed to have shown herself to a young girl in the White Mountains a long time ago. The place has since become a shrine and many sick people go there on pilgrimage, hoping for a cure. I think Simon has a distant relation still living up there. From what he's told me, I think she married a man with very strange ideas. He built an inn and Simon's relation managed it. I don't know if she still does… her husband died many years ago. Simon would know."

"What's her name?"

"Judith. I believe her name is Judith…maybe they had children….I don't remember. Why are you asking about all this?"

"Suzanna's sister is here for a visit. I heard her talking about the appearances."

"You mean Sara? She's visiting? Why didn't I know about that?" Catherine looked as if she had just received a deadly blow, but quickly recovered. "You know Aaron has been going to the White Mountains. He works as a guide for groups of pilgrims and makes good money. Helen says he's saving for the university. I don't anyone from here that has been up to the shrine — except Aaron, of course. Who can afford it? Aaron takes the well-off from the larger towns."

"I thought Aaron was still working on the farms. How long has he been going to the mountains?"

"Nearly a year, I think."

"A year!"

"You can't ask him what he knows about those appearances — he's not here. Maybe Jeremiah knows something — or if he doesn't now, he might. Suzanna pays him to come up with a poem for her special family events. A visit from her sister Sara is usually such an occasion."

Lucia longed to hear more. She wondered if Simon's relation, Judith, was still living near the shrine and if she needed help running the inn. She thought it would be exciting to live in the mountains and visit with people who came from distant places. And she thought that maybe in the White Mountains, she would get to see the Woman. When she approached Simon and inquired about the possibility of working at the inn, he told her that as far as he knew, Judith still owned the inn, and he suggested Lucia write to her.

"You thinking about working for her?"

"Yes."

"Well, don't tell Catherine until you're sure. No use upsetting her needlessly. You know how she is."

Lucia searched out Jeremiah. When she found him, he wouldn't look her in the eye. He had been doing this for months now, and it irritated her. She was also annoyed by how he was always picking at his sleeve.

"No, Suzanna hasn't asked for a poem yet, Lucia, and I haven't been able to learn anything more about those appearances."

"Couldn't you find out more for me? Couldn't you talk to Sara about what she knows when Suzanna is not around? Offer to put it in a poem for her."

"You're scheming. It isn't like you. Why don't you ask Sara yourself?"

"She's leaving in a few days and I'm so busy. Please try for me."

"It's that important?"

"Yes. I might go to the White Mountains too. Simon knows someone who runs an inn. Maybe I could work for her."

"You're leaving? Why?"

"Please, Jeremiah," said Lucia, folding her hands together and extending them toward her friend.

"You don't know what you're asking," Jeremiah said quietly, but seeing her shoulders slump and knowing she was disappointed, he said, "All right. I don't like it but I'll do it…for you."

When Jeremiah told Lucia he had managed to speak with Sara, she demanded he tell her everything.

"Well, it *is* an extraordinary story. But that's not entirely true. It seems there are actually two stories: one told by the priests and the other by women who claimed to have known the young girl. In the priests' story, the Virgin Mary appeared to a young girl in a grotto. The Virgin told her that if human beings continued their present course all the nations of the world were headed toward many years of great evil and suffering. She said we could spare ourselves destruction if we changed what was important to us. If all nations first sought to nurture the young, take care of the old, and tend those who were ill, many things would right themselves. As a sign of the truthfulness of her message, the Virgin Mary showed the girl a spring and told her that if anyone bathed in the waters, and if they believed in Her son, they would be given a sign of Her compassion."

"Father Ignatius told us that already. I like that story, but what about the story Sara heard…the one the women told?"

"Sara heard it from a woman who heard it from her great-grandmother, who supposedly befriended the young girl before she became well-known. In this story, the young girl was a shepherdess who grew up frightened of everything. She was so afraid she had trouble breathing and sometimes large clumps of her hair would fall out. One day when she was pasturing the sheep in the mountains, she heard men's voices in the distance. She left her flock to fend for itself and fled into a cave. She went as far back into it as she could beyond a spring, and into a place that was completely dark. Meanwhile, because the men were worried about her, they stood shouting for her at the cave's entrance. When she didn't answer, they guessed she was terrified of them and left. The shepherdess was close to passing out when she heard a woman's voice asking her why she was afraid. The girl said that she felt a woman's presence. She said the woman felt close to her, closer to her than her own beating heart. She said that the woman held her like a mother holds an infant in her arms. The young girl began breathing freely again and felt her body relaxing and becoming strong. The young girl asked the woman who she was.

"'I have taken many names,' the woman said. 'You can call me Compassion.'

"'Where is your home?' the girl asked.

"The woman replied, 'I am everyone's home, but I myself am without a home unless you give me one. Will you be a home for me?'

"'How can *I* be your home?' the girl asked.

"'Work with me,' the woman answered. 'I'm trying to quiet every fear and ease the pain of every creature.'"

"According to the women's story, she told all this to her family and her family's friends. They were all impressed by how different she seemed. When strangers started coming to the door wanting to see the cave, she never refused to take them or tell them her story. One day, a young boy with many sores on his skin went with his family and the girl to the cave. He got thirsty, drank some of the spring water, and then washed his face with it. In three days, when his condition had remarkably improved, his family declared him cured and ran to tell their priest. The priest told the bishop and he ordered an investigation.

"During the investigation, the priests working under the bishop became uneasy about what the young girl said she'd heard from the woman. They tried to put words in the shepherdess's mouth, tried to get her to say that the woman who had appeared to her had called herself Mary, but the young girl insisted that the woman had many names and that she was told to call her Compassion. The bishop and priests lost their patience with the girl and were disturbed by her; she seemed fearless and was not awed by their authority. By this time there was so much excitement in the neighboring villages and towns — and so many examples of genuine cures — that there was no possibility of absolutely denying that something extraordinary was happening. So the priests changed the story to their liking — according to Sara — and their version was the first story I told you."

"What happened to the young girl?"

"In the priests' version she entered a nunnery, lived a brief but devout life, and died after she courageously endured a painful illness. In the other version, when the priests asked her to confirm their story and begin leading processions to the spring, she refused. Even when great pressure was brought to bear on her and her family, she remained adamant. Three devout, elderly sisters, who lived together, took her in. She stayed with them for a little while and then left because she yearned to tell as many people as she could about the Woman who had spoken to her, and because she wanted to work with Her to quiet fear in the world. No one knows what became of her after that."

Jeremiah stopped speaking and waited for Lucia to say something.

"Which story do *you* think is true, Jeremiah?"

"Maybe it is better not to choose. It's unfortunate when people want to hear only one version of something so important."

"I like both stories, but they both can't be true – they are so different!"

"You sound like Aaron. That's something he would say," Jeremiah said, sounding irritated.

"But both *can't* be true."

"Perhaps neither one is perfectly true without the other," said Jeremiah. "Maybe one is for the outer self and one for the inner…. All our stories, even the best of them, are like clothes we put on and wear. And that is a good thing, Lucia. If only one dress was the right dress, if only one story was the right story, you would have so little to wear. As it is, you have a wardrobe fit for a queen, a dress for every circumstance and condition. But remember, what's most important are not the clothes you put on, but the body that lies hidden underneath them."

As soon as he said this, Jeremiah's ears reddened. He grimaced and walked away. Lucia did not see him again for a very long while.

Chapter Sixteen

Lucia had known about a woman's moon rhythm for several years. Soon after she had moved into her godmother's house, Catherine had thoughtfully anticipated her questions about a young female's physical changes, and she and one of her daughters had talked to Lucia about the swelling of breasts, the flow of blood and the new appearance of hair so that when these changes occurred they had seemed natural.

Now that she was sixteen, Lucia found herself more curious about the experience of the other young women in the village. She listened when they talked about the inconveniences of their moon blood, the size of their breasts, or which boys noticed them – and which parts of them the boys were noticing. Sometimes Lucia was intrigued by their talk, other times she was bored or felt out of place. In Lucia's eyes, the physical changes of womanhood, while significant, seemed inconsequential compared to the transformation she had felt when she had named and released her desire for adventure by the river. She never understood why her female friends paid so much attention to what the young men desired and so little attention to what it was they wanted for themselves.

One afternoon when drawing water from the village well, she was joined by a group of young women all eager for gossip and buzzing like bees. She heard the details about a liaison with a young man from a neighboring village and then someone began telling the long story of a woman who was desired by two brothers and could not make up her mind which one she wanted more. Lucia had filled her bucket, and having already heard the latter story, was about to return home. She had taken a couple of steps away from the well when the chatter took an interesting turn.

"If I could have a secret lover, I would choose Aaron."

"Aaron! He's handsome, all right, *very* handsome. But he isn't the marrying kind. My mother says he's a heartbreaker."

"And your mother knows a great deal about having her heart broken...and a few bones besides!"

Lucia was shocked; some of the other girls laughed.

"Who knows what he does when he's on the road? He lives like a monk when he's here, but maybe he acts like the devil himself when he's away. He might have a mistress or two in one of those towns he passes through. Maybe he goes to prostitutes."

"A man can't have a mistress if he's not married."

"I still think Aaron is the handsomest man around here."

"And what good is it? Has he paid attention to any one of us? No. Why not? Aren't we good enough for him?"

"He reads a lot. Maybe I should read more," a young woman said wistfully.

"And would you be willing to travel all the time, sleep on the ground, get rained on, and probably go without food? I *hate* sleeping on the ground."

"You wouldn't mind so much if you were in his arms. Imagine him bending down and kissing you while you were both lying in soft field of grass...." The young woman who was talking dramatically puckered her lips, leaned toward the young woman who had just spoken, and made a loud smacking sound. Lucia laughed with the others, but felt uncomfortable.

"I would wager that Aaron has kissed more books than women. It's because he was raised by that priest — the one who left."

Ten days later, Lucia was sitting alone in the church after work when Aaron strode in. One moment the church was empty — and in the next — so full. Lucia could not focus on anything else. Aaron stood close to the altar, hat in hand, and bowed toward the crucifix. Lucia waited a short time so as not to give her agitation away, then quietly left the church. She had gone only a little way when she heard his voice behind her.

"Hello, Lucia. I hope I didn't disturb you."

Lucia stopped and turned around slowly, afraid of what her expression would give away.

Her entire body warmed and stirred like some beast coming out of long hibernation. It was as if she had never known her own body until now. She felt wetness between her legs and then an ache and a strong pull to surrender utterly. No one had told her that physical desire could be so overwhelming — that it could completely take over. In her wildest fantasies she had not imagined either her body's power or its eagerness to worship another's. It took every ounce of her strength to keep herself still, but that strength was limited and her body's craving, limitless. In the midst of her struggle, a struggle she did not think she could win, she became aware of a completely detached and watchful intelligence that let her know very clearly it was not yet time for such physical yielding. That intelligence tipped the balance more decidedly toward restraint, but even so, she did not risk looking at Aaron directly. She simply shook her head in answer to his question about disturbing her.

"I didn't want to bother you. I haven't been in a church for years. I don't know why I felt the urge to go in and pray just now. Maybe it was because I saw *you* go in.... I'll be leading another group of pilgrims up the mountains in a few days. I know what you must be thinking: *Why does he do this when he himself doesn't pray anymore and when he doesn't believe in the religion he was taught?* I do it, Lucia, because it pays well and it allows me to see the world. I hear you're leaving the village..."

He paused, took off his hat and smoothed it, waiting for her to say something, and when she didn't, he told her that he had met Judith and seen her inn, and that he thought Lucia would like both the inn and the innkeeper. He paused again, and when Lucia did not say anything or look at him, he twisted his hat in his hand and cleared his throat.

"Well, goodbye then. Maybe I will see you up there sometime...unless I'm accepted at the university before..."

Lucia was so surprised that she looked up at him. He leaned forward and was looking into her eyes. His intentness was exciting. She squeezed her hands into fists and forced herself to lower her gaze. He gave her a slight bow, turned, and quickly walked away.

In a daze, Lucia climbed the hill above the church. Her legs and hands were trembling as she sat down on a fallen log and began to take stock. She was surprised that she was not disappointed at how things had gone, and that she felt no fear or embarrassment either. Even more astounding, her body did not seemed harmed by the restraint her mind and will had forced upon it, nor were her thoughts in the least disturbed by her body's passion. It was as if mind and body had exercised each other and were now pleasurably spent and resting comfortably together. She was perfectly at ease and felt joined to everything in a new way. *Timing is important*, she said to herself, remembering how she had known it had not been time to yield to the desire of her body. She was pleased with herself – that she had known what to do in the moment – and pleased as well, because on her own she had discovered something important about being a woman in the world.

II.

Underground Journeys

Chapter Seventeen

Judith had written back saying that she did need help and would be happy to have Lucia come and work for her. Lucia both hoped for and dreaded the possibility that Aaron would be back in time to lead her group. However, a little while before her departure, she heard a rumor concerning Aaron: he had been accepted at the university. When Lucia asked Aaron's mother, Helen, she confirmed it and said he would not be coming back for a long while.

"Aaron's a solitary, independent fellow," Lucia overheard Catherine telling Simon later. "He comes and goes like some wild creature. I don't know if he realizes how much female attention he attracts."

Lucia realized she contributed to that female attention and tried not to feed what seemed like hopeless fantasies, but she was unsuccessful. Thoughts of Aaron preoccupied her, though she knew they were making her less attentive to her godparents and their feelings. She felt guilty sometimes — when she was not thinking about Aaron — because they had been so good to her and she knew they would miss her. She knew Catherine was making a heroic effort to appear cheerful. And Simon, he was moving about the house like a timid boarder afraid to draw attention to himself. He insisted on taking Lucia to the town where she would meet up with the other pilgrims, even though his back pained him and the road was rough. It was Simon's wanting to do this for her that brought home the kindness of her godparents and made her realize how much she would miss them.

The day before she left, Jeremiah appeared at Catherine and Simon's door, his beard trimmed and wearing a new shirt. No one had seen him for several months. He politely declined Simon's offer to enter the house, and asked to see Lucia. When she stood before him, Jeremiah tried looking directly at her, but could not manage it. For the last several months, they had spoken only in passing and when they did speak together, Jeremiah was guarded and self-consciously polite. It hurt and bothered her that his reserve was even more noticeable now that he knew she was leaving. Lucia — who had always felt they were good friends and wanted to remain so — was devastated by his aloofness. She had spoken to Catherine about it and Catherine had asked her if she had ever seen Jeremiah at ease with women, other than those who were young or very old. Lucia understood Catherine's point, having sensed his painful and awkward feelings about women. Her tender feelings and respect for Jeremiah had grown, not lessened, with her new understanding of him. She wished he knew this.

Now he was asking her if she'd meet him by the church in an hour and she agreed she would, though she felt a vague uneasiness and wondered what he wanted to say. As she was approaching the church at the agreed-upon time, she saw Jeremiah standing by the church door, repeatedly shifting his weight from one foot to the other. He stopped when he saw her and asked her if she would be willing to walk up the hill with him. Though Lucia had misgivings, she followed him, not wanting to hurt his feelings and believing he would never hurt her.

At the top of the hill, Jeremiah stepped behind some trees. Lucia hesitated, but then followed him. He turned and came toward her, grabbing her fingers and kissing them, before she knew what was happening, before she could move her hand away. Then he knelt before her.

"Lucia, when you were a child I told you many times that you were the joy of my heart and the delight of my eyes. I say it again, today, because it is still true. But now you also torment me. I can not imagine living without you. I beg you, don't go. When you are around I am not so lonely....You cannot go." His voice trembled, as did his fingers. She pulled her hands away, not as gently as she would have liked. He fixed his gaze on her, silent.

Lucia's legs wobbled. She wanted to sit down, but dared not. She could not think of what to say or do. The naked longing in Jeremiah's expression disturbed her — his need for the whole of her, soul and body. She took a step back and said, "Oh, Jeremiah....No!"

"No," Jeremiah repeated. He closed his eyes, then opened them and looked at her, grief-stricken; the hands he stretched out to her, offering, fell to his sides. "No," he said again, this time with horror — whether it was her horror he was expressing or his own at what he had just done was not clear to her. He threw himself face down on the earth, his arms over his head, and writhed on the ground.

Lucia wanted only to be gone, wanted this not to be. She had wanted to be loved entirely, but never suspected how painful it would be if she could not return that love equally; nor had she known how traits so endearing in a friend would seem repulsive if that friend presented himself as a lover. Inwardly, she recoiled from him, from his intense and transparent need, and she hated and condemned herself for feeling cold and disdainful toward him and for not knowing how to soften the blow of her inability to reciprocate his love. He was a beloved friend and mentor, and all she wanted was for him to disappear.

She wept, frustrated, unable to move, unable to say anything, agonizing. And then he lay still. "Jeremiah," she whispered. She thought he might have died; he was so quiet, but then he moved his head slightly. Hoping he wanted her to leave, and dreading having to face him or speak to him again, she left.

She did not sleep that night. The next morning, she was relieved when Jeremiah did not show up to see her off. However, she feared this meant their friendship was irretrievably lost. Her godparents observed how distracted and tired she was and surmised it had something to do with Jeremiah, but they did not question her about it. As Lucia was saying her goodbyes, Catherine kissed her cheeks and held her to her breast until Simon said that they should be going. Lucia climbed onto the seat of the cart. A gentle rain began to fall and Simon pulled her cloak's hood over her head. When the sun came out again and they stopped to eat, Lucia felt a need to share what had happened with Jeremiah, but it seemed too intimate and terrible to speak of. She knew Simon was curious and suspected something had happened between her and Jeremiah, but she also knew he would not pry. Simon said only how much he appreciated Catherine and what good food she had prepared for them.

When they arrived at the town from which Lucia would set out, Simon helped her down from the cart. After he had handed her the satchels with her clothes, some food, and her two favorite books, he surprised her with a package containing a new pen, more ink, and paper. "For you to write down those thoughts of yours. Send some of them to us."

"Thank you, Simon." Lucia kissed him on his firm, wet cheek. Later she would regret not being more profuse with her gratitude. It was such a thoughtful gift.

"All right then. Catherine and I will keep you in our prayers."

After a few days on the road, Lucia knew that she would always love traveling. It was both exciting and strange. She felt she was finally going forward to meet her future, and her past was rushing to accompany her. The simple act of walking, with no particular task in mind, summoned memories that came and went as swiftly as the high, gray-edged clouds that moved above their heads. She thought first of Jeremiah, for that pain was still raw. She tried to imagine what Aaron was doing, and what it was like being at a university. Then there were memories of Sophia, Father Lawrence, Catherine, and Simon. Occasionally, the image of a scarred face disturbed her. At first, she could not identify it; but then she recalled the man in the barn during the storm and knew it was his face.

Her group was traveling in late summer. For days they walked on a high plain where the earth and the very air were golden. The grass, growing light in its dying, sang in the wind. As the sun set, it planted terraces of color. And when night came, the stars were luminous seeds resting securely in a fertile darkness. One warm afternoon, the White Mountains appeared on the horizon for the first time. Excitement spread among the group. The nearer they came, the more Lucia felt the mountains drawing her.

In the early mornings before the others were awake, Lucia found a place — usually a small rise or promontory — and gazed at the peaks, watching as the rising sun cast a soft nimbus around their ragged heads. In that light, it looked as if the mountains were walking into this world from another world – a world without time.

One morning, a man in his middle years approached Lucia when she was eating her breakfast. He asked if he could join her. Lucia nodded and pointed to a place opposite from where she was sitting. When he offered her a cup of warm milk, she thanked him and took it.

"I've noticed how much you like looking at the mountains," he said.

"They're magnificent."

"They are that."

Lucia had already learned that when one traveled with strangers, the usual rules governing speech did not apply. There was more freedom on the open road. An alliance was assumed rather than carefully constructed.

"Are you ill?" Lucia asked the man. Not all those who were traveling with her were hoping for better health. Some were accompanying loved ones who were sick.

"I have numbness and tingling in my legs, sometimes pain. I'm hoping that bathing in the waters will make it go away. But if it doesn't, I won't be too disappointed. Who knows what's truly best?"

Lucia nodded. "Is someone traveling with you?"

"My two sons. One is seventeen, the other only eight. When I was the age of my youngest, I saw these mountains for the first time. I believe it's your first?"

"Yes."

"The first time is special. I was awed when I saw the mountains as a young boy. I had never imagined anything of such size and grandeur, but while I was looking at them I saw something so much more immense and vast behind them. Next to the mountains, and especially next to what was behind them, I felt infinitely small. And I was not intimidated by this — on the contrary, I was the happiest I have ever been."

"Feeling small made you happy?"

"I did feel small. I was small. But I was also the vastness behind the mountains and so I was even bigger than the mountains. And something moved back and forth between my vastness and my smallness. My whole body pulsed with power. I felt so alive, and so capable of being in this world."

He smiled at the memory. Lucia didn't know what to say, but the man didn't seem to expect a response.

"I hope my sons experience something like that.... Amazing, isn't it — how children experience the deepest truths?"

Lucia drank her warm milk and the man wrapped both hands around his cup and looked off to the side without saying anything, as if he was deciding something. When he turned to look at her again, she noticed how fully he was giving her his attention.

"Why are you going to the shrine?" he asked her. "Have you lost a loved one?"

Lucia immediately thought of Jeremiah. The man saw how she was trying to compose herself. "I'm sorry," he said.

"I'm not going for that reason," Lucia replied. "I'm going to work at an inn up there. I wanted to leave my village."

"You're looking for adventure, then?"

Lucia nodded.

"Good for you. My grandfather used to say that having an adventure was not what people thought. He said it's not about something happening to you that you didn't plan for; it's about finding out that *you* are nothing like what you assumed or imagined yourself to be."

The man's older son came wandering between them to say that the younger son was looking for him. Lucia handed him back his cup. The man excused himself, wished her a good day, and left. Lucia watched him go, watched as he put an arm around his son, and wondered what it would have been like to have had him as a father.

Chapter Eighteen

The snug, solid, comfortable inn was situated in a cluster of other such inns catering to the more well-to-do, about three miles from the shrine. It was smaller and less elegant than the others, but seemed to do a brisk business. Lucia had heard that Judith's energy and warm hospitality had much to do with its popularity.

Judith was busy when she arrived and Lucia was directed to wait for her in the parlor. Lucia took the opportunity to look around the large, cozy room and soon noticed a strange figurine standing on a ledge directly above the hearth. It was of a kneeling woman, about two feet tall, with large, starkly outlined eyes, gazing sideways. In addition to her slender arms, she had golden wings that stretched out and curved upward, until their tips almost touched. Lucia went over to it and gently ran her finger over a wing.

"That is Isis, the greatest of the Egyptian goddesses. She is the holder of the key of life, protector of the dead."

Lucia turned around and saw a tall, well-built and well-dressed woman with a self-assured and confident air.

"You must be Lucia. Welcome."

Judith approached her and took Lucia's hands in hers. She gave Lucia a steady gaze, making Lucia feel as if she was being closely examined. "Come sit down on the sofa with me. You must be tired."

They sat on the sofa and Judith asked Lucia about Simon and Catherine and about life in her village. Then she talked about the inn and the sleeping arrangements. She told Lucia that for half the year she had four employees and when things slowed down in late fall and winter, she would let one go. She said that one of her long-time employees had left to tend her sick mother and the temporary employee had also gone, finding the work too demanding.

"Before I show you the rest of the inn, do you have any questions for me?"

"Yes. Could you tell me more about that statue...about Isis? I've not heard about goddesses before."

"Of course. I'm pleased to see you are curious. Isis was both the sister and the wife of Osiris. She was a partner, equal to him in every way. When Osiris's body was torn to pieces by his enemy, she gathered up all his members and made him whole again. They didn't speak of goddesses in your village? Was it a Christian place?"

"Yes," Lucia replied.

"Ah. You must think it odd then – having a goddess here in a holy place of Christendom. But my husband, Richard, didn't think so. He believed that the honor and devotion given to Mary, especially in this place, was the Christian way of worshipping the goddess. It was hard to argue with him." Judith stood up. "Now let me show you the rest of the inn and your room. You should settle in and rest for an hour or so and then come down to the kitchen and join Martha and Grace and myself for afternoon tea."

When Lucia entered the kitchen, Martha, Grace, and Judith were nearly done with their tea. Martha and Grace introduced themselves. They seemed very amiable and comfortable with each other. She understood that they roomed together. Martha got up and poured Lucia some tea.

"I'll go over your duties tomorrow, Lucia," Judith said. "Is your room sufficient? I know it's small. It will seem even smaller when I hire another woman."

"It's larger than I'm used to and the bed is quite comfortable."

"I like to think this inn has rustic comfort," Judith said. "It doesn't have many fine things, but I've learned to see that as an asset. Coming here helps the rich believe they are willing to sacrifice their luxuries for the sake of their souls, but of course I try very hard not to let them suffer any inconvenience. So they enjoy themselves here and don't feel overly guilty about doing so."

Martha and Grace laughed and looked at each other. Judith placed a sweet biscuit on a plate, handed it to Lucia, and asked if she wanted more tea. "You passed my test, Lucia."

"What test?" Lucia asked.

"Excuse us, Judith," Martha said. "Grace and I have something to do before dinner."

"Yes, yes. I know you two have heard this before. Go on about your business."

Martha winked at Lucia; then she and Grace left.

Lucia looked at Judith. "The test was that statue of Isis above the hearth. I watch how my guests and new employees react to her. If they are bothered, I know I have to be careful about what

I say and more meticulous in how I care for them. If they say something witty or curious, I know they're more open-minded and will probably enjoy lively conversation. If they don't notice my Isis at all or pretend they don't, I know they're more easygoing and will be forgiving of small lapses of my attention."

"Does it work?"

"You'd be surprised by how often. If my statue really shocks them, I pretend ignorance and tell the offended person that it is only a sentimental gift left by guest for whom I once had a passionate regard. Only rarely does someone guess that I mean my husband!"

"Your husband gave the statue to you?"

"Oh, yes. He was quite a collector. He was an importer and fairly successful at it. But I always knew it was just his excuse for roaming about the world in search of artifacts and images of the goddess. Now it's time for me to start dinner. Someday, when I can afford it, I need to hire a cook."

Lucia soon learned that Judith relished problems, believing that there was no problem too small or too large for her to solve. Judith's attentive and active mind consistently evidenced a remarkable ability to organize a multiplicity of details and demands. One guest told Lucia that Judith's talent was comparable to the great astronomers who had looked upon the vast scattering of stars and ordered them into constellations. Judith was always busy. And though she anticipated tasks, she was never frantic or rushed. She met the next moment confident that it would bring further proof of how things always worked out in the end.

While she was not bossy and always respectfully delegated tasks to her workers, she had to know everything and have an opinion about everything going on in their lives. After working for Judith for a couple of months, Lucia found this trait disconcerting and annoying. For a time she tried simply avoiding Judith when she wanted privacy and tried not to be obvious about it. Judith, however, was too discerning and asked Lucia why she was avoiding her. Lucia decided to be honest and told Judith she was bothered by how Judith invaded her privacy – how she insisted on knowing everything.

"Well, I apologize. I'm aware I'm too persistent and ask too many questions. My husband, Richard — God bless him — used to say I was a force of nature whose equivalent was found only in a bad storm at sea."

After this confrontation, Judith made clear attempts to curb her curiosity and she was successful at it – nearly half the time. Lucia's admiration of Judith grew steadily. She noticed how attentively Judith listened and how she knew how to ask the question or interject the brief comment that would keep a conversation, flowing. Watching her speak with the guests, Lucia knew that Judith was picking up clues about them. Judith had an understanding of people. From little things they let drop, she gleaned their likes and dislikes, and being a sound and caring businesswoman, she would translate that knowledge into action if she could. From admiration came affection. Lucia began feeling fond of her employer and thoroughly enjoyed conversing with her. Judith also seemed to enjoy it when they could take advantage of a few free moments to talk.

Once as they were preparing dinner together, Lucia asked Judith "Was your husband a Christian?"

"How can I answer that? Richard believed in *his* version of the Christian religion, one I doubt the priests would approve of.

He kept journals. You are welcome to read them if you like. Some day I will show you his collection. It takes up an entire room."

"I would very much like to see both."

"I will put one of his journals by your door this evening. I think my husband would have liked you and wouldn't mind if you knew his thoughts."

"I think I would have liked your husband too," Lucia said. "The way you talk about him makes me feel he was an adventurous person!"

"That's one word for it. I found him exasperating. Sometimes I wondered why I stayed with him. He loved me — I know he did — and he appreciated women as few men do, but he didn't have a domestic bone in his body. He wasn't content unless he was leaving me to travel to some exotic place. And when he was at home, he was preparing for his next trip or doing research on the artifacts he brought back with him. I was more lonely, Lucia, than most unmarried women."

Lucia thought of Aaron.

"It was wonderful," Judith continued, "for those first years before the children came, when I could go off with him; but then someone had to stay behind and raise them, and it wasn't going to be him."

Judith raised the lid of a pot and took a whiff. She seemed to be savoring a memory. "Once, when he returned, I told Richard that while he was off searching for his goddess he left one in his own home who ran his household, raised his children, helped him with his various enterprises, and endured his long absences. Did he beg for forgiveness? Say that he would stay at home for more than a few weeks at a time? Oh no! He knelt before me, took my hand and kissed it. 'You are indeed my Hestia,' he said, 'the goddess of my hearth.' What could I do with a man like that?"

"Did you love him?"

"Passionately…. But we were so different. He loved it best when things were stirred up and disorderly. He made huge profits, then lost everything — and did both with equal ease. He said when we lost the goddess we lost a sense of creative chaos and the needful play of opposites. When he was in a certain mood, he would make dire predictions about the future. He said that unless we acknowledged and served the goddess we would find ourselves living in a drab and dreary world. That was my husband.

"When he died, how I suffered! The thought that I would never welcome him home again made me fall to pieces. I let things go. I would spend days in bed or staring out the window when I could. I even consulted mediums, hoping for a message from him even though I had considered them all frauds before. I lit candles and would sit still for hours before his collection of goddesses, hoping to sense his presence. But nothing brought him back. Sometimes I felt he must be laughing at me. And once I had the clear impression that he believed he had won, that I finally had to admit that there were many things in this world that couldn't be domesticated. *That* brought him close to me again."

That night Lucia was about to extinguish the candle by her bed when she heard a quiet knock. When she opened the door, Judith was standing there in her red velvet sleeping gown. "Richard's journal. I almost forgot. Have a good night."

Tired, but curious, Lucia slipped into bed, drew up the covers, and randomly opened the journal. Richard's script was easy to decipher. It was bold and large and all the letters carefully rounded. She would read just a page or two before falling asleep.

The learned and powerful men of the church have created subtle distinctions between who Mary is and who or what God is. Their mental contortions are nothing more than a poor attempt to keep her in a lower place. But the people, knowing better, have continually worshipped her in their hearts. The people's love for Mary has proved more powerful than the fear of the church's ingenious gatekeepers. Time and time again the theologians have had to yield to the people's intuitive reverence.

When I studied the history of the church, I found that scholars were always inventing new doctrines, doctrines that acknowledged yet one more quality that sets Mary apart from the rest of us. What a clever strategy! By giving her an abundance of titles, but refusing to say she is divine, the theologians thought they could both appease the people and protect their one-sided and self-serving idea of God. And their strategy served another purpose. It attempted to separate us from Mary by telling us that she was a privileged being: the only mother of Christ, the only one besides Christ who was completely pure. But Mary continues to show herself to us in ways that clever definitions cannot keep up with. She is our mother, our sister, our daughter, our beloved. She is not separate from us, from our sin and suffering, our grief and hope.

I am planning on purchasing an inn near one of her shrines in the mountains. My wife and I will extend hospitality to those who come seeking her aid. Something numinous has happened in that place. I sense it everywhere, particularly in the cave itself. I have no doubt she has been there. And I sense she will be revealing more of herself soon. Her power and beauty and imagination will make all our dreams of perfection appear small and silly — the dreams of infants....

Lucia's heart pounded in her chest and she felt on fire. A

guest had once regaled Judith and her employees with stories of how he had circumnavigated different regions of the world. Lucia felt that Richard had circumnavigated stories of the goddess his whole life and had come close to finding the passage to a new world. Something like lightning flashed inside of her and she recognized that what mattered most was not that she have and enjoy a private vision of the Woman, but that everyone and everything that breathed and moved on earth see Her. That would be the most fulfilling adventure of all.

Chapter Nineteen

There was a great deal of work involved in running an inn, even one managed as efficiently as Judith's. Lucia was busy from sunup to sundown six days a week, and was worn out by the time she went to bed. Martha and Grace had worked for Judith for nearly twelve years and seemed to have found a rhythm acceptable to their employer and not overly taxing to their constitutions. Lucia tried to learn to find her own rhythm by observing them. For three years, Lucia ended up sharing a room with a succession of seasonal workers, one of whom was Lea, Judith's daughter. Lea was married, but couldn't get along with her husband. She lasted about four months.

"She's strong-minded and stubborn, like her mother," Judith told Lucia. "Her husband's a decent man. His only flaw is that he has his own ideas about things and won't go along with hers all the time."

Judith treated her help more like family than servants. Because she worked so hard and was involved with everything, formal distinctions between employer and employee were not the rule. When Lucia took time to entertain the children that came to the inn, Judith had only good things to say about it even though it meant additional work for her.

"You make me realize that I've neglected the young ones. I *do* like hearing a child laugh, especially one who is ill."

Lucia was free on Saturdays and would use most of the day to write letters to Catherine and Simon, read – Richard had also collected many books — or hike in the mountains. When she finished the journal Judith's husband had written, it inspired her to start her own. What she did not do during her free time was visit the shrine. She did not understand why, but she was afraid — afraid that something might happen there or be asked of her that she was not prepared to give. When Judith asked Lucia why she didn't go, she told her she didn't know; and though Judith was not happy with the answer and started probing and speculating, she never found out anything more.

After Lucia learned her new tasks and settled in, she had hours, sometimes days, when she was overwhelmed with homesickness. She had wanted to leave the village and live another life. However, she felt a growing appreciation for what she had left behind. She was in a new place and was always meeting interesting people, but she missed her village. And there were other days when she felt stuck in a cage and knew that going back to the village would not change that. Both the village and the inn would always be too confining. She wanted to expand, soar, and penetrate every part of the world. And she wanted something even more, something she could not define or name. She began wondering if she would ever be happy with her life, if she would ever feel it measured up to her desire.

On her days off, she started roaming farther up the mountains. She discovered many caves, each with their own shape, character, and smell. She was always afraid of them, of the wild and poisonous creatures they might shelter, of the ease with which she could lose her footing and possibly fall into some even darker hole, and of the power she sensed around even the most insignificant cave. But while she was afraid, exploring them gave her a sense of freedom. During her third summer at the inn, she found the courage to venture deeper into them, and in each one she would sit for a while. Caves were like the "nothing" Jeremiah had talked to her about. They appeared empty, but when she sat in them she sensed a presence, a palpable will, as if the silence that filled them was not an absence of sound, but a being that was unlike anything that walked the earth.

One day, a summer storm quickly blew in when she was high up, near a pass. Thunder drummed against the peaks, reverberating down the mountain. While little rain fell, lightning struck the ground close to the summit, sparking fires in the low, dry brush. Lucia sought shelter in one of the caves. Its opening was narrow and slanted downward, but once inside she felt air moving about as if she had entered a large space. The floor was relatively smooth, and scattered with small bones. The roots of a solitary, ancient tree hung from the cave's ceiling. She sat on a rock, near the cave's mouth, her knees drawn up. Even with eyes closed, the intense flashes of light were blinding. Thunder struck like a mighty wave, unveiling the cavernous nature of the world. She fell into synchronous rhythm with it. She was the center of an explosive, focusing power that diminished peacefully as it was drawn back toward an equally powerful silence. She lost all sense of time.

When she opened her eyes again, she saw grey and white clouds playfully nudging each other in a field of blue. It was hard to believe there had been such wild weather. She knew she had to get back before nightfall, but her legs refused to obey her.

She had been frightened by the storm, more frightened than she realized.

Sitting there, something pressed in upon her, a vague image of a scarred face and then the frightened visage of a young boy. She knew she was remembering the time in the barn, the time before Sophia found her. Then, for the first time, she remembered what she had felt: fascination, repulsion, fear, powerlessness when she could not help the boy. She recalled feeling guilty as she ate his bread because she did not know what else to do and was afraid of the man with the scarred face. She remembered her terror at being left alone, how she had run after the man when he left the barn despite how he had treated her.

She did not want these to be her first memories, but when she tried remembering further back, straining to recall her parents' faces, she came up with nothing. What had happened in the barn was the beginning of her remembered self. She wondered what that meant. Jeremiah had taught her that the beginning of every story was important, that it already contained the middle and the end in a secret, hidden way.

Thinking about this, she got up from the rock, left the cave, and scrambled down the mountain. By the time she arrived at the inn, night had fallen. Judith was entertaining two elderly gentlemen with stories of her husband's travels. When she saw Lucia come in, she excused herself and followed her into the kitchen. "Are you all right?"

"I'm fine."

"You certainly don't look it. You're wet....You've been crying."

"Don't worry about me. I'm sorry I interrupted you." Lucia tilted her head toward the elderly gentlemen.

"Those two? I'd wager they're grateful for an opportunity to gossip about me. Let's have some tea; then you should get to bed."

That night as Lucia lay in bed unable to sleep, she heard voices. She got up and went to the open window and leaned out a little. The sky was clear and the moon was rising. The two elderly gentlemen were conversing under a tree while enjoying their pipes.

"If you ask me, it is not seemly or safe for a young woman to be out alone after nightfall."

"She's young and the young are foolish. I blame the innkeeper. What a lamentable lack of good judgment!"

"And propriety."

"I have to say that Judith manages things quite well, but I agree with what you said earlier; she's a bit forward and free in her manner and her taste in statuary is abominable. I'm sure you know what I mean."

The next morning after the gentlemen left, Lucia told Judith what she had overheard and the two of them shared a long, irrepressible laugh at the expense of their oblivious guests

Chapter Twenty

Lucia was preparing a light lunch for those staying at the inn, when Judith came into the kitchen, sat a letter on a table, and stood waiting for her reaction. "It's for you."

Lucia examined the writing. "It's another letter from Catherine." Lucia looked at Judith.

"Go on. Read it. I'll finish here."

Lucia took the letter up to her room. She smelled it before opening it. Enclosed in Catherine's letter, she was surprised and excited to see one from Father Lawrence. She read the letter from Catherine first.

Dear Lucia,

Thank you for your last letter. Simon and I are proud of you and happy that you are doing what you wanted and seeing more of the world. To be honest, I could never understand why people, especially young people, have such wandering feet when they have a good home and loved ones who care about them, but it seems there are many kinds of people on this earth of ours. Simon and I have always preferred to remain close to hearth and home, but others choose differently. I am glad you get along well with Judith and that she treats you fair, but remember we are your family and you will always be welcome.

Simon is well, although his back continues to bother him. Jeremiah is not his usual self. Few people ever see him regularly, and it has been a long time since he's shared a poem or told a story. I wonder where he goes off to when he disappears. Simon is keeping an eye out for him. As soon as he has the opportunity, he will invite him to dinner again. I know he isn't eating well.

Helen told us that Aaron is doing well at the university and has been working for nearly two years with a bookbinder. He is making a good wage and sends her money every few months. He has no plans for returning soon. I must say this was disappointing news to several young women, who for all their complaints about him like him very much and had their hopes up. "Good for him," is what I say if anyone bothers to ask my opinion. He was always reading and wanting to share his thoughts with Father Lawrence, who said that he had a fine mind. Maybe those learned men in that big city will see that we country people also have intelligence...

There were a couple of pages describing several conflicts and dramas going on in the village. And then:

I am enclosing a letter to you from Father Lawrence. It was apparently misplaced, then sent here. I imagine it is old news now. I myself received a brief letter from him in the same package your letter came in. He mentioned that he wants to return to the village now that his health has improved. He has been waiting for permission from the bishop. I hope it comes soon. Father Ignatius is a decent priest, but he is not Father Lawrence. Father Lawrence always made me feel worthy of God's attention. Not many people in this world make you feel that way.

You know Simon and I keep you in our prayers. We speak of you often, wondering what you are doing and whom you have been meeting since we last heard from you. We miss you terribly. Simon wanted to know if you have enough ink and paper. I think he would be tempted to travel all the way there if you said you were in need of anything. Speaking his feelings is a difficult thing for Simon, as you well know, but he loves you dearly.

God's peace be with you.

Lucia next opened Father Lawrence's letter:

My dear Lucia,

I have remembered you and Sophia every day even though I have not written. And for not writing, I apologize. My health and my state of mind made it difficult, but that is really no excuse. I cannot explain why I did not write as I thought about doing, so many times. I can only ask your forgiveness for not doing so.

You must be a lovely young woman by now, and I hope you will show me the kindness I did not show you, and will write to me and let me know how you are and what you are doing. My memories of you and Sophia and our times together are among my most treasured. Every time I saw you both, I felt as if I were waking up from a long sleep. I suppose, without being aware of it, I imagined God as a fairly serious man, like myself. You and Sophia helped cure me of that erroneous and unhappy idea.

It has taken a long time, but my overall health is steadily improving. This I attribute to the influence of two people, a husband and a wife I began living with about a year ago. The wife, Maria, has a younger brother who is a priest. When he became ill, he went to stay with Maria and her husband Gabriel until he recovered. Maria's brother recognized early on that she and her husband had a gift for healing, and after he was made a bishop, he sent other priests who were suffering from various maladies of body or soul to stay with them for a time. I am one of a long line of fortunate priests. I went through a very dark time after Sophia died. Something I had struggled to contain and manage for years, something that Sophia had helped me with through her sheer presence, nearly overwhelmed me. My heart and mind took time to heal.

Maria and Gabriel live many miles from the nearest village, just off a road that winds along our northern coast. They raise sheep for wool and raise most of their own food. Their cottage sits on a slightly elevated grassy table of land, about a mile from the sea. There is a path, well-worn by hooves and shoes, leading to a small, sandy cove. At first, I would go down there only to stretch my legs and was too restless to stay for more than a few minutes. I preferred helping in the garden or working with the sheep. I needed to feel useful. But after a time, I would spend many hours on that little beach with one of their dogs, named "Sabbath." When Sabbath tired of chasing sticks, he would sit near me while I listened to the surf and watched the giant seabirds fly in low over the waves.

When I first arrived, I learned that I was expected to bless the animals every Sunday. On my first Sunday, I went with my hosts to the sheepfold and proceeded to raise my hand to recite a blessing over the entire herd as I had done in the village. But no, that was not what they meant. I had to bless each one individually. And then I had to bless the dogs, the cats, the chickens, the cow, and the geese. It took almost an entire morning!

It took me awhile, but I pieced together their story. They told me they felt a special kinship with me, because of what I had told them about Sophia. This is what I learned. They were once well-off and lived in a large home with their three children. Two of Gabriel's brothers lived fairly close. One night, hearing that the elder brother had just returned from a long trip, they left the older daughter in charge while they went to visit him. A fire that started in an adjoining house quickly spread to theirs. The children were sleeping upstairs in their room. None survived.

Maria wanted to die. She considered poisoning herself, but her faith and her love for her husband kept her from doing it. They decided to leave the city and make a new life. With much hard work — work that left them too tired to remember and too exhausted even to speak much to each other — they built up the place where they are living now. After many years, they had a house and a farm, but Maria said it was not really a home. Though they had a little more time, Maria kept up her habit of not speaking. For Gabriel, the silence between them had become unendurable. He had no one to talk to — only the travelers that would stop by. Gabriel wanted to sell their place and look for a new place close to his brothers and their families, but Maria did not want to discuss it. Maria knew her silence was hurting Gabriel, but feared the greater hurt she would cause him if she spoke; she was afraid of the words that would come pouring out.

One evening, during supper, I described how Sophia wandered about at night. Maria told me she had done the same. "I would walk for hours after nightfall," she said, "while Gabriel sat here alone waiting for me, worrying about me. I had to do it. Sometimes when I walked, I could feel the earth crying. Her sobbing rose up through my feet and legs and into my womb. And sometimes the grief and longing in my empty womb was pulled down, taken from me, held in the womb of the earth." She said this went on for a long while.

Then Gabriel shared this, or something like it: "Just when I thought I could bear the silence no longer, something happened. One evening when Maria got up to go outside, a strange impulse came over me. I stood up and without asking her permission, took her hand and went with her. We walked for hours without speaking. I just held her hand until she broke down in tears and I did the same. We felt weak because of our grief and lay down on the ground. We stayed there on the ground the rest of the night, her hand in mine and the earth holding the both of us. We were awake when dawn came. When the sun rose, it felt like its light and warmth was coming from inside of me and when I looked at Maria I sensed she felt the same thing. I kissed her and then we both kissed the earth. After I helped her up, she said that she was ready to live again."

Between Gabriel and Maria there is a great deal of grief, peace, knowledge of the earth and its creatures, an intimate knowing of each other and care for the stranger — so many wonderful and deep things. Their house is a home in the fullest sense of the word and they graciously open it to others — not only to priests like myself, but also to any traveler who happens to stop by.

Once, a young, poor scholar, a student of languages, stopped by and asked for food. Gabriel insisted that he not only share dinner with us, but that he stay the night. The next morning, I asked the scholar if I could accompany him on the road for a while; I wanted to stretch my legs. He readily agreed.

"They are such hospitable people," the young man said when we were out of Gabriel and Maria's hearing. "I rarely have come across such kindness."

I told him why I was staying with Maria and Gabriel and that I had found the kingdom of God in that little place, and in that marriage. The scholar turned to me and gently said, "You should not say, 'kingdom,' when Jesus meant 'queendom.' In Aramaic, Hebrew and Greek, the word that is translated as kingdom is of the feminine gender. Therefore, the better translation is queendom."

I confess I laughed at the young man's earnestness, perhaps I was remembering my own seriousness when I was his age. He mistook my laughter as an insult. Wanting to make amends, I quickly thanked him for such valuable knowledge and asked him how he would describe "queendom" and what difference it made. He told me he would need to tell me his story to answer that.

"I have always been good with words," he said. "When I was still living in my father's house, I would help him write his speeches. He was a government official charged with convincing others of the inevitability of the last war. I enjoyed the challenge of bringing people around to a point of view they had initially opposed, as well as the even greater challenge of winning my father's admiration.

"When I was twenty, I fell in love with a strong-willed girl, the daughter of one of my father's friends. Soon after we became lovers, she told me that she was not comfortable with what I was doing and she asked me if I truly

believed what I wrote or if I was only trying to please my father. I laughed at her, and when she asked me why, I remember saying that she was lovely, but being a woman, she didn't know how the world was run. What a condescending fool I was! I will never forget her reply: 'That's not how the world is run; it's how it falls apart. What is deepest in your heart — that is what you must bring out into the world.'

"At that moment I was invited to enter the queendom, Father."

I told the young scholar that he had given me much to ponder and asked what had become of their relationship and the young woman. Tears flowed down his face, tears he did not try to hide.

"She left me and married another man. She had given me time to make a choice and change my ways, but by that time I had grown greatly attached to the favorable opinions of others, to the money and power. Only after losing her did I begin to free myself from all of that."

I asked him what had led him to study languages and although I already had some idea, his answer struck me, "You should understand, Father…. I'm making atonement."

Since I am feeling better, I sometimes spend a couple of weeks in town. I have been assigned to a parish and given the task of visiting the sick and dying when I can. On my rounds, I have begun touching the trees as I pass. I put out my hand for dogs to sniff. I see the beauty of people without having to look for it. I used to tell Sophia how I was tormented by ambition and a sense of uselessness. I still am…after all these years, after all that has happened; but I see my struggles differently now and I do not lose hope.

Before I close, I ask your prayers for Aaron. I know you have heard that he was accepted into the university and is doing well. I should feel proud of him, and I do. He has a keen mind, a kind, responsible nature, and good intentions; he still wants to make the world better. He also says he has lost his childhood faith and doesn't know what he believes in anymore. I tell myself that this is probably a passing stage, but I fear for him…

Chapter Twenty-One

S now knee deep covered the ground. The inn was nearly empty. Most of the travelers seen on the road were hardy young men, many of them soldiers, and typically none of these could afford to stay at any of the inns. They would room together in the plain and simple lodge run by an order of religious brothers whose mission was to provide hospitality to pilgrims and to the poor who had no shelter in inclement weather. During winter, the inn was thoroughly cleaned, linens were mended, accounting books checked, and the inventory of needed supplies was updated. Judith let her fourth helper go and gave her other workers extra days off.

On one such free day, Martha and Grace talked about shopping even though it looked like it was going to snow again. They invited Lucia to come along, but she felt like staying in the inn with a good book. She was reading by the fire in the parlor when Judith sat down next to her. Her face was flushed and her arms were full of newly mended towels.

"I've been promising to show you my husband Richard's collection. Would you like to see it now?"

Lucia immediately shut the book she was reading. "I would love to."

Judith set the towels on her chair, grabbed the set of keys always about her waist, and felt for the one that would open the largest room on the first floor. It faced south, had only one small curtained window, and was always locked. With the key in the door, she turned toward Lucia. "There are only two others besides myself and my daughters who have ever seen this room. You'll see why."

Judith pushed open the door and stepped inside with Lucia right behind her. Lucia smelled stone, clay, old paper, and the wax of many candles. She sensed a presence, much like the presence she felt in the caves. When Judith lit lanterns positioned on either side of the door, Lucia saw how the walls were covered with paintings and tapestries, while the room contained dozens of small wood and stone pillars on which stood artifacts she couldn't quite make out. Judith went around and lit several more candles, then stood by Lucia's side, waiting for her reaction.

"I've never seen *anything* like this before."

"It *is* amazing...they're from all over the world. I fixed it up like this after Richard died. I thought it would help me keep him around, but of course it didn't. Go on, look...touch whatever you want."

Lucia went up to one of the large artifacts. It was a rock carving showing a faceless woman with ponderous breasts, huge hips and belly, and holding a crescent moon up with one hand. She ran her fingers over it and over a nearby statue. It was only a few inches tall, was also faceless, and around the head were seven rings. Although small, she appeared solid and powerful. She noticed a large vase. Painted on it was a woman seated on a throne with a green snake in the background. Beside her was a horned man, also sitting on a throne, and between the man and the woman, a tree. There were several statues of women with bird-like heads, a woman with a fish in her womb, another who cradled a bear cub, and several who were giving birth surrounded by leopards or lions. One carving showed a snake emerging from a woman's womb while simultaneously it suckled at her breasts.

Judith took her over to a corner. "This is one of my favorites."

Lucia saw a carving of a woman sitting on a throne. She was holding a child while both she and the child were enfolded by two spiraling snakes. Lucia next inspected the paintings and tapestries on the wall. Many of them were of Adam and Eve and the Virgin Mary. There was a woodcut of the Virgin standing among sheaves of wheat. Lucia had seen similar likenesses in church. Hung among the more ancient depictions of women and goddesses, they seemed to have new meaning. Between the paintings and tapestries were female figures of dark wood standing on stone pillars. They were seated on thrones with a child seated or standing on their lap.

"The Black Madonna," Judith announced following her gaze.

"Why are they black?" Lucia asked.

"Richard said black was for the depths of the mystery of the heavens, for the dark soil of earth, and for the sorrow and woe of all creatures."

Lucia knelt down on the floor and sat back on her heels. She quietly wept, overcome by the knowing that emanated from everything in the room, a knowing that resonated with an inner knowing of her own. "Why did your husband collect all of these? What was he going to do with them?"

"Come to the parlor. We'll stoke up the fire, have some tea, and I'll try to explain. First I have to find a letter." Judith rummaged about among some loose parchments on a shelf. "Found it."

When they were settled comfortably in the parlor, Judith took a sip of tea and smoothed her skirts as she always did before a guest.

"I don't know what Richard was planning on doing with his collection, but I'll have to do something. I know that what's in that room is too precious to be kept locked away. And you asked why Richard collected the images. I think it was because of his grandmother."

"His grandmother?"

"His father's mother. She came to live with his family when he was only three. She was a well-traveled woman with a good head for business. I heard she had a few affairs, smoked, and could speak several languages. She had only one child, Richard's father, and never had any interest in raising him, but she was very interested in Richard for some reason. When she came to live with them, Richard's parents were going through very difficult times. They were in debt and were always fighting. His grandmother helped them out financially, and Richard used to say that things started to calm down in the house even though he never recalled his grandmother interfering or saying anything. Many times Richard overheard his parents speculating about why his grandmother had moved in with them. They wondered if she was ill, lonely, or simply feeling the aches and slowing down of advanced age. Richard believed that none of these was the reason.

"My husband asked her once why she had stopped traveling and whether she missed it. She told him, 'I haven't stopped traveling; I have just changed conveyances. I've outgrown ships and carriages. Now I travel in stillness and silence, and the more I abandon myself to them the more astounding and exotic everything appears to me.'

"When my husband told her that everything wasn't so wonderful, she took a piece of parchment and with a needle made a small hole in the middle of it. She took him into the garden and put the paper about a foot away from his eyes and said he had to look at the garden through it. She asked him what he saw. Richard told her he couldn't see anything. His grandmother took the needle and made the hole much bigger and asked again what he could see. Richard told her he could see the color green. She told him, 'You can see everything around you if the hole is big enough. It all depends on what you're looking through.'

"Richard asked his grandmother if she was ill. He told her that he had heard his parents talking about her. His grandmother told him that she was very well and more important, so was the world. Richard was surprised by this because his parents, particularly his father, spoke about the world as if it was diseased and ruined. But his grandmother held up the parchment and reminded him of the lesson of the needle. She said, 'It all depends on what you're looking through.'

"My husband said he could tell his grandmother everything. She would listen to his dreams and tell stories to his friends. She never cooked and rarely sewed, and would spend long hours just sitting still in the garden or walking in town. Richard told me that wherever she was, she brought out the magic in whatever was around her. He said he would take one of his toys and put it by her feet or ask her to hold it. He swore, even as mature man, that his toys came alive in her presence. She died when Richard was eleven and it seemed to him as if the hub of a wheel had cracked and all the spokes had flown in different directions. I believe that all the traveling he did later and his obsession with the goddess was his way of remaining in his grandmother's presence. She was the goddess in his life, the mystery he was always trying to understand. Sometimes the thought crossed my mind that Richard married me because I reminded him a little of her. He denied it, swore up and down it wasn't so, but the more he insisted the more I knew it was true."

"Did he ever have a vision of the goddess or of Mary? Did she ever speak to him?"

"Not that he ever said, but Richard felt she was always directing his thinking and that knowing her was something like breathing, something natural and close." Judith dabbed at her eyes. "Something remarkable happened to him near the end. There's something about it in his last letter, the one he wrote just before he set sail to come home. He was lost at sea...seven years ago next month." Judith pulled a letter out of her skirt pocket.

My Dearest Hestia,

I hope you are well. I am in Egypt. I went to see the apartment where my grandmother lived for several months. Although it was very small, an entire family of six was living in it. The wife remembered hearing my grandmother sing when she was a little girl and recalled how loudly she would laugh.

The other evening on the way to a tavern for supper, I almost stepped on a snake. It hissed and I jumped, but calm was restored when we acknowledged our respective boundaries and inwardly I wished it good evening before walking away. When I got to the tavern, I remembered how afraid I was of snakes in my youth and how surprised I was when I had learned that my grandmother was not afraid of them. I remember trying to convince her how my fear was quite reasonable, because even the priest said that the serpent was the one that brought evil into the world and made Adam and Eve suffer. This made my grandmother shake her head. "How can one have adventure without suffering? How can one learn to walk carefully if there is no danger?"

Then Grandmother talked to me about snakes as if they were tutors she admired. "Take a good look at the snake, Richard. It has no legs or feet, but it still moves. By concentrating its energies and by patiently working its way back and forth, it can get to where it wants to go. The snake has no arms or hands, but because it is intelligent and courageous, it can defend itself. It will often alert other creatures to its presence, but if its warning is not heeded, it will gather up and direct all its energy and strength and strike at its enemy. Even a man who is practically sleeping on his feet will immediately give a snake his full attention. These would be reasons enough to admire the snake, but there is another, and perhaps the most important of all: the snake renews itself continually. It can slough off what is old and create a new skin, a new way of sensing the world around him. And the snake does that in such a way that the pattern of the old way is clearly seen."

I know my mental meanderings are not always welcome, but I have to tell you, Darling, that for many hours I sat in the tavern and recalled my various encounters with the serpent. Remember the first statue of the goddess I brought home, the one where she holds a snake in each hand? When I first saw it, I was nearly overpowered. I didn't know why. It seemed to have a meaning beyond my grasp. I remembered how little sleep I got in the next few weeks as I tried to work out in my mind the source of the power in that little statue. I never did completely. But tonight I understood that the serpent is the symbol of the mind and its power. What my grandmother admired in the serpent could be said to exist in some fashion in the mind. When I saw this, I was humbled by what the ancients knew. They appreciated the power and magic of mind, but they did not perceive mind as the ultimate power. She was the ultimate power. She had the serpent in hand; she wielded it. In one carving, the serpent is emerging from Her womb and suckling at Her breast, showing us how She is the origin of mind and it is Her substance alone that truly nourishes it.

I recalled many more things, but I will write no more about these matters tonight. I know they tire you...these enthusiasms and reflections of mine...I am grateful that you have put up with them patiently these many years. Few would have done so.

I miss you dreadfully. I am more homesick than I ever remember being.

"Lucia, I won't read the next part. It's private and I would only bawl if I read it...but here is the last part."

I woke early this morning after a night of strange dreams and wandered about the narrow, winding streets, thinking. When the sun came up and lit the tops of the roofs, it was very beautiful. It kept becoming more and more beautiful until I was completely dazzled. And then I suddenly knew my grandmother was with me. Her presence was quite vivid and distinct, but not separate from the sunrise or its effect on me. My heart overflowed and I called out to her. I shouted her Christian name; my breath mingled with the sound of it. And then she was gone.

My beloved wife, I have been given so much. I have been honored in a manner that makes me conscious of my lack of personal merit, while freeing me from all concern about it. I am anxious to see you again. Perhaps, like my grandmother, I am finally ready to settle down. What will the goddess teach me then?

As Judith read the last letter from her husband, Lucia felt the stirring of a great, unseen company in the room. She asked and was given permission to copy the letter except for the page Judith wanted to keep private.

Spring came and guests began arriving. Lucia wanted to continue talking at length with Judith, and Judith had a like desire, but they were too busy for leisurely conversation. Lucia had shared many personal things with Judith during the less busy winter season and had told her stories about Sophia, Father Lawrence, Catherine, and Simon. She also spoke in great detail about Jeremiah; however, she never shared with Judith what had happened between them the day before she left her village. She also told her what little she knew of Aaron, for Judith had told her that the young man had impressed her.

Judith listened attentively to her stories and was especially intrigued by Sophia. She eventually coaxed Lucia into telling her the story of Sophia's dream and how the Woman had revealed Herself to her mother. Afterward she told Lucia, "My husband would have loved speaking to Sophia. I always thought he was the only one searching for the goddess, but I was mistaken." Conversations like this strengthened their friendship. Though Lucia and Judith made an effort to keep a semblance of an employer and employee relationship, it was impossible to hide their special affection for one another.

As the work increased again, Judith hired a fourth worker, Louisa, who would prove so capable and friendly that she was not let go even for the winter season. Lucia liked Louisa very much and they got along well together. Louisa was a gifted seamstress and it was a pleasure to watch her working. Calmly, Louisa would watch her fingers as if she entirely trusted their intelligence, and to Lucia they did seem intelligent; it was as if her hands could see – they moved with such skill and grace.

"In ten days, a special guest will arrive," Judith announced one morning as they were preparing breakfast in the kitchen.

"Who?" Martha asked.

"Esther."

"Esther! It's been years! Is she well?"

"She's nearly blind, but otherwise I hear she's quite well...given her age."

"Lucia, Louisa...you'll love Esther. She has such stories," Martha said.

"The best ones are about herself," Grace piped in.

Later, Judith told Lucia that Esther was one of the few whom she had allowed to see her husband's collection.

Bad weather delayed their anticipated guest for a few days. When Esther did arrive, Lucia observed how quickly she settled in and was impressed with her confidence and ease, despite her blindness. Esther would simply ask her maid or the staff for assistance, graciously thank the helping person, and then clearly signal that she could safely be left alone.

One Saturday, when Lucia was free and about to leave the inn for a walk, Esther, who was sitting in the parlor drinking tea, heard her and called out, "Is that you, Lucia?"

"Yes, do you need anything?"

"No, no. I was just going to ask if you weren't busy or going anywhere, if you wanted to have a chat."

"Certainly," Lucia said, sitting down carefully next to her.

"Judith tells me you've seen her husband's collection. What did you think?"

"It was so extraordinary! What did you think?"

"It felt like I was in the presence of a remarkable, wise, and very interesting relative whom my family had kept secret."

Lucia laughed. "It did feel like that."

"Judith tells me you haven't been to the shrine.... don't be upset with her...she didn't offer me that piece of information, I wheedled it out of her when I was asking about you. Of course it's your business, but if you would permit me, I would like to share something with you." Esther held out a plate of biscuits to Lucia. "Would you like some?"

Lucia took one. Esther smoothed her skirts.

"People know this place is special, but many of them don't really know why. I didn't when I first came here. It is not about the cures — they do happen, but not very often. It's not about repentance — despite what the priests say. And it's not about being cared for or even about caring for others. The secret of this place, Lucia, is suffering. Not suffering we're supposed to overcome or avoid, not suffering as a punishment we're supposed to accept, not suffering as evidence of our evil nature, and not suffering we're supposed to cure, but suffering as a mirror – a mirror that lets us see ourselves. For suffering to be a mirror we have to keep it out in front. It can't be forgotten, put behind us, nor will clutching it to our bosom work — which is what I did for years and years.

"Maybe you haven't gone to the shrine because you know that suffering is a mirror and you are afraid of looking into it. I don't know that of course, and it's not my place to say.... But I want to tell you that there is nothing more freeing than looking in that mirror. I know what I'm talking about. I've experienced it. I would like to tell you the story of my first visit here, if it is all right with you."

"Please," Lucia said eagerly.

"Good. Well...I first came here many years ago...when my eldest daughter was eight. She was born with a cleft palate. I thought her the ugliest child I'd ever seen." Esther took several sips of tea. "I wondered if there was something repulsive, something evil in me that had come out in her. I knew it was ridiculous, but it didn't change my feelings. It pained me to be around my own daughter. My husband was wealthy and he offered to pay someone to care for her, and that's what we did. I thought when she was out of my sight, I would feel better, but I didn't. Then I thought that after I had healthy children, I would, but that didn't happen either. Before I made the pilgrimage here, I had two more children…sons. For many years I rationalized that my boys would be tormented and held back by the presence of their sister, so I never mentioned her and told my husband not to either.

"The guilt never left me. It ate at me and my marriage like a maggot, compelling me to seek forgiveness. That's why I came here. I wanted forgiveness, but I didn't really want to change the arrangement my husband and I had made; I just wanted to be able to live with what I had decided."

"What happened?"

Esther laughed. "I thought it was possible to go on as I had been doing, but then I met the vendor."

"Who?"

"I didn't even find out her name. I was on my way to the church when I noticed a foreign-looking woman selling rosaries on the side of the road and stopped to buy one. They were made of dried petals from different flowers and had a wonderful scent. I took my time. I fingered and smelled many of those rosaries and asked the vendor if she made them herself. She nodded but looked disinterested, and that made me uncomfortable. I've always prided myself on my ability to engage others and to please them.

"I asked her if she sold many rosaries and she shrugged. I thought maybe she spoke another tongue and didn't understand me, but then she asked, 'Are you buying or not?'

"'I will,' I told her, 'but I want to find just the right one.'

"The vendor laughed and I felt uneasy again. 'And how will you know when you find the right one?'

"'By how I feel when I look at it and when I touch it,' I told her, thinking she would be impressed. Instead she snorted and laughed; I remember thinking she sounded like a pig. People turned to look at us and I was very embarrassed.

"She said, 'You put a lot of work into picking out a little rosary!'

"I remember saying, 'I want to be careful about how I spend my money. What's wrong with that?'

"She looked at me very intently...I felt she could see right through me, and thought she might be a gypsy or a witch. She asked whom I was buying it for. I surprised myself and told her I was buying it for my daughter. She asked me how old she was and what flowers she liked. I told her that she was eight years old and that I didn't know what kind she liked. She shook her head and her lip curled up and she told me, 'You need to look and feel every rosary very carefully, but you don't know your own daughter's favorite flower!'

"At this point, I broke down in tears. The vendor didn't pay attention to them, so I cried louder. Then I remembered I was in public and tried to collect myself. Stupidly, I asked the vendor if she had a mirror I could borrow. I wanted to see what I looked like before going into the church. The vendor laughed so hard *she* started crying. I remember her saying over and over, 'A mirror, she says. A mirror! She wants a mirror before she goes and sees the Virgin!'"

"I was ashamed, so ashamed — and I realized then that I was being ridiculous and started to walk away, but something drew me back. When she saw me coming she shouted at me, 'Don't come back unless you want to buy a rosary.' As she was repeating this, I knew I was returning because I didn't want her to think me a complete idiot, even though I *was* being a complete idiot.

"'I was going to buy one, if you had been kind.' I was yelling at her because I was angry. 'A little kindness would help your business!'

"'Kind,' she said, 'I'm trying to sell rosaries. Kindness is between family and good friends. You're a stranger.'

"When she said, 'You're a stranger,' calm came over me. I knew she was right and I knew that I was not only a stranger to her — I was a stranger to myself. I saw very clearly that I had been acting like a madwoman — not just then, but for a long while; and I saw just as clearly that I knew I was acting like a madwoman because there was an unshakeable sanity inside of me. I remember looking at the vendor as if I was seeing her for the first time. I calmed down.

"'I'll buy two rosaries,' I told her, 'one for my daughter and one for myself. You pick them out.' The vendor chose two rosaries, wrapped them in a soft cloth, and handed them to me.

"'I have rosaries for sale, but no mirrors,' was the last thing she said to me.

"As soon as I bought the rosaries, I turned around and went back to the inn. I didn't have to go to the shrine...all I wanted was to see my daughter, and I did, as soon as I returned. My husband and I brought her home after we had prepared our sons, and every night she falls asleep with that rosary I bought for her wrapped around her hand."

"I had clasped suffering to my bosom and nurtured it for years. Nothing could pry it away from me until I came here. The vendor managed to wrest it from my grasp long enough for me to catch my own reflection. What I saw was terribly unpleasant. I saw a woman who made molehills into mountains and who expected other people to do the same. I saw a crazy woman who went around creating suffering. But I also saw the eyes I was seeing all this with…and they were extraordinary."

Chapter Twenty-Two

Inspired by Esther, Lucia decided it was time for her to see the church and the cave where the woman had appeared. She told Judith she was leaving, and was headed out the door when she ran into a messenger delivering a small package with her name on it. Inside was a letter from Catherine and two thin, planed boards bound together with twine.

My dearest Lucia,

We are well here. Simon sends his love. He has a harder time getting around, but refuses to hire anyone to help him. He says his back hurts whether he is sitting down or working, so he might as well take care of things. Jeremiah finally showed up and Simon invited him to dinner. He looked ill and ate like a bird, saying he had grown used to eating very little. He was grateful for everything and seemed in good spirits. After dinner, he handed me his gift to you. Simon and I guessed it was some of his poetry. Over dinner, he asked about you and seemed embarrassed whenever he said your name. He has great affection for you, and as is his way when his affection concerns a woman, he carries his regard like a millstone. I feel for the man; so does Simon.

Simon reminded me that Jeremiah had come to see you the day before you left, but he never returned to see you off. I will not ask you what happened when he met you at the church — that is for you to tell or not tell. I only hope he did not burden you, and if he did, I know he never would have deliberately done so.

There are changes in the village since the beginning of March. We have had to pay a special tax. Knowing our reluctance to contribute when we cannot see the benefit, the magistrate brought eight soldiers with him to help convince us. He says that the tax is necessary, that the country is being attacked and we need to defend ourselves. But you know how we are in the village. Unless we can see enemies with our own eyes or hear them with our own ears, we will never quite believe they exist. So far no one has refused to pay, but there has been a lot of grumbling and haggling. The magistrate looks quite worn out!

When the Bishop was here, we asked him what was going on. All he knew was that people living near the border are fleeing into safer areas, into the countryside. Even though we are far away, Father Ignatius believes we will see refugees before the war's end. He hopes nothing worse befalls us, that none of our young men will be forced to fight. When the soldiers leave, they will take three of our young men with them. They volunteered – like Jude did. Why are young men attracted to danger like moths to flame? War fever is spreading quickly like the plague. Have you heard news where you are, and are you affected in any way? God protect you. God protect us all...

Lucia was disturbed by Catherine's report. She remembered how a guest, a colonel in the army, had mentioned to Judith several months previously that war was a possibility. While the colonel obviously said what those in charge expected him to say — that war would be used only as a last resort — his shifting glance and his twirling of his wine glass expressed contrary thoughts.

As Lucia ran her finger over the twine that bound together Jeremiah's gift, war receded into the background. Untying the twine, she lifted up the top board carefully and saw a beautiful piece of parchment on which a circle had been drawn in gold leaf. In the center was a white flower with five petals, a flower like the one he had given her when they had spoken about Sophia's revelation. It was pressed and held in place with a little piece of wax. No letter, no poetry…only this wordless message. Lucia held it in her lap, wondering how he had been able to procure the parchment and especially the gold leaf. As she looked at it, shame and worry dropped from her like ripe fruit from a tree. What remained was love, bare and sorrowing, in unconfused poignancy.

Chapter Twenty-Three

As Lucia was setting off to the shrine a second time, Judith suggested she wait and go with the guests. Hearing that rain was likely, they had ordered a carriage. Lucia thanked Judith for her consideration, and said she wanted to go alone.

"Well, you'll need a warmer cloak, then." Judith took her own off a hook and wrapped it around Lucia. "If you can't get back before dark, stay at the hostel for women and children. We will muddle along without you tomorrow. You'll have to tell me all about it....You know that, don't you?"

Lucia laughed and told Judith she was planning on it. The road was empty when she stepped outside. Looking up at the storm clouds, she put the cloak's hood over her head, got a firmer grip on her small satchel containing some food, and hurried off. After a half mile, drops began to fall which quickly turned into a downpour. Catching sight of a three-sided shelter set back from the road, Lucia ran toward it. Underneath the roughened beams were other bundled-up people. They stood quietly together, watching the torrent.

"It doesn't look like it'll let up for a while," one man said.

A young girl asked, "Mum, does the Holy Mother Mary bless the rain?"

People began chuckling and passing along what she had said to those who had not heard. An older boy stepped outside the protection of the shelter. Holding up his arms, he spun around. "If the Holy Mother blesses the rain, then we don't have to go to the shrine. A miracle can happen right here!"

Lucia had started moving to join the boy, when she heard a sound of deep displeasure. The boy stopped spinning, but remained standing in the rain. Lucia had checked herself and, smiling at the boy, stuck her hand beyond the shelter. The boy's father, a stocky gruff man, shouted, "Get back in here and stop embarrassing me. You're too old to be playing around like that."

When the boy returned, his father cuffed him and said, "Show more respect." Lucia caught the boy's eye and smiled again, trying to encourage him, but he hurriedly looked elsewhere.

People were murmuring and pulling nervously at their clothes, as if they had been the ones rebuked. Though it was still raining, several headed toward the road. Lucia looked up, and seeing how the sky was clearing, ran to join them. No one greeted her, but she felt welcome, embraced by their silence. They walked slowly, at a pace comfortable for the young children and elderly, moving as one body toward the church.

When the group arrived at the church steps, Lucia hung back. A young woman turned around and looked at her. No one else noticed. Lucia stood on the bottom step, her heart racing. The massiveness of the church overwhelmed her. She felt that its size was a reflection of the enormity of the mystery that awaited her inside.

Remembering what Esther had said, she forced herself upward, heart pounding. Entering the church, Lucia was struck by the sheer number of people – there must have been nearly a thousand. They were kneeling on the cold, damp floor; many had rosary beads entwined in their fingers. The air vibrated with the steady, flowing sound of their prayer; Lucia felt her own body vibrating with it. She stood at the back of the church, not sure about what she wanted to do or why she was there.

Above and behind the altar, Lucia noticed an immense painting of Mary, rendered in an artless style. Her arms were outstretched and her head bent as if she was taking in all the misery and heart-ache of the world. At her feet were a cave, a stream, and a young female supplicant, while above her head was a dove surrounded by rays of light. From Lucia's readings of Richard's journals, she knew the dove was an image of the Goddess. She stared at this painting and thought about it, trying to distract herself from vague and conflicting pulls she had begun to experience.

One by one the people standing around her began to kneel when they saw how crowded it already was in the church. Lucia alone remained standing. A young girl kneeling near her looked up and whispered that there was room next to her. Lucia thanked her but remained standing. The longer she stood, the lonelier she felt — and the lonelier she felt, the more determined she was *not* to kneel. Kneeling down only to ease her sense of loneliness seemed beneath her. And yet by not kneeling, she felt as if she were saying that all those kneeling around her were beneath her, and she did not feel that way.

Lucia felt a tug on her sleeve and turned to see an old woman, who signaled her need for assistance by pointing to the floor. Lucia knelt down first, then gestured for the old woman to lean on her shoulder, holding out her arm in case the woman would need it to steady herself. The woman tottered and nearly lost her balance, but Lucia held her firm. Safely on the floor, the older woman gave Lucia a toothless grin, then took out her beads and made the sign of the cross. Lucia smiled back, then closed her eyes.

She was kneeling, but she could not pray. Although she had often gone to the church when she still lived in the village, she had never asked God for anything. She had always believed that God already knew what she needed and that suffering was something she was either meant to bear or learn to overcome. She had never asked God or the Virgin to free her from it. So even though the concentrated force of prayer entered her and moved through her like a river in flood, she did not add her own prayer to it. Instead she simply continued to listen to it, and while she listened she heard how the people's lament was full of longing. She remembered what Jeremiah had told her about the stream of longing that flowed through the world and now she knew that at some point the stream of longing and the stream of lament intermingled. For a moment she felt the sorrow of the world gushing through everyone in the church like blood from an open wound. *When will the wound heal?* she asked herself.

The old woman was tapping her on her shoulder. Lucia, not knowing how much time had passed, stood up and helped the woman to her feet by firmly grasping her under an elbow. A young man, seeing what she was doing, had rushed to help pull the older woman up.

As she left the church, Lucia noticed that though the sun was obscured again; beams of light streamed through the clouds. Children were jumping up and down the steps. One bumped hard against her, quickly apologized, and ran off. Vendors had set up their booths near the church and were hawking their wares. Lucia wondered if the one who had helped Esther was among them. She looked at their faces and glanced at their wares until she learned that any sign of interest made them focus all their energy on her. She asked a nun for directions to the cave and was told to follow a group of pilgrims just a little way ahead.

Hundreds of people were at the cave when she arrived. Men, women, and children were arriving on the backs of strong men and women, or in handcarts pushed by others. Only the wealthy few arrived by carriage. A long line snaked around the entrance. Nuns were examining and ministering to those in immediate physical distress. They led the ones they judged the most ill to the front of the line and no one argued with them – not even those who were in the habit of receiving preferential treatment. Lucia stood quietly, wondering where all the people had come from and what stories they had to tell. Despite their weariness and the long wait, almost everyone looked expectantly at the faces of those leaving the cave. Lucia also looked, noticing that though those leaving seemed relieved and lighter, there were no celebrations of cures, no shouting about any miracle.

As she came closer to the entrance, Lucia felt her knees grow weak and it became harder to swallow and breathe. It was as if she was a small child with a storm coming, and it was not the cave she was approaching, but the barn. She wondered why she was nearly overwhelmed with fear and shame and thought that maybe it was because something would happen in the cave that would definitely cut her loose from that horrible time. Hoping for something like this, she stepped inside. Immediately, she felt a draft and heard rivulets of water flowing over small stones. The cave was larger than she thought and was lit by many candles. Crutches and letters hung on a wooden wall lodged against the rocks. Behind tall screens, people were putting on or taking off shapeless tunics. When it was her turn, Lucia took off her clothes and put one on. It was rough but light and was still damp from a previous pilgrim. She was given a burning candle.

A priest blessed her, and a nun led her further into the cave, near the spring. The nun then took her candle and gave a signal to another woman. The woman was barefoot and wore a garment similar to the ones worn by the nuns, but she had no veil. She took Lucia down some brick steps that went into the spring. A half a dozen women were already in the water. It smelled fresh and was very cold. Lucia's teeth started to chatter. Lucia knelt down while the woman dipped a ladle into the water and poured it over her head. It was over so quickly. The woman led Lucia back up the steps. When there was room for the two of them to stand together, the woman turned toward her, took her hand, turned it palm up, and tenderly placed her own on top of it. At that moment, Lucia remembered how she had felt for the boy in the barn. She had not helped him, but she knew he was afraid and she had not wanted to eat his bread. At the beginning of her story, she had been truly powerless, but she had also been compassionate. Lucia raised her hand with the woman's still on top of hers and bent down and kissed her hand, because the woman's compassion had served as a mirror of her own. The woman whispered a blessing.

A nun appeared, handed Lucia a damp towel and her candle, and led her back behind the screen. It was all over so quickly.

When Lucia stepped out of the cave, it was twilight. Two men were preparing to lock the iron gates barring entrance into the cave until morning, and were starting to turn away pilgrims. They said good night to her and wished her a safe journey. Lucia got directions from them to the women's hostel.

A full moon lay between the mountains, like a pearl. Lucia often stopped and gazed at it, remembering Sophia. It was late when she finally arrived at the shelter. An elderly woman kindly directed her to a small cot among sleeping women and children. Lucia felt grateful for all these women and for all the women she had met that day. After pulling a scratchy woolen blanket up to her chin, she quickly fell asleep.

Just before waking, Lucia had a dream. She was standing on the little hill above the church in her village. It was twilight. The evening star was visible and the trees were turning into shadows set within the deep blue of the sky. Sophia stood by her side. The two of them did not say anything. They simply watched as the barest sliver of a crescent moon rose just above the curve of the hills, its hollow side turned upward like a bowl or shallow cup. After a while, Sophia raised her arm and pointed to the new moon. Lucia looked more attentively and saw how the moon was surrounded by a perfect circle of stars, stars that had not been visible before. She knew they were the sign of a full and perfect protection.

Suddenly, the sky was full of bright, blazing stars moving at incredible speed toward the new moon. Lucia knew that the beauty and power she saw and felt would kill her, and though she was afraid, she was willing to die. And then as if a lamp was being deliberately dimmed by another's hand, the innumerable and brilliant lights slowed and muted; the mobile and incandescent stars became nothing more than cold, grey smears lying motionless in a colorless sky. Lucia had gone from witnessing the radiant and unbearable splendor of an onrushing life to being the witness of an inconceivable slaughter.

Why had her awareness dimmed? And who had decided it was necessary? Grief-stricken and wanting to know who wielded such intimate power, Lucia turned to face Sophia, but her mother was gone.

Being alone with the weight of what she had seen was intolerable. Lucia walked through a village, knocked on doors and asked if anyone had noticed anything unusual. No one had. Lucia was shocked by this. Eventually, a child opened a door, invited Lucia in, and told her that the old woman who lived in the cellar might be able to help her. Lucia made her way through a long tunnel and into a large cave that was lit up, not by candles or lanterns, but by the radiance of a woman seated on a simple wooden chair. It was Sophia, and Sophia was looking directly at her. She appeared firm but kind as she often did when she was alive —only more so of both.

"Mum, something wonderful happened and then something horrible."

"I know."

"I couldn't stand it. I thought it was going to kill me."

Sophia held out her hands, palms up, and stretched them out to Lucia as if she was giving her something. Lucia noticed they were no longer bent and swollen.

"Learn from Her," Sophia said. "Let Her teach you how you can grow into Her. Then you will be able to bear Her light." Lucia knew immediately Who her mother meant.

Chapter Twenty-Four

Lucia was at a table in the parlor copying a passage from Richard's journal into her own.

"Aren't you tired?"

Lucia jumped. She had been so focused on what she was doing that she had not noticed Judith coming into the room. "What time is it?" she asked Judith.

"It's late. Everyone's in bed. Would you like some warm milk, or tea?"

"Tea would be nice." Lucia gathered up the journals and followed Judith into the kitchen.

"Which part of Richard's journal were you copying?"

"The part where he wrote about the mind."

"Would you read it to me while I make the tea? I enjoy hearing what my husband wrote. Would you like a sweet roll?"

"Yes, and thank you."

It took Lucia only a moment to find her place. She cleared her throat and began:

We are still ignorant of the mind and its capacities. We use it as if it existed solely for our survival, defense, and benefit. In doing this, we severely restrict and confine what is naturally unlimited. The mind is a fully fitted ship, but we treat it as if it were only cargo space. We keep it safely anchored near familiar shores and work hard to protect its contents. We do not dare unfurl the mind's sails or take it out to the open sea, and therefore we never discover its possibilities and its higher functions.

But what if we did? What if we realized the mind must serve something greater: it must serve Her. And it must serve Her without demanding the reward of comprehending or possessing Her. This is what raises the anchor and steers the ship out of its narrow harbor. And when we recognize that She is the heart, the heart of all possible worlds, and that it is the heart that must steer us toward understanding Her, then the magnificent sails of the mind are released, and open out to the carrying winds.

A mind that is used only as a cargo hold, and not as an active member of Her fleet, eventually becomes infested. Such a mind is dangerous, no matter how strong and clever it is, or how much it holds. It will do and permit great evil on this earth while believing its intentions good and just. It will seize upon what is beautiful and marvelous, the inner workings of the world that She has shared with us, and will use them to destroy what it cannot control and to reshape what it has never appreciated. I would despair, anticipating the suffering the mind will unleash in Her world, if I did not have the certainty that the time of Her revelation is drawing near....

Judith poured the tea and sat down across from Lucia.

"Richard could be very grim."

"I think he was being hopeful."

"Why were you copying that part of my husband's journal? What happened at the shrine?"

Lucia told Judith about the boy who twirled about in the rain and how she had felt an impulse to join him, but didn't. She had been afraid and had only stuck out her hand to feel the rain.

"Richard would have gone out and danced with that boy…
and me…if I had been there watching him, I would have been
so embarrassed and so proud. I never knew there were two such
contradictory creatures inside of me until I met Richard. My
heart and my head were never as easily joined as his."

"I have felt that too — how my heart wants to do one thing
and my mind another. When I entered the church, my mind didn't
want me to kneel down and pray like everyone else, but my heart
was moved by the prayers of all those people."

"Sometimes don't you envy those who believe that all they
have to do is show the Virgin Mother their pain? I've never had
faith like that. Have you, Lucia?"

"No, not like that. But I think I have faith."

"Richard's faith wasn't so simple either, but I don't think it
was a lesser kind. Now, go on. Tell me more."

Lucia continued her story. When she got to the part about her
dream, Judith rubbed her arms. Lucia asked if she was cold.

"I'm all right. It's not the cold; it's your dream making the
hairs on my arms stand up. I'm a practical woman and don't worry myself about dreams, but some part of me knows that dream
was special. So why were you copying that part of Richard's journal? Was it because of your dream?"

"Yes. I was wondering what my mother meant about learning
from the Woman and becoming like Her. In my dream, Sophia
didn't say. I think Richard knew something about it."

During the next weeks, Lucia thought long and hard about
her dream and all that she had experienced at the shrine. Thinking
sometimes frustrated and exhausted her, but at other times she
felt she was close to unearthing a treasure, and that drew her to

think more. When she was not working, she read and reread several of Richard's journals and made many attempts at writing a letter to Jeremiah. She wanted to thank him for his priceless gift, but the right words did not come. One morning she woke up knowing what she wanted to say, and quickly wrote a letter.

Dear Jeremiah,

I must first thank you for what you sent me. It moved me greatly. It was a silent gift, but it spoke so eloquently of the greatness of our friendship, a friendship I will always value as one of my most precious.

Since I have been here, I see how much suffering is part of life. Affliction is not something we can escape. Even Sophia continued to live a hard life after her wonderful revelation, and I know that you, despite your beautiful visions and your poetry, also find life difficult. I know I have been loved dearly, but I still feel lonely and I get so restless. I feel as if I am confined in an unbearably small space, as if I were a large bird in a very small cage.

Here, I have seen how much other people suffer too. I've seen children with tumors, heard the stories of women who miscarried, and helped men who once provided for families but now cannot even remember their names. On the road I have seen soldiers who move about like puppets with broken strings. And in the church there are hundreds of people pleading to the Virgin for relief. So much suffering!

You know how I have always loved stories. My employer has many books — most of them are her deceased husband's. Among those books are several about Parzival. He was a knight who went in search of the Holy Grail and ended up in an unknown land after many adventures. The Grail was there and it fed people in a marvelous way, but the men and the women suffered greatly — their king especially. He had a wound that tortured him day and night. Parzival could have ended their sorrow if he had only asked why the king suffered, but he was silent. He had been told that asking too many questions was not courteous. And so Anfortas, the king, and his loyal people had to suffer many more years. And Parzival did as well until he returned and finally asked the question: "Why are you suffering?" When Parzival finally asked the question, joy returned to the kingdom. The story does not say what the answer to the question was. After so many pages, that surprised me. But maybe that is the point: there is no answer. So why is it important to ask a question when there is no answer? And why does just asking the question end the suffering? I have been thinking a lot about that and it has given me many headaches.

From what I have seen, most people who come here do not ask why there is suffering, or if they ask, their heart is not in it — I can tell. Most people simply want to feel better. They want better lives and they believe the Virgin Mother can help them. I have been with them when they prayed and I have never experienced anything like it. The closest I have come to praying like that is in doing what you suggested. You told me to say what I desired and then let it go as far as it wanted. You told me it was important to keep watching it. Remember? I've done that. Is that prayer?

I think about Sophia often. And when I think about suffering I think about her revelation and how she said when she heard that one word, "Woman," she was willing to die a thousand deaths. She knew something that made pain and suffering seem like nothing. Will the Woman have to reveal herself to everyone to end our suffering? Will it take all of us praying together like the people do here at the shrine? Or will we all have to ask why we are suffering, like Parzival did in the story of the Holy Grail? What will end it?

I always wanted adventure and knew that it came with hardship and suffering, but I never knew how much. Sometimes there seems to be no balance. The suffering is so heavy and I have no sense of adventure at all. After reading about Parzival, I realized that for many years it was the same for him. Maybe if you can always remember that you are having an adventure, you aren't, really – having an adventure, I mean. And I remember something you told me about Eve – about how she reached out to the not yet despite the pain she knew it would cause. We are all children of Eve, aren't we?

I have many thoughts and questions. Sometimes I imagine I am sharing them with you, like I used to. Remember how I would badger you? I miss those days. Thank you again for your gift and all you have given me. Sophia loved you a great deal and told me that she admired you for your fearless heart. I do too. No pain, no suffering, no shame either one of us has felt could diminish that love or that admiration. I will always consider you a friend and I hope you will consider me one too.

A week after Lucia sent out her letter, Martha told her that the hostels for the men were filling up with wounded soldiers. And as the days passed, reports about these veterans from guests and visitors became the main topic of conversation at the inn. Some of the veterans had no families to go back to or had found the relative quiet of their homes incapable of containing the explosive rage and terror the war had unleashed in them. They had left hearth and home and were drawn to the shrine in search of peace. Many of these ex-soldiers had visible scars or had lost parts of limbs. A few were blind or were missing an ear. All carried a burden they believed they would never be able to lay down. As their numbers grew and the hostels filled up, a shelter was hastily constructed and several religious brothers were assigned to care for them. There was much talk about what more could be done for them.

Within a few months, the rocks inside the cave were scrawled with the names of hundreds of soldiers. Many not only scrawled their own name or their mark, but also the names or marks of comrades that had been killed, wounded, or who had disappeared.

Most of the soldiers were grateful for any kindness shown them and chose to stay for several months before moving on. There were a rowdy few who drank too much and caused trouble, but the other men took it upon themselves to see that they did not do too much damage. A few chose to remain at the shrine to help their comrades.

The priests gave sermons about man's need for Divine redemption, insisting that the war was further proof of human-kind's depravity. A wealthy merchant and thoughtful man, who came to stay at the inn, took issue with the priests and once at dinner reasoned aloud that if God was good, he was incapable of loving what is evil. Therefore, if as the scripture said that God loves man, man must not be evil. He granted, however, that there was something about human beings that made them susceptible to evil influences. His train of thought created a stir among the other guests and led to a heated discussion. Lucia tended to side with the merchant, but felt that he too was missing something. For days she pondered it, and although she knew she did not fully understand the nature of love, she was somewhat satisfied with a few sentences she had written in her journal: *If God is incapable of loving what is evil, He does not love everything that exists, and that means love has limits. I do not believe that love has limits; love has to include every-thing — even evil. If love includes evil, perhaps evil is not what we think it is, or perhaps love is more powerful than we realize.*

Judith had her employees give food to any soldier who knocked on the door, and she began collecting blankets and cloaks to give to them. She asked her guests to help pay for them and many gladly did. Lucia liked preparing meals for the ex-soldiers and would sometimes invite them into the kitchen if they appeared particularly weary and were willing. She listened to their stories when they chose to share them and never ceased to be astonished at what they had experienced: horror and beauty, blood lust and tenderness, hatred and loyalty. How could one person encompass so much? Sometimes she wept as she listened, but she learned that her tears stopped the flow of their stories if the men noticed them, and so she tried not to cry.

The world she saw through their eyes could not be explained. These men had experienced things that eluded and defied reason. After they had eaten and were on their way, Lucia wondered what had happened to Jude and to the other men from her village who had thrown in their lot with the army.

One evening, as she was in the kitchen cleaning up with Martha and Grace, Lucia began trembling. She was frightened at first and had a fleeting thought she might be having a seizure, but she did not say anything. Neither of her companions seemed to observe anything amiss. Lucia's curiosity was piqued as the tremor persisted. It was a fine, delicate tremor, involving her whole body, and was accompanied by a vague sense of distress. She knew, without knowing how, that something mysterious and powerful was at work. When the clean-up was finished, she immediately went to her room. Louisa was there, about to go to bed, but she did not observe anything alarming about Lucia either. The tremor continued through the night, and the distress intensified. Her nerves began thrumming and kept her from sleeping.

The next morning she was still trembling. The others did not notice, but they sensed she was not herself and asked if she was ill. She did not know what to tell them, and so she said that she had had a restless night and would be fine. Around midday, when she was in the kitchen cooking for the guests, she heard a knock at the back door. When she opened it, a man in tattered uniform and large, sad eyes stood before her, hat in hand. "Are you hungry? Would you like some food?" Lucia asked.

"Please. I would be very grateful. But that is not why I'm here. I'm here to deliver a message to Lucia. Does she work here?"

Lucia's trembling and her distress merged, causing her knees to buckle. She clutched the door frame with her right hand. "Do come in. I'm Lucia," she told the man. When he was in the kitchen, she held out a chair for him to sit on and then offered him a plate of food. Afterward, she sat down, unable to stand any longer.

"Thank you. I appreciate your kindness. But before I eat, I want to deliver the message I was given. I know it's important."

"Who's it from?"

"Aaron. He said you would remember him."

Lucia folded her arms tightly across her chest. "I do. What is the message, sir?"

"Aaron told me to tell you that he has not forgotten you, and that you came to him in a dark hour."

"That's all?"

"Yes."

Lucia wanted to find out how the soldier knew Aaron, and if he knew what Aaron had meant about having a "dark hour," but the trembling in her body had become excruciating. She yelled for help, but fled through the back door before anyone else got to the kitchen. She ran up the road and up the mountain, not caring who was looking at her or the alarm she was causing. She didn't slow down until she was high up, close to her favorite cave. There she collapsed on a patch of grass near a small creek, curling up on her side like an infant.

As soon as the soldier had mentioned Aaron's name, she had known without a doubt that her tremor was tied to him. "He's dying," she told herself, "or he's in terrible pain." Anguish seized her. She wrapped her arms around herself and rocked on the grass. But there was no defense against what she was feeling. Inspired, she lifted herself off the ground and knelt. Opening wide her arms, she invited the anguish to fill her. She would not defend herself against it in any way.

She cried out inwardly as she felt Aaron's suffering move through her, but she soon realized that his suffering was linked to others'. The pain of many people seemed to be forcing its way into her consciousness. Her skin was no longer a boundary, her body no longer hers. What belonged to others, belonged to herself. She bore everything. Their pain was her pain. Many hearts were pounding in hers. Her cry contained many voices. And then, both she and the tormented multitude disappeared. There was only one who was suffering, only one who was crying out, only one who was opening up completely. She knew it was Christ. As soon as she realized that, He disappeared and there was only an awareness of a Presence that saturated her with bliss so intense she fell into unconsciousness...

When she came to, she was lying on her back. The sky was cloudless, the shade of blue that signaled the arrival of evening. Near her head, several birds hopped about, pecking in the grass. The tremor had gone. She sat up, half expecting to see a crowd around her, but she was alone. For a while, she could not think. She sat savoring the peace inside of her. With each breath she took, the peace grew, as if the very air she was taking in and breathing out was peace. She did not want to leave. Only the thought of Judith and her co-workers and how they were probably worrying about her forced her to her feet. She also had a passing thought about the soldier she had abruptly left alone in the kitchen.

The sun was setting as she walked down the mountain. She wondered what had happened to Aaron and the others. How was his suffering and theirs connected? Could such suffering be survived? The possibility that Aaron might be dead shook the calm she felt. She realized how deeply she cared for him. *No...it's more than that*, she thought, *I long for him. I want to be with him.* Lucia hoped that whatever had happened, Aaron's anguish had passed quickly. With her whole being she wanted him — and all those others — to experience the same Presence, the same bliss that she had.

Chapter Twenty-Five

Eighteen months earlier, Aaron had been deep in his studies. Lacking money, connections, and even experience living in a large city, the first months had been difficult, but determination, hard work and resourcefulness had eventually paid off.

Aaron had found employment with a stationer who did bookbinding. The stationer had not intended to hire anyone else. He had one employee who had worked with him for many years, and had no thought of expanding his business. Aaron, however, had convinced the stationer to take him on for four weeks as an experiment, saying that the man did not have to pay him during that time. It did not take long for the stationer to discover that Aaron was a quick learner, had a steady character and good ideas, and was well-liked by his customers. He hired him. Aaron's tasks included delivering sections of the manuscripts to the illuminators, cutting and smoothing the wood covers, and stitching the various sections together to create a firm spine. He gave himself the additional job of advertising.

Through the university, Aaron met young men, idealistic like himself. They gathered nightly at a tavern popular with students and local workmen. The tavern keeper served cheap and not bad-tasting food, and good ale. And there were always a few women about, available to provide pleasure — for a price set to accommodate the meager means of the tavern's regular customers. But for Aaron and his young friends, the primary source of pleasure was conversation. They thoroughly enjoyed satirizing the more politically minded of their professors and pointing out the absurdities and contradictions of the current government and of religion. Along with his friends, Aaron relished the opportunity to exercise his wit, and usually held nothing back, only drawing the line at priests. His classmates would call them unthinking sheep, wolves in sheep's clothing, but Aaron's loyalty to Father Lawrence and the image of his mentor's goodness would not permit him to add his own scornful comments or even to laugh at those of his friends. His silence on the topic of priests was observed by his companions and became a target of their playful derision and humorous speculation. Aaron did not satisfy their curiosity. He said nothing about Father Lawrence, but would laugh with his friends as they made fun of this peculiarity and others of his character and person, as he would laugh at theirs.

Aaron was liked by his classmates and by nearly every person who knew him. People found themselves well-disposed toward him as soon as they met him. He did not hide anything: his irrepressible confidence, his unquenchable optimism, his capacity for quick and unstinting affection, his hunger for learning, or his desire to change the world. Everyone knew he had come from a poor village and most knew that what he earned had to be sent to his mother because his father had abandoned her. And it was also common knowledge that Aaron rented a tiny back room whose only furniture was a narrow bed, a wobbly table, and a plain wooden chair. He never portrayed his condition as being better or worse than it was. His classmates knew how he was barely scraping by because he had to support his mother, but they also knew that he had a good job with an employer he respected and who paid him well. Aaron was a young man whose judgments and opinions were listened to by other young men, young men who would also unconsciously imitate him.

When Aaron suggested that the times were requiring more seriousness and threw out the idea that they begin talking about what constitutes a good society and what they could do practically to bring it about, his friends objected, asking him if he wanted to steal from them their few moments of fun. They called him a secret priest, a destroyer of human happiness; but when rumors of war multiplied and its imminence could no longer be ignored or rationalized away, their conversation did take a more serious turn.

In academic gatherings, Aaron frequently spoke up, uninhibited by considerations of his class or lack of connections. His questions were always pointed and well-articulated, and he could think well on his feet. He quickly had a firm grasp of the central points of any argument or position and was unerring in sensing the unfounded assumption. His natural facility for many subjects: philosophy, logic, mathematics, science, and the law was so evident that respect was paid him even by those professors who used wealth and connection to weigh the worth of students. It was universally assumed he would do well even with his glaring disadvantages, and that he would eventually marry a woman whose station in life would further advance his prospects. Aaron was aware of what people were saying about him, and if he did not quite believe the world was his for the taking, he did believe it was his to change. Rumors of war did not extinguish his confidence; they only altered its form.

Despite his optimism about his course in life, there were moments when he felt an empty hole in his chest as if his heart had been scooped out. He began to experience strange aches and pains and wondered if he had contracted some disease or if he had weakened his constitution with lack of sleep, poor air, and the hours he spent in intense concentration. His employer, observing that he had become more distracted, inquired about the reason. Embarrassed, but worried enough to say something, Aaron told his employer how he felt. His employer immediately arranged for him to be seen by his own physician. After a thorough examination, the physician declared him fit and able, and recommended a week's rest.

The feeling of a hole in the middle of his chest persisted, but Aaron said nothing more about it. He did not want to be seen as hysterical or obsessive, even by himself. For several months he tried ignoring the feeling – that made it worse. Then he tried acknowledging its presence but without worrying about it or trying to figure out what it was. When he did that, his thoughts changed. He began thinking more about his mother and Father Lawrence and Sophia. He remembered the village and the White Mountains. But most of all he began thinking about Lucia. Whenever he thought of her, the feeling of that hole in the middle of his chest disappeared. Instead, it was as if his heart was wide open, spacious. He imagined her standing before him outside the church, how she had glanced up at him. He remembered how he had wanted to hold and touch her. From thinking of her, he would question himself about how he thought about the world. He realized he still believed in the power of the world to change, but sometimes it was as if all his ideas about the nature of that change and its imminence had evaporated.

With increasing talk of war, the ubiquitous presence of soldiers, and the requisitioning of local supplies and services, the climate of the university changed. Students wanted to know where their professors stood regarding the war and whether it had a legitimate rationale. Most of the professors were reluctant to share what they thought with the students, and told them not to distract themselves from their studies. These admonitions stirred up suspicion and distrust among the students, for every day they observed the cold silence that lay between professors who once enjoyed arguing with each other. It was obvious the professors held and expressed opposing positions with regard to the war, and as time went on, it was also obvious that among the students themselves there was a range of opinion. Passions were easily roused and tempers flared more frequently whenever students gathered, leading many to speak more cautiously — if at all — about political matters. Aaron refused to be affected by the silence of others, and continued to speak openly. Meanwhile, the strange ache in his chest intensified. There were days when his optimism wavered, when his ability to influence circumstance seemed nonexistent. But in a few days, his confidence would return.

The group of friends continued to meet and their lively discussions began to attract others. The tavern became known as one of the few remaining places where men spoke their minds and discussed what was to be done. One evening, a tall, muscular, fair-headed soldier came into the tavern accompanied by two others who kept an obsequious distance. He was a low-ranking officer, but carried himself like a general. Aaron's friends immediately picked this up and mocked his pretentiousness; but Aaron felt there was something perilous about the man, something that made him avert his gaze. He thought about warning his friends off, but did not want to appear less emboldened than they. The tall soldier motioned for the tavern keeper and leaning in close to the tavern keeper's face said something, his back to the group. The tavern keeper looked frightened and shook his head. The soldier turned around and pointed toward Aaron and his friends.

Timothy, a member of the group, and an especially close friend of Aaron's, stood up with an untouched mug of ale and walked toward the tall soldier. He placed the mug on the counter next to the officer's elbow. "A welcoming brew, General, from our group," he said, waiting for a look, an irritated response, some acknowledgment, but there was none. Catching Aaron's eye, he shrugged and returned to the table.

The tall soldier crossed his arms over his chest and stared directly and pointedly at Aaron. It was an appraising look that offered nothing. Aaron did not want to look back, but knew that looking away would be interpreted as a sign of weakness. He stood up, mug in hand, and invited his friends to stand, which they did. Aaron led them in a toast to reason and the common good, angling his body deliberately in the direction of the officer. The officer tipped his hat to him, said something to the two other soldiers, and abruptly left. After a few minutes, the tavern keeper approached the group and told them that the soldier had asked what was discussed in his establishment and if he knew the names of those in their party. He was particularly interested in Aaron.

"I told him I was partly deaf, and that I minded my own business as long as the customers paid, but I don't think he believed me," the tavern keeper reported.

For a couple of days this event put a damper on conversation, but when the officer did not appear in the tavern again, Aaron and his friends grew even more brazen. They began piecing together what they believed were the real antecedents of the war. They based their theories on observation and reflection, what they had heard from credible, knowledgeable people and their intensifying political skepticism. They readily shared their theories with whoever was interested and began writing them down, hoping to get them published, perhaps through one of Aaron's contacts.

They held that it was their own leaders who had fomented the dissension and riots within the country on the western border. Their leaders were bent on overthrowing the country's ruling class and seeing that it was replaced with men more amenable to cheap trade, willing to sell off the country's resources at a lesser price. From credible sources, Aaron and his friends had learned that the plot had been discovered, several of the rioters and dissenters killed, and there was a retaliatory raid on a few of their own cities near the border. The burning, looting, and loss of life were exaggerated by their own government and had been put forward as signs of the neighboring country's determination to occupy and ravage theirs.

As a formal declaration of war drew closer, Aaron and his friends had a new, urgent topic to discuss: conscription. Aaron was the first to say he would refuse to fight in a war that had no justification. They all agreed, but secretly most of the young men hoped their resolve would not be tested, that their status as students would protect them. Their hope was soon swept away. War was declared, and on the same day, conscription was announced. University students who had no connections were not exempt — they were required to show up and register at the local military post. Names of the non-exempt students were posted near the entrance to the university. Aaron and most of his friends were included in the list.

At first, not registering seemed to be of little consequence. Things were disorganized and chaotic. But soon soldiers appeared in the classes and told the professors, in front of the students, that they were required to turn in the names of all non-exempt men or be forced to resign. A few professors refused to comply. Among them was a professor of philosophy whose name was Frederick. Aaron had heard about Frederick from his friends. Frederick had been at the university only a short while, but had already gained a reputation for his unique teaching methods. Aaron had heard that his classes were not so much lectures as conversations, and each conversation had a life of its own. Rumor had it that he also taught female students on the sly and treated them as equals, and that it was his insistence on teaching women that had made previous universities let him go, despite the protests of his students.

The government increased its pressure; the governing board of the university was forced to expel the non-complying professors. The students who refused to register were threatened with imprisonment, and any who harbored them were threatened with the same. Aaron stopped going to his classes and left his small room. He tried living in the streets. It did not take his employer long to figure out what was going on. "You'll stay with us," he said. "And you won't take manuscripts to the illuminators. There's plenty for you to do here."

The group of young men no longer met. Most had fled the city and returned to their families; two had gone ahead and registered. As the war effort faltered, notices were put up on every corner that those who refused to register in person would be executed. Strict punishments would be meted out even to those who only abetted the "traitors." Aaron knew he had to return home until the war ran its course, hoping that even if men were being conscripted from his village, it would be easier to hide in the countryside or in the surrounding forest. In the city, it was impossible. He was putting his employer at risk.

Aaron's friend, Timothy, one of the few still in the city, told him that there were some professors, including Frederick, who were meeting with students in their homes. Aaron found this tempting. He wanted to hear Frederick. He and Timothy talked it over and decided to participate in a conversation at Frederick's and then leave the city together the same night, after packing the food and extra clothes they had stored at the bookbinder's. He and Timothy would travel together for several days before separating. Aaron was relieved that they had a plan and looked forward to the evening. He felt in need of inspiration – something that would nourish both mind and heart and would give him the courage he sensed he would need in the days and months ahead.

Chapter Twenty~Six

Aaron's employer and his wife, Anna, were upset when Aaron told them his plans. They pleaded with him to reconsider going to Frederick's. Aaron expressed his gratitude to them for all that they had done, but told them it was something he felt he had to do, and that other students had been taking part in similar conversations with Frederick for months without detection.

Anna reminded him that young men were being picked up by roving patrols and were never heard from again. "If that happened to you, my husband and I would be in danger. They have a way of getting information from everyone. If you still insist on going, disguise yourself. Let me help. In my younger days, I worked in the theater. I still have a few wigs and costumes lying around somewhere. But the clothes and hair are not everything.... You have to change the way you walk. Your stride is a dead giveaway." She demonstrated a stiff-jointed, old man's shuffle.

And so, disguised and walking as an old man, Aaron made his way slowly to Frederick's house and knocked on his door.

"What do you want? Why are you here?"

"My name's Aaron....I'm a student, a friend of Timothy's. I've heard about the professor's conversations."

He heard voices behind the door, and when it opened there were three young women. They stared at his grey wig and laughed.

"That makes five old men, and three men dressed as women," the tallest one said. "Come in. Make yourself at home. My name is Cecilia. We're just being careful."

Aaron stepped inside and immediately straightened up, removed his wig, and thrust it in a pocket. The small parlor was packed with students sitting on the worn rug. There were not enough chairs. Twice as many women as men were in the room, and they were mixed comfortably together. There was a fire in the hearth, and food on a small table. Aaron helped himself before sitting down on the floor toward the back. The professor, while conversing with a young woman, caught his eye and nodded in greeting. Aaron was speaking with Cecilia when a small black cat leapt onto his lap. Aaron jumped.

"That's Sophia, the professor's cat," said the young woman, laughing. Aaron ran his hand over Sophia's arching back and scratched behind her ears. "I knew a woman named Sophia. She lived in my village."

"Sophia is the Greek word for Wisdom. The professor says that the cat was wise in choosing him. She sensed that he would spoil her, and he has."

The room was quieting down. A few students near the front were overheard urging the professor to leave the city as soon as possible.

"Why? You're still here. I see no reason to leave when there is work to do here...not yet, anyway," the professor said, waving a hand in the air. That gesture brought a complete silence in the room. Aaron's thoughts about the upcoming weeks dropped away and he listened as if he was incapable of doing anything else. Looking around the room, he realized that everyone else was also paying close attention and was waiting for the professor to speak. As the professor sat quietly, Aaron studied him.

Frederick was a large, broad-shouldered man, with a full head of hair and a magnificent beard. Both were reddish brown and streaked with gray. He had a prominent forehead that would have made him appear stern, but for the eyes that danced beneath his bushy brows. Frederick sat straight in the chair, but his limbs were relaxed. He seemed at ease with himself and quite pleased to be sitting with them. Aaron found this intriguing, given the circumstances.

Frederick looked around the room and began. "How do we come to Wisdom?"

A young man answered, "By thinking and reflecting."

A young woman quickly added, "By thinking and reflecting on our experience."

"That's the common understanding of things," Frederick said. "Let's look at the various parts of that proposition before we decide what value it has. Let's begin with experience. What is it?"

"Experience is something we undergo, something that happens to us," the young woman said.

"Like a trial or a test," a young man near Frederick added.

"Are you saying that experience is *not* something we determine?" Frederick asked.

"We can plan to do something, but we cannot plan the experience of doing it. That is not in our control," the young woman answered.

"That's a good observation," a young man said, "but can we

do something that would make it more likely for us to have experiences of a certain quality?"

"Yes," Cecilia responded, "but it is not we who decide the specific form, and sometimes we may have experiences that seem opposed to our actions. A person doing a good deed may experience feelings of loathing or vanity, and a person doing evil may experience momentary tenderness or a longing for goodness."

"Are you saying that the specific form of our experience is not something we decide?" Frederick asked.

Another young female student spoke up. "I don't agree with what Cecilia just said. I think how we interpret an experience changes that experience. If I like a young man and he falls in love with my best friend, how I interpret it will matter a great deal. If I believe that my best friend deliberately seduced him, I will feel anger and jealousy. But if I believe they're a good match and could not help falling in love, I may still feel abandoned and sad, but maybe I will even be happy for them. My interpretation will change the original experience."

"What would prompt someone to alter their interpretation?" Frederick asked.

The room grew very quiet. Aaron sensed the young woman's example was not purely theoretical. The woman took time answering, and when she did there was a quaver in her voice.

"What would prompt someone? Probably not wanting to suffer or to cause suffering to others."

"And what prompts *that* desire?" Frederick asked. "Is that desire, itself, an experience or a self-generating act?"

Again, the room was very quiet.

"Ah," the professor said.

A young man with a wig askew on his head spoke up. "We

can't hold on to any experience. It's like trying to hold water in our hands, or air."

The flow of the conversation surprised Aaron. He took pride in his ability to follow and anticipate the thinking of others, but with Frederick and these students he was lost. They veered away from well-worn paths and were striking out in entirely new directions. The fact that they were not clear about where they were going did not seem to trouble them greatly. He noticed Timothy slipping in and felt him squeeze his shoulder in passing. Timothy went to sit across the room in the only spot available.

A young female student said, "We're back to saying that we do not really determine our experience, that it's something we undergo. I find that scary. I don't like feeling I have such little control."

"Those feelings are common," Frederick responded. "Perhaps that is why fully entering into any experience is so difficult. There seems to be an element of suffering in every experience."

Timothy spoke up. "How do we get past that, Professor? How do we enter our experience? Is it a matter of accepting suffering first?"

"What do the rest of you think?"

Aaron jumped in, "Isn't there something in us that fights suffering: a need to act, to better things? Wouldn't accepting suffering contradict that need?"

Frederick looked intently at Aaron. "Where did that need come from? Did you create it?"

Aaron felt disoriented, shaken. He wanted to affirm he had, but it seemed false. "No, I don't think I produced it, at least not entirely. So are you saying that even that need to fight suffering is itself an experience?"

"I think I am saying that," Frederick replied.

A woman, who appeared older than the rest, spoke up. "I used to think I could have experiences where suffering didn't exist. Love, joy, beauty…. You would think those are free of pain. But if that were true, why do we find them unbearable? Why do we weep when we are experiencing them? And why is there relief when they pass?"

"What has all this got to do with Wisdom, Professor?" another young man asked.

Several students laughed.

"Thank you," Frederick said. "Every conversation needs someone who remembers how it began. What was our original question?"

"I think it was: how do we come to Wisdom," the young man answered.

"Ah, yes…and how does what has just been said about experience relate to Wisdom?"

"I don't know."

Everyone laughed, including Frederick, and the laughter continued for awhile.

"Well, let me try to summarize. We come to Wisdom through experience, and it seems that all experience has an element of suffering about it. So Wisdom is not something we can simply have for the wanting. I want to look some more at experience. Is there another common element in it, other than suffering?"

Cecilia answered, "There has to be awareness. If there is no consciousness, there is no experience."

"Ah…and can we be more or less aware?"

"Yes," she answered.

"And can the degree or intensity of awareness shape experience?"

The older woman spoke up, "It can…it does…." She paused, reflecting. "Or is it that awareness helps us enter into our experience more deeply, and so the experience seems different?"

Aaron could feel excitement building in the room.

"Can we choose to become more aware?" the Professor asked.

"Yes," Cecilia practically shouted. "We can't directly determine our experience, but we can choose to be more aware of it — and that awareness transforms experience, doesn't it?"

"Does it eliminate the suffering of experiencing, Cecilia?"

"No, I don't think so. But it's different somehow."

Heads were nodding in the room.

"We were reminded that we began our conversation by asking how we come to Wisdom. Someone said that we come to Wisdom by reflecting on our experience. I think the common understanding is that over the course of years of experience, we may discover patterns and rhythms, which if we reflect on them, lead to Wisdom. We can explore that possibility. But there are other possibilities we have begun to look at. I want to suggest that looking closely at the nature of experience, as we have been doing this evening, is a path to Wisdom. And I want to hold out the possibility that one experience undergone fully — with awareness and attention – is a meeting with Wisdom."

Aaron could no longer follow the conversation. He had a very fleeting and paradoxical impression of an immobile presence, moving at great speed through everything. This presence was unimaginably intelligent and generous. And then his mind went blank. When he came to, he thought maybe he had fallen asleep. He looked over at Timothy — he appeared completely absorbed.

He did not know how much time had elapsed when he heard

Frederick say, "Next week, if we meet, we will continue looking at the nature of Wisdom. For now, be safe…all of you."

Most of the students stood up and either talked among themselves or approached Frederick. Cecilia, who had been sitting next to Aaron, turned to speak to him. Aaron tried to listen to her, but could not focus his attention. After a few minutes, she said that she was glad he had come, and got up and joined the group of students around the professor. Timothy sat down next to Aaron, peered at him, and waved his hand in front of Aaron's eyes.

"Are you all right?"

Aaron slowly came to. "I want to thank him."

"We really should be going. Write to him."

"It will only take a minute."

Aaron stood up and moved toward the professor; Timothy followed. It was obvious that the students gathered around Frederick did not want the night to end. Several of them began expressing fears about not being able to meet again. Rather than allay their fear, the professor just listened. Other students began saying how much they would miss the gatherings. Tears began to flow. The students began sharing memories.

An hour went by before most of the students had left and Frederick was free. Aaron went up to Frederick, and Timothy introduced them. Frederick held out his hand, and after Aaron shook hands with him, he followed an impulse and bowed to Frederick. There was so much he wanted to say, but nothing came out. Frederick seemed to sense the amazement and appreciation Aaron was feeling and warmly pressed his hand again. "Come back, if you can, young man. You and Timothy are welcome."

Timothy carefully placed his wig on his head and tugged at Aaron's sleeve. "Time to go."

Reluctantly Aaron turned from Frederick.

"Put your wig on, Aaron."

Aaron ignored him. Timothy was more insistent. "Put your wig on!"

"I will," Aaron said absently, to put him off. He wanted to savor what he was feeling and was annoyed that Timothy kept harping on the wig. He strode out of Frederick's house.

"What are you doing, Aaron? There are always soldiers around at this hour...you know that. Put it on and slow down."

Timothy loudly whispered this last request as Aaron quickly turned a corner. Timothy saw Aaron's wig still dangling from his pocket. He ran to catch up with him.

Chapter Twenty-Seven

"Stop!"

Aaron heard the shout, though he was still engrossed.

"Stop," he heard again. He kept moving forward, telling himself that the command was directed at someone else.

"Stop or I'll shoot!"

The muscles in his legs twitched; he wanted to run, but his mind, now sharp and clear, forbade it. He held himself back and turned around. He guessed there were a half a dozen soldiers. Aaron looked around for Timothy. His friend had already been seized, and in the torchlight he could see Timothy staring at him. Timothy's eyes bulged and his jaw was pulled downward. Terror had so altered his friend's countenance that Aaron hardly recognized him.

"Stand still," one of the uniformed men said, rushing up. "Put your hands in the air."

Aaron obeyed. His hands were roughly pulled back and tied, and then he was searched for weapons. One of the soldiers plucked Aaron's wig from his pocket. Another soldier had torn Timothy's wig off his head and was dangling it mockingly in front of his face. The soldiers laughed, and the one in charge barked another order. Aaron and Timothy were marched toward an old, thick-walled fortress near the government offices. Aaron felt his legs buckling and tried counteracting the physical evidence of his fear by throwing his shoulders back and holding his head higher. A soldier behind him gave him a hard smack on his head for his effort. He heard Timothy take a blow, too.

He wanted to remain with his friend, but as soon as they passed through the heavy, uninviting gate and crossed the court-yard, they were separated. Without thinking what he was doing, Aaron shouted after him, "Timothy, I'm sorry." He did not know if his friend heard him or not. As he was being led down a nar-row, dimly lit hall, he felt as if Timothy was being cut away from his own flesh. One of the two soldiers escorting him rapped on a solid wooden door. "Enter," Aaron heard.

"Captain," said the soldier who had knocked, "a traitor and deserter. We arrested him with another young man. He had this in his pocket." The soldier thrust forward Aaron's wig. The well-dressed captain was sitting behind a table, writing. Without looking up he pointed to a corner bare of documents. The sol-dier placed the wig there and stepped back.

"Did he say anything? Has he already confessed?"

"When we took the other man away, he said he was sorry."

"Wait outside."

The two soldiers left after shoving Aaron down onto a small stool so short that his knees nearly came up to his chest. Aaron sweated profusely as the captain continued writing, though the room was cold. It seemed that hours had gone by before the captain put down his pen, blew on the paper, placed it meticulously on a stack, and looked up. Aaron's mouth went dry. It was the tall, fair-headed officer from the tavern — the one Aaron had not wanted to look at.

"No toasts today?"

Aaron said nothing.

"I would wager that you're poor and from some decrepit village. So what are you doing here? Looking for better women? A better world, perhaps?"

Aaron winced.

"Well?"

He wanted to answer, but no sound came out.

"Your courage seems in short supply. Or perhaps you've been up to something and know you don't have the wit to throw me off."

Aaron sat as erect as he could. "You're assuming. You have no proof."

The man expelled a short, loud burst of air. "The precocious and superior law student finally finds his tongue." The captain stood up and walked between Aaron and the table where he had been sitting. He stood with his legs astride and his arms crossed over his chest as he had in the tavern, and looking down at Aaron named three professors, including Frederick.

"You've studied under them, haven't you, after they were forbidden to teach?"

Aaron said nothing. He shifted on the stool, trying to center himself.

"Your book learning has turned you into a fool and made you an inferior man. Are you aware of that? Do you know what it means? It means you will be giving me names. You'll betray whatever friends you have. You've already had one of them arrested. You know that, don't you? Would he be here if you had looked out for him?"

Aaron felt as if the point of a sword had sliced him to the

core. *I have betrayed Timothy*. He had understood that immediately, as soon as they had been arrested, but fear for his own life had made him incapable of fully taking it in. Though he had shouted *I'm sorry*, he had only begun to understand what he had done. Now he knew that Timothy would pay for his poor judgment, carelessness, and pride – possibly with his life. The thought was unbearable. Aaron told himself he would not betray anyone else, but doubt that he would have the fortitude to withhold incriminating information crept into his heart like a cold draft.

"I know enough to have you and your friend executed."

The man moved closer to Aaron. Aaron leaned away from him. "Don't move, or you won't leave this room alive." The Captain unsheathed a knife and placed it on the table within easy reach. He searched Aaron's face for a reaction and then put his own so close to Aaron's that neither of them could see anything else. Aaron felt the man's image penetrating him, filling him — and protectively closed his eyes. The captain roughly forced Aaron's left eye open and spat in it. When Aaron flicked his head, the captain struck him twice on the mouth with the back of his hand. Blood spilled over Aaron's lower lip. His teeth and jaw ached.

"Think about what you did and why I should let you live. Now I've got work to finish," the captain said, straightening up. "Guards!"

The soldiers who had brought him in reappeared.

"Take him to the post."

Although he did not know what the words meant, Aaron felt an urgent, uncontrollable need to relieve himself. The soldiers forced him to his feet and through a series of halls and then entered a courtyard. A searing stench filled Aaron's nostrils and throat. In the center of the court stood a gallows, and in the half-light of early morning, he saw a body, hanging. Not far from the gallows was a tall post. One of the soldiers directed Aaron where to stand while the other held a sword to his throat. The first soldier wrapped a rope through the one that already bound his hands. He tied that one tightly to the post. Then he placed another short rope around Aaron's neck, and twisted. Aaron thought he was being strangled and struggled to move his head.

"We're not trying to kill you, but we will if you don't hold still," the guard with the sword yelled.

Aaron stopped fighting, but when the guard who was tying him took the twisted rope and drew Aaron's neck back toward the post, he instinctively thrust himself forward. The rope pressed hard against his throat, cutting off his breath, and he felt the sword nick his throat. He quickly leaned back.

"That's better," the soldier tying him said.

Aaron was facing the corpse. The rope around his neck was tightened until breathing became difficult. When his head moved even slightly forward, his breathing was cut off.

The guards left. He was alone in the empty courtyard. He could hear screams coming from inside the building and told himself not to think of Timothy. The gallows squeaked, and as the sun came up, he could see the large, thick stones that made up the courtyard walls. There was nothing green in sight. The ground was hard and compact, like fired brick. Beyond the gallows, in a far corner, he saw a raised pit that was covered with an iron grate, and next to it a large anvil. The anvil had iron hoops on its sides and attached to the hoops were leather straps. Aaron forced himself not to imagine what it was doing there.

As the day wore on and the courtyard heated up, the buzzing of hundreds of flies maddened him. They lit on his face and neck and on his hands. Aaron tried closing his eyes. That kept the flies out of them and shielded him from the revolting sight of the corpse, but it made him more aware of his labored breathing, the nauseating stench, and his inner tumult. The terror he had been pushing down was pushing back — hard — and was forcing his body into an unholy alliance with it. Thought, will, and intention seemed mere children in front of an avenging and ruthless army.

He tasted emptiness — saw the bareness of his essence. Though his heart was beating strongly in his chest, there was nothing in it to protect him. He was doomed — as sure as the seed that fell on barren ground or as a thin-shelled egg that had fallen from the nest – he was doomed. How he had once imagined himself was a dream. This twitching, vulnerable body was who he really was. *No,* he shouted within himself, *I am not this. I am more. I am more.* He almost believed it.

When his eyes were opened it was easier to think that the horror had nothing to do with him. It was the world that was more hostile and antagonistic than he had realized. There were evil forces in the world against which human beings had no defense. *I could leave it,* Aaron thought. In the next moment he felt something like sleep steal upon him. *You must not withdraw.* This last was not a thought. It was a voice speaking within him, and it was as if everything had come down to those words and what they meant. They bore an implacable truth.

The impossibility of his situation clawed him, ripped him open. He had no defenses against the cruelty of men, but he could not withdraw. Bound to the earth he was nothing, but he could not leave it. Whatever residues of strength he had left withered under the pitiless light and the merciless command.

He closed his eyes again and let himself fall forward. Father Lawrence appeared before him. His face and hands were bandaged, his face shone with love. He was blessing Lucia, who knelt in front of him. Lucia turned and looked at Aaron and began speaking to him, but he could not hear her. He had to hear her. Though he had not noticed that his breathing had stopped, he pulled himself up and leaned back against the post, gulping for air. He had to know what Lucia had said to him. From the depths of his being he cried out, desperate, his voice raspy but forceful and clear enough to be heard if someone had been near, "Lucia! Lucia!"

As he spoke her name, he felt his entire body penetrated by golden light down to his bones. He could not tell if he was coming from the light or the light was coming from him. The whole experience was over in the blink of an eye. Everything was the same — the gallows, the corpse, the buzzing of the flies. Breathing remained difficult. His fear was still there, the revulsion and guilt, but everything was also different. Something new had entered into him. Whatever it was steadied him, gave him a sense of space, and seemed to radiate out from his chest. Marveling at his own sudden transformation and full of gratitude for it, he wept.

Hours passed and the sun had almost set when the same two soldiers approached him, one carrying a sharp axe. Though Aaron assumed he was going to die, he felt surprisingly calm. The soldier with the axe held it up level with Aaron's chest, then stepped sideways and took a swing. When the axe was less than a foot away, the guard stopped, but rested the tip of the axe hard against Aaron's ribs and rubbed, drawing blood. "The captain gives you a choice. Join the army and bury its dead, or be sliced open and hanged like that fellow over there." The guard pointed to the corpse still hanging on the gallows.

"What about my friend?" Aaron's voice was hoarse and no louder than a whisper.

"What did you say?"

"He asked about his friend," the other guard said.

The soldier with the axe turned and scowled at the other. The shoulders of the second slumped and he said no more.

"The Captain wants your friend....I would forget him if I were you."

Aaron swallowed hard. He wanted to offer himself in Timothy's stead and opened his mouth to do so, but nothing came out.

"So what's it going to be? Will you join the army?"

Without thinking, but knowing it was what he needed to do, Aaron nodded.

"Just like the captain thought." The guard with the axe forced it into the ground. The other cut Aaron's bonds and released him from the post. Aaron stumbled forward and landed face down in the dirt. The guard with the axe had drawn his sword, ordering the other to bring a ladder to the gallows. When the ladder was set up he told Aaron, "You are to start now. Pick up the axe and cut down the body over there and bury it...bury it deep, but don't disturb any bones you might find."

Digging was difficult in the hard ground. When night came, two new guards with lanterns took over. They sat and ate and did not offer Aaron anything, not even water. He was so parched he could not think of anything else. When he came across bones, he would have to rebury them and dig a new hole. There were numerous bones; many men had been executed in that place. When morning came, he had only the shallowest of trenches to show for his efforts. His body, weakened by hunger and thirst and the emotions of the last 24 hours, was on the verge of giving out. His hands were raw and bleeding, and his whole body ached.

The captain appeared at midmorning, standing in the half shadow of a doorway. He stared at Aaron for several moments, saying nothing. Fear, anger, and a deep loathing rose up in Aaron like bile. He recognized their danger, knew that if he nursed them, the captain would triumph, that his perverted will would have succeeded in subjugating him. He took a deep breath and inwardly repeated Lucia's name over and over again with his full attention as he hacked at the ground. He soon forgot everything: the captain, his situation, and his physical pain. He remembered how his body had become light when he had said Lucia's name when he was tied to the post and he felt that again, though less intensely. Lucia had offered him a priceless gift. It would be his task to care for her gift and make himself worthy of it. That would be his hope and his salvation.

Having an uncanny sense for when a man was nearing his limit and the cruelty to deny him the relief of passing out, the Captain ordered Aaron to stop in midafternoon, although the grave was only half dug. Aaron plopped down on the unyielding dirt, realizing too late that he had sat in the sun. Too weak to move, he sat glazed-eyed and burned in the hot sun. His guards finished burying the corpse, occasionally showering him with dirt and small stones. He was beyond caring. When the corpse was buried, he was dragged back inside, locked in a small, airless room without windows, and given a little food and water. He drank but was too exhausted to eat. He fell asleep on the smelly floor and woke only when a guard kicked him. He was given some bread and water mixed with sour wine and had barely finished eating when he was marched back out to the courtyard.

It was late morning, nearly noon. The first thing Aaron noticed was another body hanging from the gallows, and his first thought was of Timothy. But when he looked up at the bloated face, he saw with great relief that it was not his friend. Flames leapt up from the pit in the corner while nearly thirty defeated-looking men stood in a line that began near the anvil. Almost as many guards stood around with swords and clubs. A few had guns. Aaron was told to stand behind the last man.

One part of his mind guessed what was going to happen while another denied it. A non- uniformed man strode to the fire pit with a branding iron. Some of the men, seeing this, began to shout. They were struck with clubs and quickly quieted down. The iron grate over the pit was lifted up and the brand was placed in it. The men were forced to stand as the iron heated up and the sun rose mercilessly above their heads. After an hour, one of the soldiers walked past the men into the building. When he returned, the captain accompanied him. The soldier yelled for the men's attention.

"You men are traitors and will be branded as such," the captain said as if he was observing a slight change in the weather. He nodded and the soldier standing behind him took his sword and wrote a large "T" on the ground. "We want your right hand."

The captain went to the head of the line. The first man was forced to kneel and his hand was strapped down across the anvil. His agonized scream and the sound of sizzling flesh echoed off the walls. Aaron felt for the man as he underwent this procedure twice, for the captain, examining the first mark, did not think it adequate. The first four men were branded twice. All but one had to be dragged back to their cells. Aaron told himself he would keep his legs. He imagined that it was not a "T" that would be burnt soon into his hand, but Lucia's name.

When it was his turn, he knelt down and never stopped repeating her name. He did not scream and fought to stay conscious, but the pain severely narrowed his attention. He heard the captain complaining, "Why did you mark him with an L?" And he heard the man who wielded the brand insisting he did not know how it happened, perhaps because he had branded so many men, a piece of wood had stuck, or a roll of skin. He asked if he should brand him again. "No, do the next man," the captain ordered. Aaron was dazed, but was able to walk back to his cell without aid.

For the first few days, the pain made him retch. More sour wine was added to the water, which made him retch more. After three days, someone checked on his wound when his slop bucket was emptied. He poured liquor on his hand without saying anything. Aaron told the man his name and asked for his, but the man ignored him. Being isolated in such complete darkness was horrible. His thoughts tortured him, making him grateful for the distraction of physical pain. He wondered what would happen to his mother. He knew the village would not let her starve, but he also knew her life would be harsher without him, and she would worry and grieve if she did not hear from him. Day and night he heard screams and though he listened closely, he could never be certain if he was hearing Timothy or not. He often thought about the moment when he had meant to offer himself in his friend's stead and wondered why he had not spoken up. His throat had been parched and constricted, but was that the only reason? Could he have been too terrified to actually make the offer? And there were thoughts of Frederick, his employer and his helpful wife,

Anna…people dear to him. Now because of his carelessness and lack of good judgment, they were at serious risk. He wondered what would happen to them. He thought often of Lucia and how he might never see her again. He imagined himself dying alone in prison. The relentlessness of his regrets and dark conjectures took him to the edge of madness.

He struggled to control his thoughts and spent hours re-constructing the entire conversation that had taken place at Frederick's, and reflected at length about each part. Gradually his thoughts ceased their compulsive turning and began to branch and stretch like living things. When he recalled what one of the students had said about the impossibility of holding onto any experience, how it was like trying to grasp air with one's hand, he groaned aloud. That was what he had done that night. He did not really hear Timothy telling him to slow down and put on his wig, because he was trying to hold on to the experience of the conversation. That was a painful realization and Aaron did not want to think about it further. For days he resisted looking more deeply into his own insight. But then he remembered the courage Frederick and the other students showed, how they would keep inquiring into their experience though it was difficult, and he de-cided to do the same.

His thoughts then took a surprising turn. He had assumed the pain came from his being the careless author of so much misery, and that certainly was a large part of his suffering. But what he discovered, as he reflected on what he felt, was that he felt not only guilty; he was also angry and lost. The world was not how he had dreamt it to be. It would not be shaped by his ideas or will, nor would it be forgiving when he most wanted and needed mercy. He felt as if he had been living drunk for many years, and now that his suffering was beyond bearing, he was being forced by the world into painful sobriety.

How do I live in such a hard, unfeeling world? he asked himself. *How can I endure this hell?* For the next several days he thought about these questions. When he remembered Lucia and the light that had entered him when he was tied to the post, he realized that what he had experienced then was also the world. That led to thoughts and memories of Father Lawrence, his mother, and the people in his village. And he recalled how his jailor would sometimes tell him about the weather when he brought him his food, or give him news about the course of the war. Suddenly he saw how little he knew about the true nature of the world. It was a mystery that encompassed and embraced what could never be reconciled: evil and good, ugliness and beauty, lies and truth. The world was deep. What it was about, what it was doing, was beyond his comprehension.

His question about how to live changed when he saw how little he understood. Instead of asking how he could live in such a harsh world, now he asked himself: *How can I live in a world I do not know?* He pondered the latter question for what seemed a long time and then laughed out loud when he realized that the answer all along had been in that conversation among Frederick and his students. Experience — that was the key. The world meant for itself to be experienced and that meant it had to be undergone, suffered. Although men — including himself — fantasized otherwise, the world could not be controlled nor grasped entirely. For a brief moment, Aaron then had the intimation of something wonderful: the world was an unknowable mystery because it was a living being. And even more astounding, as a living being it was not unlike a man. *And less unlike a woman*, Aaron said aloud, surprised that he had said that.

One day afterwards, when he was eating another meager and unsatisfying meal, a line from the gospels he had avidly read as a young boy came to mind: "It is easier for a camel to pass through the eye of a needle than for a rich man to enter the kingdom of heaven." He thought about that phrase, "the eye of a needle," and realized that fully entering into the experience of the world was like passing through the eye of a needle. To fit through such a small opening, he had to be willing to let go of everything. He had to go through the particular experience of each moment with nothing more than the intention to do so, for that was the only thread that passed through the needle's eye. That is what he had not done that night at Frederick's, and that was what he had to learn to do.

Aaron calculated that he had been in his cell three months when his cell door opened and a soldier threw some clothes at him, telling him to get dressed and come out. Aaron found even the dim light in the hall painful, and covered his eyes, and though he had exercised his limbs and muscles as well as he could, his legs wobbled as he walked. He stole a look at his right hand. It *was* an "L" that had been burnt there. It was a livid rose in color, more striking because his hand was so pale, and it was not fully healed. Because his shirt sleeve was short for him and did not cover the length of his arm, he noticed how thin his wrist and arm had become. He glanced at his clothes. He had put on an ill-fitting and badly stained uniform. Aaron suspected at least some of its stains were blood.

He was led down a hall into the courtyard where other men in tattered and dirty uniforms stood at attention. Black ribbons were being tied around their arms. They were told these designated them as responsible for the burial or burning of corpses and if they were ever discovered without them, they would be flogged. For the next several days they received more food and spent a couple of hours marching together in the courtyard. Aaron relished the warmth of the sun and the feel of the slight wind. And it was good to be near people again, even if the men were not permitted to speak to each other. But while he was grateful to spend at least part of the day outside his cell and would not ever choose to be locked up continually again, he missed the intensity and clarity he had discovered in his solitary cell before there was any reprieve. Already, he sensed a dulling. He spent much of his time alone anticipating his release or fearing that it would never come. Catching his thoughts wandering like this, he realized he was already getting too big for that eye of the needle. One morning after an hour of marching, a young officer, not much older than Aaron, introduced himself to the men. He would be their commander and they would be leaving for the front the following day. Each man would be given a sack for few provisions, and a coat. The men did not say anything, but Aaron felt the general sense of relief. Like himself, they had probably thought they would never leave their prison, that they had been forgotten.

Winter was coming. The march to the front was long, cold, and arduous. Although there was more food, there was barely enough to sustain the men, who walked nearly twenty miles every day. Three men became ill and were left behind despite the protests of Aaron and a few of the others. At the front, they joined another burial unit and were immediately set to work. Aaron dug holes for the dead, the countless dead, nearly every day for almost a year. When there were too many, or the front was moving too fast, he helped burn them. Among his comrades were men not fit for soldiering. There were some who were able-bodied but dull-witted or slightly crazed. There were also several criminals and some older, working men with grown children. He found himself drawn at first to the students who had refused to register or who had actually written articles in opposition. But he soon discovered that they had succumbed to the temptation to think too far ahead. They also seemed in a constant state of bewilderment. One of the criminals told Aaron that the students were unable to accept the fact that they could be treated inhumanely indefinitely. "Their former privileges mean nothing now, but they refuse to see it." Aaron tried to share with the students what he had thought about and learned since his arrest, but they scarcely heard him. He ended up befriending a couple of the older men and would sometimes speak with the young officer.

The burial unit was never given supplies. It was understood that they would take what they needed from the dead: food, water, boots, and clothes. Often that was sufficient, but if they were on the move, the men went hungry. Aaron convinced the young officer to let him use his foraging skills, and with the help of a workman or soldier, he would scavenge the countryside in search of food, especially when a number of men were ill.

Thievery, fighting, and refusal to work began to plague the unit after the first few weeks. The young officer meted out frequent and progressively severe punishments. Aaron saw that the officer was not happy doing this, but had no idea what else to do. One evening Aaron found himself alone with the young officer, who took the opportunity to confide in him.

"I always wanted to be an officer in the regular army...not over a unit like this. These men are not soldiers. I don't know how to handle them."

"Soldiers are men too, and need managing. Many don't want to fight."

"Are you saying this unit is not that different?" the officer asked.

"We have something to do and we have to look out for each other while we do it. That's the same as any unit," Aaron answered. "If you do not see that we look out for each other, who will?"

After this conversation, the young officer spoke more to his men, and became more observant of their moods and energy. There was still trouble, but there was less dissension and the officer slowly won the respect of the older men — even the students mocked him less behind his back.

From the moment Aaron touched the first dead body, he knew he was being initiated into another mysterious aspect of the world. For several days he thought about this as he separated out tangled bodies and rolled them into graves; it helped him overcome his abhorrence of decaying flesh and of the men responsible. He was reminded again of how the world was to be undergone, suffered through — and he remembered how one of the students at Frederick's had called all experience a trial. He laughed as he recalled this, though at that moment he was burying a man's face with a shovelful of dirt.

After this there were days when he allowed himself to perceive the vast difference between living bodies and corpses. He tried to put the difference into words, but knew it was impossible.

The difference transcended thought and speech. Life and Death were irreconcilably different and yet both, once again, were encompassed within the mystery of the world.

Though he did not like to see it happen, there came a time when, like the other men, Aaron grew inured to the sight and smell of rotting human flesh. The men argued, told stories and jokes, and would sing ribald songs as they buried or burned bodies, as if they were merely stacking wood.

One especially cold and snowy day, Aaron felt a strange impulse. He did not want to act on it, assuming that the men, if they saw him, would think that he was growing soft. The impulse remained and grew more urgent. Aaron sensed he would be refusing an important service if he did not follow it. He whispered, "Lucia," then knelt down in the snow. He turned over a body of a soldier. He appeared to have been years younger than himself, a mere boy. Rummaging through his rucksack, he set the boy's food aside and kept looking. He found a letter, folded many times. Although his hands were stiff with cold, Aaron worked at it and eventually opened it. It did not take long to read. There were only a couple of lines of poorly written script: *We love you William and every day we pray for you. Your brothers and sisters miss you. Take care of yourself and come home safely.*

Aaron refolded the letter, and opening his coat, he placed the letter over his heart, holding it there with his right hand. He closed his eyes and sensed where his fingers touched the letter, sensed the letter's weightlessness, and sensed his heart taking it in as if it had been meant for him. He wept for the first time in months. He placed the folded letter within the boy's coat and then buried him. That night, around the fire, he knew that in the future he would have to find some way to connect himself to every dead man he buried.

And he did. Sometimes it was a letter he found, other times it was a ring, a lock of hair, a rough drawing of a house, a miniature portrait, a book. Twice he found a small child's tooth wrapped in cotton. His private ritual did not go unnoticed. He was not mocked as much as he had feared, however, and many of the men wanted to know the meaning of his actions. Aaron told them he didn't know, but he felt something moving him to do this. When he shared that he sometimes felt the presence of the dead, a few were horrified and went to the young officer, complaining. The young officer, who had seen for himself how Aaron had begun behaving around the corpses, took him aside one evening and told him that he had no objections, but that the men did, so he needed to be more discreet.

When spring came and the weather warmed, Aaron would sometimes move away from the other men when it was time to sleep. Lying on the ground, he would gaze at the stars and think of his village. He remembered his mother, Sophia, Jeremiah, and Father Lawrence. His imagination lingered longest with Lucia. He kept going back to that time in front of the church and wondered if Lucia had desired him...he remembered feeling something. But then he would wonder if it was a fantasy of his, something he wanted so much that he created it.

Sometimes, lying sleepless for the entire night, he would wonder and agonize over what had become of Timothy. He had not seen his friend since their arrest and thought it unlikely that he was still alive. *Why did the captain spare me and not Timothy?* He asked himself this question many times. *He,* not Timothy, had seemed to attract the captain's sadistic attention. So why did the captain let *him* go? There were no answers. And then there was Frederick, the other students, his employer...what had happened to them?

Sometimes he remembered the presence he had sensed so fleetingly at Fredrick's, how it moved so fully and so quickly through everything, and how he had experienced his body as light when he had said Lucia's name. He knew with ever greater certainty that the presence and the light were inseparable, and that his impulse to connect himself to the dead belonged to that presence and that light. For hours he would ponder the relationship that bound these experiences together and wonder what their unity meant. Reason did not take him far. However, he discovered a power of the mind he had not known existed. It could see. It could simply gaze upon the relationship between his experiences as his physical eyes could gaze at the stars. The effect of his contemplation was a new feeling and sense of the world. The world moved in hidden ways and acted in a manner that surpassed the thinking and imagining of men, and yet he sensed the world needed men. That gave him heart.

Aaron knew some would call what he perceived "God", but he believed the word was like an illiterate's mark and said nothing meaningful. Perhaps, Frederick would call it Wisdom. For Aaron it was simply the whole of the world. Whatever *it* was, it could not be pinned down and limited by a word.

The bodies needing burning or burying multiplied. The war seemed to be intensifying, not winding down, and the men grew despondent....

When he had been digging graves for eight months, Aaron's

unit entered a fortification that had been reduced to rubble. There were many bodies, some crushed beyond recognition. The young officer was told that any man still breathing had been already moved behind the line. Aaron looked through the ruined maze of damaged rooms, until in one scattered with cutlery and pots and pans, he found a body with a nasty gash on its head. As was still his practice, he knelt before it. There was no rucksack nearby, so Aaron tore off a dangling button from the man's shirt and held that close to his heart, closing his eyes. He thought he heard the slightest of sounds coming from the supposed corpse. He pocketed the button and opening his eyes, bowed over the body, putting a finger underneath the man's nostrils. He felt for a pulse around the neck. The man was alive. Aaron yelled for help.

That evening, as Aaron cradled the wounded man's bandaged head, trying to feed him some broth, the man's eyes opened. Aaron smiled. The man closed his eyes again, but swallowed the liquid. The next morning, the young officer told him and one of the soldiers to take the wounded man back behind the lines where he could hopefully benefit from a physician's skill. It took a full day and a half before Aaron and the soldier, carrying the wounded man between them on a dirty blanket, found a place where the injured were being attended to. The cries of these men were harder to bear than the silence of the dead. Before he left the man, Aaron knelt down, took the button out of his pocket, and held it to his heart. The wounded man had opened his eyes and was watching him do this. Afterward, he motioned to Aaron to come close.

"I want to do something for you," the man whispered.

"It's not necessary," Aaron said gently. "I was told to bring you here."

The man shook his head. "I have no family; my friends are dead. Give me a reason to live."

Aaron sat back on his heels and thought a moment. Then he bent over the man. "Have you heard of the shrine of the Virgin Mother in the White Mountains?"

The man nodded.

"There is an inn there, about three miles from the church, run by a woman named Judith. A young woman works for her. Her name is Lucia. Tell her that Aaron sent you. Tell her that she came to me in a dark hour and that I have not forgotten her."

The man nodded once more and reached for Aaron's hand. "Thank you," he mouthed.

As the war progressed, Aaron and his unit pressed further into enemy territory. At first, the towns and villages they passed through were empty except for dead soldiers of both sides of the struggle. The young, the old, and the women had fled their homes ahead of the bloody war. But after a while, some bodies of non-combatants were also found rotting in the hot sun of late summer. Orders came from the front *not* to bury them, for they were enemies and not worth the trouble. They would act as a warning. Anyone who disobeyed and tried to bury them would be shot. And then one night, with the fire and smoke of battle visible to the grave-digging unit, Aaron felt a growing agitation in himself and in his comrades. No one slept that night. A painful sense of foreboding had overtaken them all.

The next day they walked into a burnt out town and saw hundreds of corpses of old men, women, and children; some had been hacked to pieces. Although the men had already seen many horrible things, they felt their stomachs turn and tried avoiding looking at this new display of human ferocity. The silence as they walked through the town was an oppressive weight. A few of the men yelped at the top of their lungs, either in an attempt to prove they were not ghosts themselves, or to scare off the dead. Aaron felt a cold creep up his limbs, as if he had been bitten by death itself. He watched as the young officer slowed down and shook his head as if he had just realized he was lost.

One of the men was shouting. Aaron turned around, looking for him. It was one of the dull-witted soldiers. He carried the body of a dead girl in his arms. His intention was obvious —he was going to bury it. The officer had come out of his daze and was yelling at him to put the body down, but the man ignored him. The officer screamed more loudly and threatened him, and still the man continued walking. And then a young soldier, without an order from the officer, unsheathed his sword and, approaching the man, ran him through. As the man fell with the dead child still in his arms, the young soldier looked blankly at the officer. The men in the unit had watched it all, unbelieving.

Aaron had another impulse. He was done with madness, with war. He took off running and he ran for what seemed like hours. He ran through a forest, through deserted villages. He ran while the evening star appeared in the sky. He ran until it was so dark he could not see his own hand in front of him, and then he collapsed under a tree. His body shook and his stomach heaved, and he knew that he could die from disgust and exhaustion.

He did not remember falling asleep, but when he saw the sun he realized he had just forced himself awake. He had been having a dream. In his dream, he had stood on a high mountain. He had heard a woman screaming, and knowing it was Lucia, it ripped the heart from his chest. He lay there spent, despairing.

He was startled by the touch of a leaf falling on his face. He held it by its slender stem and ran his finger over it. He moved it over his cheek and then opening his shirt, laid it on his bare chest, over his heart. He found himself growing steadier as the sun rose in the sky, as if he was righting himself after entirely losing his balance. Aaron put the leaf carefully in his pocket and sat up. He ate some dried bread he found in his small sack, and then assessed his situation. He decided he would return to the city where he had attended school. He would hopefully find out what had happened to Timothy and see how Frederick, his employer, and the other students were doing. Then he would return home to his village.

For the next two months, he tried to sleep during the day, and traveled at night. He scavenged for food, was twice almost killed for it, and spoke to a young soldier he surprised on patrol. When he had first come upon him, he had instinctively recoiled, now wary of young boys with weapons.

"Where are you coming from?" the young soldier had asked him. When Aaron did not answer, the young soldier looked him over carefully. Aaron was holding a staff and the soldier could see that the hand that grasped it was branded. "Are you a deserter?"

"Yes," Aaron had replied, noting the boy's harmless tone and manner.

"Think you'll make it back home?"

"That's my intention."

"Has it been hard, running away?"

"Very, but better than staying where I was."

"I know what you mean. Would you like something to eat?"

"Yes, but I can't stay. It would put us both in danger."

"I understand. Good luck to you."

As Aaron approached the border of his own country, he began to question his original plan. Whom could he stay with, once he arrived in the city? Whoever gave him refuge or food would be putting themselves at risk. He sat down and tried to work out a new plan, but nothing came to him. He needed to eat soon; it was getting difficult to think. Once he crossed the border, he became obsessed with finding out what had happened to Timothy and the professor. A few hours before dawn, he slunk into the city, wishing that it was his old village. No one was about and there were no patrols. It took him hours before he could remember and locate Frederick's house. He knocked on the door for what seemed a long time, and then a large presence filled the door frame. Though he could not speak or raise his head, Aaron sensed health and vigor radiating from the man. He fixated on a small, broken piece of pottery hanging around the man's neck until leaning against the door frame, he slid to the ground. He felt himself being dragged into the house.

"Who are you?" Frederick asked.

Aaron knew he answered and wondered why Frederick's ear was so close to his mouth. Then he thought about the other students and wondered where they were. He heard Frederick asking again, "Who are you?" The strange thing was he did not know anymore, and did not mind not knowing. He remembered the professor had a cat and tried to remember what it was called. He mumbled many names, hoping to stumble on the right one, and grew agitated when the name eluded him. Finally, he knew what it was.

"Sophia," he sputtered, triumphant, and then passed out.

Chapter Twenty-Eight

When Lucia arrived back at the inn, she slipped in through the front door, hoping to go unnoticed. She had taken only a couple of steps when she heard the swooshing of skirts in rapid motion. Judith, Martha, Grace, and Louisa all came running and soon surrounded her.

"What happened? You had us all worried to death. I was about to send Martha and Grace to look for you," said Judith, fanning her face with a feather duster.

"I can't explain…I needed to be alone."

"Was it Nicholas? He said his message disturbed you. He said he thought you were going to faint."

"Nicholas?"

"Nicholas is the name of the messenger," Grace said. "He told us what he said to you, and we couldn't figure out why that would make you so upset."

"Were you worried about Aaron?" Judith asked. "I didn't realize he meant so much to you."

"Yes, that was it…that was part of it…. I'm sorry, but I'm so tired. I need to sit down."

"Oh yes," said Judith, "let's all go into the kitchen."

Judith took Lucia's arm. As soon as Lucia opened the door, she gasped when she saw Nicholas cutting up vegetables and putting them into a pot, looking as though he'd been standing there doing that for years. He gave her a concerned look.

Lucia approached him and held out her hand. "I apologize if I gave you a fright, Nicholas. I'm better now."

Nicholas put down the knife and shook her hand awkwardly. "No apology needed. It must've been shocking, my appearing at the door like that. I overheard what you said in there and I want you to know that when I last saw Aaron he was neither ill nor dead and I saw no wound upon him except a brand."

"A brand," Judith repeated. "I don't believe it. Why?"

"I don't know. In these times men get branded for many reasons, not all of them something to be ashamed of. I could never figure out what he was supposed to have done, unless it was lying or lechery, two vices I doubt he indulged in. He had an 'L' branded on his right hand."

"An 'L,'" Lucia said, amazed.

"Ah," exclaimed Nicholas, "that's the first letter of your name, isn't it?"

"How do you know Aaron? When did you last see him?" Lucia asked.

Judith interrupted, "Before we get into this, let's sit down. Martha, please put a kettle on to boil. We all could use some tea. Nicholas, do you want to sit?"

"I'm good here, thank you, Madame. I'm used to working when I'm talking. I would probably clam up if I sat down."

And so over tea, and with Nicholas stirring and tasting and adding herbs, his story came out.

He told them that Aaron was part of a burial unit and that

Aaron had found him in the ruin of his kitchen, and had determined he was still alive. He told them how Aaron had taken charge of him when he was incapacitated and how for nearly two days he and a regular soldier had carried him to safety. "He held my head and fed me broth," he concluded. Nicholas wept as he shared this detail.

"I still don't understand why you're here, Nicholas," Lucia said. "Why did you come, and why would Aaron send you such a long way to deliver a message?"

"He saved my life. And I wanted to do something in return… I asked him to send me." Nicholas wiped his face with the apron he had on. "Excuse me," he said, embarrassed.

"You don't have to be embarrassed here, Nicholas," Martha said. "You're not in the army anymore."

"Who is Aaron, Lucia?" Louisa asked. "Is he the young man from your village, the one the others have met?"

"Yes."

"They told me that they were *very* impressed with him," Louisa said.

"So tell us more about him, Lucia. Now we are all curious," Martha said.

"I don't know him very well. In our village everyone knew he loved books and ideas. He lived with his mother…she was a quiet person. His father left them when Aaron was still a young boy, but the priest of our village, Father Lawrence, looked out for him. Father Lawrence was always talking about Aaron when he came to visit my mother. When he got older, Aaron went to work on farms away from the village and then he started acting as a guide for pilgrims. I heard he entered the university and that he was doing very well. However, Father Lawrence was worried about him…that's all I know."

"That's interesting," Martha dryly remarked, "but what about your *relationship* to him. There has to be a relationship, otherwise why would he send you the message and why would you be so worried?"

"I really can't say."

Martha persisted, "But you must care for him very much, and he obviously cares very much for you."

Nicholas had stopped cooking and was paying close attention, along with the women.

"I am attracted to him," Lucia said, blushing.

"So there *is* there something going on between the two of you," Martha concluded.

"Martha, leave her alone," Judith said gently. "She looks tired and needs rest. Lucia, why don't you wash up and go to bed."

Lucia looked at Judith gratefully. She knew her employer was just as — if not more — curious than the rest, and so especially appreciated Judith's bit of mothering.

"I think she's in love and doesn't know it yet," said Grace, winking at Nicholas.

Nicholas stood there, a fly on the wall, taking all of it in: the fast-moving female banter, the teasing, the quick care, the probing curiosity. It was a different world, but not unpleasant. In fact, compared to his many years as an army cook, he rather liked it.

Within a week, though the number of guests had dropped because of the war, Judith hired Nicholas on as cook, telling Lucia that he was too much part of their family to let him go. However, Judith was soon sharing with Lucia her regrets, for Martha began spending long periods of time with him in the kitchen. Judith talked to Martha about it, but it didn't change things. Martha told Judith that Nicholas needed her help because more soldiers were coming to the back door asking for food and he could not feed them all. Nicholas did not say anything; he let Martha do all the explaining.

"I hope Aaron comes soon," Judith said to Nicholas one morning when they were both in the kitchen and Martha was busy upstairs. "Lucia is not herself."

"He'll come, Madame."

"The reports have been so disheartening! I try to keep her from hearing them….She believes he's coming back. It would be so hard for her…"

"He wasn't in the regular army; he's got a better chance than most."

"Love is such torment, Nicholas."

"May we all suffer from it, Madame."

Judith caught the gleam in his eye and gave him a wry smile.

In late spring, a letter arrived for Lucia from Catherine.

Dear Lucia,

Simon and I send our love. We have good news! Some people you know have returned.

Father Lawrence is back with us! I cannot say how pleased I am about it. Father Ignatius has been asking to be reassigned to a larger parish, so everything worked out well.

Father Lawrence seems happy to be back. He's been here now for several months and has been busy repairing things. Physically, he's changed. His hair is nearly white and he has some scars, but he is the same priest he always was. Thank God for that! And then, to top it off, Aaron showed up last week with a distinguished-looking man, a professor named Frederick. Frederick is a kind and obliging man, but he stands out here like a sore thumb. The country must seem like a foreign land to him. Even though he speaks our tongue we don't understand him, and I doubt he understands us. Aaron says that the professor was beaten up once and that if he had stayed where he was, he would have been killed. He was in great danger. It seems as if Aaron was also in great danger, but he hasn't told us that story yet.

The professor is living with Aaron and his mother. Aaron has already started building a little place behind theirs for him. Father Lawrence and some of the young men are helping him out. Aaron's still handsome and not too much physically changed, though he's lost some weight. He told us he was not much more than skin and bones when he came to Frederick's house after he fled the war. He said that Frederick took good care of him. Something about him is different, though. It seems as if he not entirely here. Simon says he's grown more detached and serious, but I've heard Aaron laugh and it's quite contagious. Whether he is laughing or more solemn, he carries himself well, as you know. He is like a king. Don't tell Simon I told you this. He would only make fun of me.

Father Lawrence has asked about you and Aaron has come around here nearly every day. He asks about our health and how the grandchildren are doing and then he gets around to his real purpose, which is finding out about you. Simon was very surprised by his curiosity. He told me he thinks Aaron has intentions — as if I didn't have eyes or ears. Everyone in the village knows. Aaron has been going around showing people the brand he has on his right hand. Anyone else would be covering it up; he seems proud of it. He says it's an "L" for your name. Some have told him that it looks more like a "T," but he insists that it's an "L" and most agree with him.

When Aaron found out that I was posting this letter, he asked me to tell you that he hoped you got his message and that he would find a way to get to the White Mountains soon. He says there are still groups of pilgrims going

— 253 —

to the Virgin's Shrine. He wants to get Frederick settled first, but he is in a rush to see you.

I would love to overhear his conversations with Father Lawrence since they've both been back. I am thinking of inviting them over for dinner...and that professor, too. Simon says I am being nosy, but I tell him it's good to be nosy around people who think a lot. Maybe intelligence is something that rubs off.

I don't know how your plans might change or not, but Simon and I wanted you to know that you would always be welcome here. With that said, I also want you to know that we have been having some trouble in the village; it's not clear who or what is the cause. More people are passing through. They've been called "riff raff" and they've been blamed for the things that have come up missing and for the fires that have scorched the fields. Father Lawrence is trying to make us more hospitable toward them. He reminds us of how many of the people passing through have lost their homes and their families.

War stirs up a hornet's nest, even in such out-of-the way places as our village. The trick is not to beat the hornets back too violently. It only makes them madder...

Lucia reread that letter many times. She always had it with her. The others would tease her whenever they saw her pull it out of a pocket. She would redden and keep reading. One evening, just before dinner was served, Judith called all her employees into the kitchen. She asked Lucia if she had been noticing anything peculiar and when Lucia asked what she was talking about, the others burst out laughing. It was Louisa who explained.

"Grace said we should do a little experiment. She said that Judith should assign you most of the unpleasant tasks. She said that you were so much in love that you wouldn't even notice....

We got Judith to go along. And you *didn't* notice, Lucia, even though it's been going on for two weeks!"

Trying to collect themselves, the others headed out laughing to the dining room to serve the guests, leaving Judith and Nicholas alone in the kitchen. Nicholas leaned over a large pot he was stirring, took a deep whiff and added some herbs. Judith ran a rag over the chopping table.

"Nicholas, isn't it wonderful how love thrives even in these terrible times?"

Nicholas looked at Judith. "I'm not surprised, Madame. The heart appears to be like a good cook, and can make a meal out of anything."

III.

Lovers of Wisdom

Chapter Twenty~Nine

Although he was expected, when Judith opened the door and saw Aaron standing there, hat in hand, her mouth fell open.

"Hello, Judith. You might not remember me. I'm Aaron; I'm from the same village as Lucia."

Aaron repeated himself when Judith continued standing there, speechless.

"Were you expecting someone else, Judith?"

"Uh…no. No one else….We got your message."

"He came?"

"Nicholas? Oh, yes. He caused quite a stir. Didn't you get Lucia's letter?"

"Not yet. I've been on the road for a while. I hope you're well."

"I am," Judith said. "You look well, considering what we've heard. Would you like to come in?"

"Is Lucia here?"

"No. Today is her day off. She left early to go walking on the mountain. You're welcome to wait for her inside. She'll be home by supper. Are you hungry?"

"How can I find her?"

"Find her? Now? Well, you have to go back until you get to the crossroads. There is a footpath, marked by a little roadside shrine that will take you up the mountain. It ends at the base of a small cascade. She'll probably be nearby, maybe in one of the caves. Do you want some food?"

"No...Thank you. I want to look for her. Please excuse me." Aaron had made a quick bow and was turning to leave when Judith noticed a strong-looking black horse, hitched to the post. Aaron strode toward it and leapt effortlessly onto the saddle, snatching up the reins.

Martha came out of the kitchen wiping her hands on her apron. "Who was it?"

"Aaron," said Judith, watching him gallop up the road.

Martha crowded her at the door. "Aaron. Oh my! And what a beautiful horse! I would love to be there when Lucia catches sight of the two of them!"

Aaron had no trouble finding the footpath. He rode far up the mountain and then got off the horse as the path became narrower, steeper, and rockier. When he got to the cascade, he led the horse to a quiet pool and let him drink. He decided to wait there for Lucia, although he felt a strong desire to keep looking for her. After a short while, he bent down and studied the footprints on the softened ground, carefully tracing one he thought might be hers. Just as he straightened up, Lucia came around an outcropping of rock a little above him on the path. She gave a shout of pure joy, "Aaron!" The rocks reverberated with the sound of her voice and bore his name back to him.

She did not hesitate, but ran down to him, her reddish-gold

hair loose and streaming behind her. Aaron saw her as a comet, a light rushing toward him from another world, a being that was returning to him the fullness of who he was. He opened up his arms, knowing he had to, even though he felt his strength was not yet equal to what was being given him. And then he held her and his face was in her hair, and his body was thrilling with the excitement in hers. He was lost and knew she was also.

"I remembered you, Lucia. I saw you." He choked up.

He felt her legs give way and gently eased her down until she sat on a large flat stone. He sat next to her. When she started sobbing, he put his arms around her and said her name over and over. She spoke quietly to him. He did not hear her words as much as he heard the fluid, bubbling sound of her resonating in his chest. *How can I be given such a gift?* he wondered. She stopped speaking and reached for his hand. Feeling a ridge too straight and pronounced to be natural, she held it up and saw the "L" scorched on it. She kissed it. He then took her hand, and placing it over his chest, held it there. She looked into his eyes and opening her hand, curved it around his flesh until Aaron felt as if she was holding his heart, caressing it, touching wounds that went back further than his arrest, wounds he had borne since childhood. Tears came and Aaron felt that it was his wounds themselves that wept.

When they arrived back at the inn, it was late. Lucia had offered Aaron some food and hoped they could sneak into the kitchen to eat, but when they went around to the back she saw that lights were on and she heard voices.

Aaron laughed quietly. "Don't worry. I've faced worse. Let's go." He took her by the hand and they stepped inside. Everyone was there: Judith, Martha, Grace, Louisa, and Nicholas. Aaron stared at Nicholas. Nicholas nodded at him and smiled.

"We're hungry and wanted to eat something," was all Lucia said.

"We've been making a stew," Judith said. "Please sit down, Aaron…Lucia."

"Have we met?" Aaron asked Nicholas, looking at him intently.

"I see Lucia in her excitement at seeing you again forgot to mention that Nicholas was still here," Judith said.

"What?" Aaron said, shocked.

Nicholas held back his hair from his forehead, revealing a scar.

"He's our cook now," Martha said, "and part of our little family."

Aaron went over to Nicholas and they embraced. When they parted, the women saw that both men wept.

"We're grateful you saved Nicholas, especially Martha," Grace teased. Martha poked her in the ribs.

"Louisa," said Judith, "please get some wine from the cellar. I think it will be a long night."

It was close to dawn when they all staggered to their rooms. Aaron had narrated events very simply, had said nothing of Timothy, and had shared only a little of his inner feelings, but his story had been captivating. The hours had flown by. The others had noticed how he looked at Lucia when he spoke and none doubted he was in love with her. Judith invited him to stay; Nicholas insisted that Aaron take his room, and offered to see to his horse. He averted his gaze when Aaron warmly kissed Lucia good night.

Louisa was already in bed when Lucia entered their shared room. Thoughtfully, all she said was, "Good night, Lucia. I'm so happy for you."

Lucia undressed and got under the covers, but knew she would never sleep. She was savoring the delicious thought of Aaron sleeping under the same roof that sheltered her: safe, sound, and in love with her.

Chapter Thirty

The next morning, Judith told Aaron he was welcome to stay at the inn for a few weeks. While he was grateful for her offer, he told her he had decided to stay at the shelter run by a religious order dedicated to providing hospitality. He had come up the mountain, acting as a guide for a group of their young aspirants. They had been sent to help with the growing number of veterans who were coming to the shrine. Aaron had volunteered his services for a few weeks in exchange for food and shelter for his horse and himself. His plan had been to save as much of his money as he could, for he hoped Lucia would want to go back to the village with him.

When Aaron was seeing to his horse, Judith told him that the invitation for him to stay at the inn would stand, and that there was always something an able-bodied young man could help with — in fact, there were some parts of the roof that needed repairing. She insisted he stay for breakfast. Afterward, Lucia walked up the road with him for nearly a mile, not wanting to leave him.

"I'll come every day, Lucia. It's only three miles and with a fast horse like Thunder and a good road, it isn't far at all."

Aaron kept his promise. Every afternoon he would ride up and he and Lucia would spend several hours together. He would stay for dinner and leave before dark. Since it was summer and warmer, they would walk up the road, or even follow the footpath up the mountain to the place where they had met. On her day off and on their first full day together, Aaron told her what had happened to Timothy, about how his carelessness and poor judgment had led to Timothy's arrest, about how he felt he had betrayed his friend.

"When the professor was nursing me back to health, I asked about Timothy and he told me that Timothy had died in prison. He had gotten very ill soon after we were arrested and never recovered. Frederick didn't tell me, but I found out later from another friend that Timothy's father had stood at the gates of the garrison for days begging whoever was in charge to release his son. The captain never spoke to him and some of the soldiers began throwing pieces of brick at him to make him go away." Aaron cried. Lucia felt her own heart breaking but said nothing, and pulled her outstretched hand back before it touched him.

"I couldn't keep food down after I heard about Timothy's father. I would vomit everything up. It was Frederick who slowly made me better. He kept talking to me, asking me questions about my experience. He got me thinking again, and soon after that I found I could eat. For weeks, Frederick took care of me and never once did he mention what happened to him the night Timothy and I were arrested. When I was nearly recovered I asked him directly about it. He said that some soldiers had beaten him, and other than losing two teeth, he had not suffered any permanent damage. I asked the women who had been at Frederick's the night I was arrested for more details and found out that soldiers had started pounding on nearby doors shortly after they had seized Timothy and myself. Fortunately, when they got to Frederick's, only two of the women were still there. Frederick invited the soldiers in and acted incredulous when they asked if he was a teacher and if the women were his students. The women fell into acting the part of nieces coming to visit a well-to-do uncle. They might have fooled the soldiers...I don't know.... It didn't matter. The men were probably keyed up and under pressure to make someone pay. They said Frederick sounded like a professor and they hit him with the butt of their guns. They might have killed him but the women screamed and begged the soldiers to stop and they did...."

He had struggled to get out the last few sentences, but Lucia felt he had more to say. She waited. He looked away, rubbing the hollow under his right eye. His suffering and strain were transparent. She felt scorched by their intensity and by the guilt that had him in a stranglehold. She also intuited something else. In the effort it took for him to speak, in the clenching of his hands, the grinding of his teeth, but most of all in his wandering glance and inability to look at her, she knew he was inwardly raging and wanted to spare her the brunt of his anger, wanted to spare himself the full sight of it. He looked at her again, calmer. She knew he had decided not to say anything else about Timothy. When he asked her to say more about herself, Lucia knew he was genuinely interested in her, but also needed the distraction.

She told him about her mysterious tremor. She told him how she felt when Nicholas delivered the message.

"I knew you were suffering, Aaron. I ran up the mountain to be alone. Once I got there I realized that I was feeling not only your pain, but the suffering of many others. I could not hold all that pain; it was too much. I was inspired to let all that pain express itself through me and as soon as I agreed to do that, I started crying out — but inside of myself. And then it was as if it wasn't me any more that was crying out. It was Christ. I knew that somehow. Everything and everyone else had disappeared. There was only Christ. He was all alone and in such horrible agony. All the pain and suffering of the world was pushing out from every-where inside of him and it was Him that was crying out — not me. And then it was as if Christ disappeared too and there was only a Presence. No, that isn't right. It wasn't *a* Presence, it was just Presence. It wasn't the presence *of* anything. And then there was Bliss. But that's not right either. The Presence and the Bliss were connected, like the front and back of a hand." She held out her right hand and turned it over and back again. "When you take my hand and hold it, you are holding the palm and the back of it, even though you are only seeing one side at a time. It's hard to explain….The pain was completely gone, though, all of it in an instant — as if it had never been. There was no gradual healing, no soothing, no gradual understanding. All that suffering, it was just gone. I cannot describe that Bliss, Aaron – the power and fullness of it. I wanted you to feel it. I so much wanted you to feel it."

Aaron hugged her to himself, and while he still held her close, they did some calculating and came to the conclusion that the day Aaron and his unit had come upon the corpses of the women and children and older people — the day the young soldiers shot a man he knew and had lived with for over a year, only because that man wanted to bury a child — was near to, if not the very same day Lucia had experienced suffering and bliss on the mountain.

"I took off running after that," Aaron said. "And that night I dreamt I heard you screaming. I couldn't bear it."

"I did suffer, but only for a little while."

He told her about the leaf that had fallen on him and how he had placed it on his heart and how he had felt stronger. He told her about how he also had sensed a Presence at Frederick's and in prison, and how quickly it seemed to move through everything and how incomprehensible that Presence was.

"There are so many things I don't understand even though I've been reflecting on them for a long time," Lucia said. "I believe the Presence I felt on the mountain was connected to something my mother experienced."

When Aaron asked what she meant, Lucia told him about Sophia's encounters with the Woman. Lucia also shared how these meetings had affected her mother and what she had thought of them, and then Lucia went on and told Aaron about Richard's search for the goddess and her own dream at the shrine. "In my dream, Sophia told me to learn from the Woman and to become Her so that I could bear all the light, movement, and beauty that were approaching the earth."

Aaron listened to her with rapt attention and she listened to him, marveling. She entirely bared her heart to him; he bared nearly all of his to her. They existed in the heart's naked splendor, not in time or place. And in that splendor, when Aaron and Lucia spoke or heard a word, it did not signify a boundary, nor did it circumscribe an object. Every word was both a planting and harvesting of shared meaning. And that shared meaning was so rich and manifold, and intimated such possibilities, that by time they walked down the mountain it was as if they held the earth and its destiny between them.

Aaron seemed lighter after that day. He laughed more, would

pull pranks on Nicholas or would tease him about Martha, and when he arrived at the inn in the afternoons he would try to sneak up on Lucia before she caught sight of him, untying her apron or seizing a towel out of her hand. Then she would run after him as he fled down the stairs or out through the kitchen. Once she chased him nearly a mile down the road. He would slow down to entice her to keep running after him and then would speed up as she came closer. Sometimes he would circle back and begin to chase her. He taught her how to ride Thunder and when she insisted he dance with her on the mountain, he jumped, turned, and leapt about like a young and frisky animal, something he had never done before, even as a boy.

He was delighted when she spoke off the top of her head as they walked high up in the mountains. He found her words brave, like banners unfurling in the wind. "I feel like we've been sent out together to some far away, foreign land to do something important," she would say and he would feel emboldened. But sometimes he felt she tottered on the edge of foolishness and he would either try to joke with her or walk behind her so he did not have to reply, or even listen too carefully. Sometimes she would stop and turn around and ask him if he had heard what she had said and he would catch up with her and kiss her. "What can be more important than this?" he would ask. And if she pressed him to be more serious, he would remind her that he had had an unforgettable lesson on the cost of thinking too highly of oneself. She would hesitate when he said this or something like it, but would not be put off, and would answer him by saying that greatness was something a human being should aspire to, and that others can help you toward it if you let them.

After three weeks Aaron moved into the inn, insisting that an attic room used for storage would perfectly meet his needs. Once settled in, he and Lucia began talking about the future. Lucia told Aaron she wanted to return with him to their village and that she would live with Catherine and Simon until they wed. Aaron suggested they get married before they left. "Nicholas and Martha will be marrying soon. We can marry with them."

"But what about Catherine and your mother? They would be so disappointed. And I want Father Lawrence to be there. I'm sure you do, too…"

"You're right….We'll wait."

While Lucia found making plans exciting, and looked forward to returning to the village, she knew leaving the inn and her fellow employees would be difficult. She especially dreaded having to say goodbye to Judith. One early afternoon when Aaron was on an errand and they were both alone in the kitchen doing dishes, Judith, seeming to read her mind, brought up the subject of her departure.

"Nicholas and Martha are suited, don't you think? Martha had her eye on him from that first day. I'm glad they'll both stay here after they're wed. What about you and Aaron? What will you do? Will you go back to your village?" There was a quaver in Judith's voice. Lucia dried her hands on her apron and hugged her.

"It's too soon to start bawling," Judith said, pulling away while patting Lucia's hands. "There will be time for that later. I'm happy for you, Lucia. Let me say that. When you and Aaron are together, I sense something special. Richard would probably say that the goddess brought you together. That could be. I'm not as clear about such things as my husband was. But whatever makes your relationship special, I know it won't make marriage and family life easy for the two of you. You both are too much like Richard."

"Oh Judith, I'll miss you!"

Judith stroked Lucia's arm a couple of times. "I'll miss you too. Now, let's stop this. Time to dry the eyes and talk business. What should we cook for Martha's wedding? I was thinking a roast and maybe a pudding…"

The wedding was small and well-organized. Martha wore a new dress while Nicholas sweated profusely in a new shirt. He corrected himself twice as he said his vows, causing Martha to titter. Martha said hers quickly, unable to look at him. They both seemed enormously relieved when the ceremony was over and dinner was served. Tables had been set outside with the finest linen and candles. All the inn's guests were invited, as well as acquaintances of Martha's. Aaron had brought some of the young aspirants working at the shelter. Nicholas appeared awed by it all and repeatedly thanked Judith for the tastiness of the food and the elegance of the setting. Toward the end of dinner, musicians arrived and played for the gathering. They warmed up with sedate ballads, but as the wine, ale, and laughter flowed they progressed to more boisterous reels. Soon the company was dancing with abandon.

In the course of the evening's festivities, Nicholas toasted Aaron, telling the story of how Aaron had rescued him. He did it twice: the first time when he was still relatively sober, the second when inebriated. Nicholas had them all laughing to the point of tears, especially during the retelling when he added fantastical and lengthy details to the story of his journey to the shrine. Later, as the celebration was winding down, Nicholas raised his hand a third time to get people's attention. Everyone moaned, including Martha.

"This is my last speech," Nicholas began. The revelers cheered. "And don't worry, I'm not going to tell you the same stories or embarrass Aaron any more." The revelers cheered again, Aaron louder than any of them. "I never imagined myself a married man, or a religious man, but here I am a married one now, thanks to Martha, my wife….I like saying that, 'my wife'….And if gratitude is a sign of a religious man, then I'm a *very* religious man. All of you have made me one." Nicholas opened his arms, the simple gesture causing him to tilt forward.

Chapter Thirty-One

It was early September, a week before their departure date. Before sunrise, Lucia and Aaron put food and blankets on Thunder and left the inn. Walking silently up the moonlit road, they took the winding path up the mountain. Both felt desire and a little fear, knowing what they had decided to do.

The sun was casting a net of light on the surrounding peaks when they arrived at the base of the cascade. After a simple breakfast, they washed up at the shallow end of the pool, and Aaron let Thunder graze while Lucia took him into the various caves she had discovered in her wanderings. They would sit quietly in each one and Lucia was moved by how Aaron, like herself, also sensed something in the silence.

The sun was above their heads when they left the last cave. They returned to the base of the cascade, ate some more, and spoke about their village and what they missed about it when they were away. Afterward, they spread out blankets under a tree, and disrobing without shyness they lay down on their backs next to each other. Aaron lightly took Lucia's hand in his and she shared with him the things Sophia and Jeremiah had taught her. Then he shared with her what he had learned from Father Lawrence and his mother.

They fell silent as clouds hid then revealed the innocent vastness of the sky. Lucia rolled over on her side and began kissing Aaron's eyes, his face. He turned toward her and kissed her full on the mouth. She felt wetness between her legs, felt the stream-like nature of her body. A vast, invisible sea exerted its pull, inexorably attracting her. She yielded to it, as it rushed to meet her through him. Their bodies tasting and caressing floated willingly and entwined into passion's maelstrom where limbs and mouths, hands and eyes all woke to their separate and urgent hungers. An improvised and invigorating rhythm turned feeding and being fed into a single deed. And then he was in her and it hurt a little, but she held him close, wanting him inside of her. Afterward, they lay quietly in each other's arms and then rolled onto their backs and watched as flocks of broad-stroking birds punctuated the sky.

"Do you remember the day you found me here?" she asked him, softly.

"I will never forget that day."

She paused, relishing his response. "I was sitting in that last cave we were in when I saw you coming. I didn't see you with these eyes," she touched her eyelids. "Sophia used to tell me that we have special eyes as well as our everyday ones. She said when she first saw me, she saw me with those special eyes. I think those special eyes are here." She placed a hand over her breast. "I saw you with the eyes of the heart, Aaron. It was like I could see your soul. And I knew you were coming close to me even though I was still in the cave."

"What did my soul look like?" Aaron asked quietly.

"It was very confident, but also very humble. I fell in love with it immediately. I wasn't surprised to see you when I left the cave. I knew you would be somewhere on the mountain."

Aaron kissed her between her breasts and then stroked her face, arms and side. She moaned and felt new spaces inside of her, spaces where pleasure and sound were innocent of their difference. He was inside of her again. Even with her new spaces she could not absorb her pleasure. She cried out and then he did. They fell asleep in each other's arms. When they woke, the sun was still warm so they bathed together in the pool, splashing each other, laughing, but subdued. Afterwards, they put their clothes back on, fed the horse, gathered firewood, and ate a large dinner. As they watched the clouds scoop up the gold of the setting sun, Lucia wondered aloud how it was possible to feel so empty and so full at the same time and why that was so satisfying.

When the sun's last glorious rays brightened the rising moon, Lucia started shivering and Aaron made a fire. They wrapped themselves in several blankets and lay down next to it. Lucia told him that the stars looked like the faces of angels flickering in firelight. And he told her that the faces of the angels were shining brighter because of their lovemaking. Lucia said she liked that and kissed him good night. They fell asleep — Aaron pressing up against her back, his hand cradling her breast.

The cooing of a dove woke them in the morning.

When they returned to the inn, Aaron saw to the horse and Lucia went looking for Judith, feeling the need of a woman's presence. She found Judith, sitting in the parlor, talking to a guest. Not wanting to interrupt their conversation, Lucia stood quietly by the door. She was about to turn around and leave when the guest began looking around for something and Judith took the opportunity to glance at Lucia. Judith's face immediately softened and a knowing, radiant look came over her face. Lucia smiled, feeling her own cheeks burning. A little later, when the guest had gone upstairs, Judith invited Lucia to sit with her in the parlor near the fire.

"You gave yourself to him," Judith guessed aloud.

Lucia nodded, smiling.

"I have something for you." Judith stood up and went to the fireplace. She picked up the statue of Isis and with hands outstretched carried it toward Lucia.

"Oh, Judith, I couldn't!"

"I want you to."

Lucia traced the golden wings appreciatively with her finger. "It's a perfect gift. Thank you."

Judith placed the statue carefully on a nearby table. "I'll keep her for now. I want to pack her for you." Taking a deep breath as if to brace herself, Judith continued, "Lucia, there are few things I have ever wanted more than being at your wedding. But with the inn and all, I don't think I'll be able." Judith impatiently brushed away her tears. "I want to see you again, though. You have to come and see me."

"I will." Lucia embraced Judith. Then Judith picked up the statue of Isis and held it at eye level.

"Remember the story of Isis? Dismemberment – that is what it feels like! Love is so painful!" Judith blew her nose. "Richard said that pure love was different somehow, but I never understood what he meant by that. The way I hurt, I must be much more familiar with the impure kind," Judith said with a rueful laugh. "I do have my moments though. I know that love is the only thing that makes this strange world of ours a home."

As Lucia was packing her things the day before she and Aaron planned to leave, she came upon Jeremiah's gift – the parchment with the circle in gold leaf and the pressed flower. She sat down on her bed and thought about him, about how it would be seeing him again — and then she felt something like dread. Catherine's letters had always included news of Jeremiah, but not her last one. Why? Had something bad happened? When Louisa came in and asked if she was all right, that saying she looked shaken, Lucia said she was a little tired and had just been remembering a friend. Louisa asked if she wanted her help packing. Everyone offered assistance that last day. Nicholas cooked and baked food for their journey, while Martha and Grace packed plates, cups, and utensils they had purchased earlier for the pair.

That evening they put an extra table outside, and after the guests had eaten, they feasted under the stars. They told stories, humorous anecdotes about each other, and spoke of plans that brought a twinge of grief, because those plans would no longer include all of them. Then they said their goodbyes. There were hugs, embraces, tears, best wishes. Aaron and Lucia were sent off, while the rest took care of the cleaning up. Lucia knew she would not be able to sleep right away and suggested that she and Aaron go for a stroll. They held hands and walked up the road, where they would be headed in the morning with a returning group of pilgrims. Lucia wanted to ask him then about Jeremiah, but there was another part of her that wanted to put off knowing what she sensed was bad news. Aaron and Lucia said very little. The lively warmth, flowing up their arms and into their chests from where their hands met, made conversation superfluous.

By midmorning the following day, the small group of pilgrims they would be traveling with for nearly two weeks stopped in front of the inn. Aaron helped Lucia up unto the seat of the small cart he had bought and repaired. Judith, Louisa, Martha, Nicholas, Grace, and a few guests stood by the door and waved goodbye. Lucia blew kisses and waved back. As Thunder pulled, the cart lurched forward and Lucia felt her heart lurching with it. She placed a steadying hand on Aaron's knee.

Chapter Thirty-Two

Though leaving the inn had been difficult and she had some fear about being on the road, Lucia soon found herself enjoying the journey. Aaron and she had fallen quickly into a comfortable rhythm and the lingering and tempered warmth of early autumn, the mutual courtesy of the group of travelers, along with the absence of unpleasant encounters with thieves or soldiers raised everyone's spirits. One afternoon Lucia began laughing loudly to herself. When Aaron asked what she found so funny, she told him.

"Do you know that in the village nearly every young woman fantasized about you?"

"About me?"

"About you. But what kept the young women from pursuing you was the thought of being homeless and having to sleep on the ground. And here I am." She laughed again so loudly that the travelers ahead of them turned around to see what was so amusing. For a while afterward, she and Aaron talked about the young men and women they had grown up with, and then they lapsed into an easy silence. In the quiet, Lucia's thoughts roamed over many things. She wondered how long they would be staying in the village, if Father Lawrence had changed, what Frederick was like, and when she would see Judith and the inn again. And then she began wondering what had happened to Jeremiah. As soon as they stopped for the evening, Aaron reached into his pocket and handed her a letter.

"It's from Father Lawrence. It's about Jeremiah."

Lucia, trying to decipher the look in Aaron's eyes, took the letter and read it silently.

Dear Lucia,

I have bad news about Jeremiah. Catherine, Simon, Aaron, and I decided that the best way to tell you this news was for me to write this letter and for Aaron to give it you once you were on your way home. We did not want grief to mar your first meeting with Aaron or deepen your sadness at leaving your friends.

When I arrived back at the village, I heard that Jeremiah had not been seen for nearly two months. People were worried about him, most especially Catherine and Simon. A week after my return, he showed up in church. He did not look well and when he spoke it was with a great deal of effort. He asked if it was possible to die of loneliness. My first impulse was to say no and offer him reassurance, but I saw he needed me to speak as truthfully as I could. I told him that I imagined it was possible — that loneliness, if unrelieved, could take away a man's will to live. He did not say anything for a while. Then he told me that if he died he wanted to be buried next to Sophia. He did not want the women cleaning him up, or giving him new clothes; he wanted to be buried as he was. As he patted his chest, he said he had but one treasure, one possession he held dear. I thought he meant his gift for feeling things deeply. I thought he meant his heart.

I told him I would see that his requests were carried out and asked if he would at least share a meal with me. He politely declined, saying he wasn't hungry, and so I asked if I could bless him. From where he sat, he bowed his head as if he were too weak to either stand or kneel. I placed my hands on his head and thanked him for what he had given so generously to the village. I thanked him for the words and stories he had drawn up from the well of his heart to quench our thirst for beauty. I asked his forgiveness for myself and for the other villagers for not always appreciating the love and goodness which led him to do this for us. I wished him peace in his suffering. He kissed my hand as a thank you and then left. His sorrow was beyond anything I have ever experienced or witnessed. I was reminded of Christ. He was Christ. Christ in his agony and abandonment in the garden. Christ desolate upon the cross.

It was the last time anyone saw him. When several weeks had gone by, I told Aaron that I feared something had happened to him. We got some men together and went searching for him. We found his body in the forest, near the old ruins, many miles from the village. It had been partially eaten. From all the signs, it looked as if an animal had attacked him after he died. His clothes had been torn apart, including his pocket, which looked like it had previously been sewn shut. Aaron observed a letter poking out of the ruined pocket. He unfolded it and seeing that you had signed it, he did not read it. He folded it back up and returned it where it had been.

Catherine repaired the pocket, but otherwise we did as Jeremiah asked: we buried him as we found him, with your letter. Many came to his funeral, more than I know Jeremiah would have expected. It was a sad day for all of us. Following his wishes, we buried him next to Sophia. A few in the village resented that we gave him a church burial because they believed he took his own life. You may hear such rumors when you return, but no one knows why or how he really died. I believe it was from a broken heart. But I must add that his broken heart was no one's fault, no one's blame. Not Jeremiah's. Not anyone's. I think that Beauty wanted to burst into this world through our little village here, and Jeremiah knew that and offered himself in Her service. But it cost him dear, for it overwhelmed his ability to live a normal life and have normal relations. We wanted him to be our Moses. We wanted him to be the one to go up the mountain and hear and see God's unveiled Beauty and then tell us about it. We were too afraid or busy, most of us, to go ourselves.

I know you will miss him a great deal and I know you brought him deep joy.

There are many here who look forward to seeing you. Catherine and Simon are very eager to have you back in their home. I look forward to seeing you and hearing your stories.

Lucia had read only a little of the letter before she was sobbing. Aaron kept glancing at her, anxiously. Struggling to control her emotions, she read the letter again out loud for his sake. She did not feel like eating that evening and Aaron told their fellow travelers, when they asked about her, that she was indisposed. After the group had eaten and was settling down for the night, Aaron looked for her. He found Lucia a little way from camp, sitting on a fallen log, looking at the stars. Aaron came and sat behind her and wrapped his arms around her. She leaned back into his chest.

"Have you been thinking about him?" he asked.

"Yes. You haven't asked me about the letter I wrote – the one you found in his pocket."

"You were good friends. You don't have to tell me what was in the letter."

"I know. I *want* to tell you. I wrote to him about suffering.... I think we both suffered because of something that happened."

Quietly, Lucia told Aaron what had occurred between Jeremiah and herself just before she left the village, surprised that even though so much had happened since, she was reliving it as she told it. Aaron hugged her closer.

"There is a Jeremiah in every man, Lucia. There's one in me too. Some of us are just more successful at hiding it. Men are all drawn to Beauty even though She seems to turn us into stammering and impotent fools. I'm certain Jeremiah never wanted to hurt you. He loved you. A part of him probably knew he was behaving foolishly, but he was too enthralled with your Beauty to stop himself."

"I wished I had seen that at the time," Lucia exclaimed. "I loved him and I love him still. He knew so much; he saw so much. He was so brave. I tried to tell him that in my letter. I wanted to make up for how I acted so coldly toward him."

Aaron kissed the top of her head. "I'm sure he forgave you and would want you to forgive yourself. He would say the blame was his."

After ten days, the group began passing soldiers on the road. Once, they were forced to give up food and blankets. They heard stories of the war, how it was going badly, how more men had to help fight. During one of their last evening meals together, a heated discussion about the war got started. Trying to dissipate the tension, a woman turned to the man next to her and asked what had brought him make a pilgrimage to the shrine of the Virgin. The man spoke openly and loudly. He told her and the group that his son had killed himself the night before he was to go into battle, that he had written a letter to his father begging his forgiveness for any grief or dishonor his action might cause him.

"I went to the shrine because my wife said I had to learn how to forgive our son."

"Did you?" a young woman asked.

"No," the man said. "I didn't want to."

"What's the war about, anyway? I've never understood it," an older woman said.

"No one does," Aaron said quietly.

"Then why are we fighting?" the older woman asked.

"Our leaders know what they're doing. We have no other choice," an older boy remarked.

"How do you know that?" Aaron asked.

The man whose son had taken his own life turned to Aaron, "You refused to fight too, didn't you?"

"I didn't fight. I buried the dead. I buried hundreds of bodies. Bodies of soldiers who were still boys. I buried the bodies of men who didn't understand why they were dead. I buried bodies of men who couldn't believe that they *were* dead."

"No one can see the dead," the older boy said in a contemptuous tone.

"Now how can you say that, young man?" the old woman asked, exasperated. "You can't say a person didn't experience what they experienced."

"I felt them more than I saw them," Aaron said.

"I was taught we should pray for the dead," the young woman said. "I never understood the reason for that until just now. How terrible it must be to be so confused, so lost after you die."

"I haven't prayed for my son," said the man whose son had killed himself. "If he is wandering about lost, he brought it on himself."

"Who of us isn't lost and trying to find the way?" Aaron asked. "The living and the dead are not so different. Perhaps we can help each other."

The man expelled a burst of air as if he had just received a blow, and left the group.

Chapter Thirty-Three

As Aaron pulled the horse up near the village church, Lucia saw Father Lawrence working, lifting stones. The priest's face lit up as he caught sight of them, and he dropped what he was carrying. Lucia was immediately struck by how much he had changed. His hair was almost completely white, but his countenance was that of a younger man and he moved with a new ease and grace. Not waiting for Aaron, she jumped down from the cart and hurried toward him.

"Lucia! Lucia! It's so good to see you."

He opened his arms and they embraced. When Aaron drew near, Father Lawrence grabbed him too. After releasing them, he placed his hands gently on their heads.

"Did you have a good journey?"

"Yes. Very good," Lucia answered.

"And when you met each other…. It went well?"

"It couldn't have been better, Father," Aaron said.

"We have stories," Lucia added.

"Ah, that's the Lucia I remember." Lucia blushed. "And I would love to hear them, but I fear Catherine's wrath if I keep you too long. Perhaps tomorrow? Did you read my letter?"

"Yes, Father. Thank you for it."

"Before you leave, I want to show you something." The priest led them out behind the church where the village cemetery stretched partly up the hill, protected by a low stone wall. He stopped before a newly dug grave next to Sophia's. Lucia squatted on the ground and touched the upturned earth. Aaron quickly knelt down next to her and put an arm across her shoulders.

"Catherine and Simon took it upon themselves to see to the gravesite. This is their work," said Father Lawrence.

Lucia took in the circle of stones and the wild rosebush, blooming in the middle. Near the rosebush was a plain wooden cross that simply said, "Jeremiah, beloved storyteller." There were no birth or death dates. Aaron and Lucia stood up and Father Lawrence said a prayer of thanks for their safe return. He walked with them back to the cart, blessed them, and then blessed Thunder. The horse blew out his breath into the priest's cupped hands.

"Come and see me tomorrow, Lucia. I'll be here."

On the way to her godparents, Aaron and Lucia had to frequently slow down or halt altogether because villagers wanted to welcome Lucia back. As they drew near the home of her godparents, Simon, who was outside cutting wood, lifted his axe in greeting and then went inside and yelled for Catherine. As soon as Lucia's feet touched the ground, he gave her a fierce hug. She marveled at his ageless strength and was warmed by his unreserved affection.

"Oh my girl, we've missed you!"

And then Catherine was there waving Simon off with her apron. "My turn."

Simon shook Aaron's hand. "Thank you for bringing her back safe and sound."

Although Aaron was pressed to stay for dinner, he excused himself, saying he wanted to let his mother and Frederick know he was back. Lucia kissed him goodbye, aware of the eyes watching and appraising them.

While Lucia unpacked, Catherine prepared a special dinner. As they sat down to eat, Simon placed a flask of wine on the table, and a half-dozen candlesticks.

"My eyesight is going," he explained, lighting all of them.

After expressing her pleasure in the food and wine, Lucia began telling Catherine and Simon stories. She told them some of what had happened between her and Aaron, where they first met and how she felt. She told them about Nicholas appearing at the inn's door and what his message had been and how she had been affected. She was asked to repeat a few things for Simon. Catherine exclaimed at several points and Simon gave her a look, trying to signal her to restrain herself, but Catherine ignored him. When Lucia was telling the story of how Judith had hired Nicholas and how he had married Martha, it was Simon who could not contain himself. He slapped the table with his hand, "That's a good one! Too good to be true, some might say."

"Now who can't keep quiet?" Catherine asked sarcastically.

Lucia told them about Father Lawrence's letter. She expressed appreciation for how they had cared for Jeremiah's grave.

"I admit I didn't listen to half of what Jeremiah said," Simon remarked. "But he was a sincere and harmless man – a worthy man in his own way, and he said things that made people feel good. I couldn't believe that some wanted to deny him a Christian burial."

"I don't understand," Lucia said.

Simon looked at his wife. She looked at Lucia and said, "They found the leaves of plant in his mouth. You would know the one. It helps regulate the heart when it's taken in a small dose, but it can kill you if use too much of it."

When Lucia's mouth fell open, Catherine hurried to explain. "No one knows what happened, Lucia, or how much he had actually taken. At the funeral, Father Lawrence told us that Jeremiah died of a bursting heart. He said that Jeremiah's heart was so full of beauty and love that it could not contain them anymore. But even as we were burying him, some were murmuring about how it was all a travesty, and that Father Lawrence was naïve and lacked backbone. It was dreadful. I was proud of Simon that day. He was moving forward to say something, but Father Lawrence beat him to it. 'Do not judge, unless you want to be judged,' he reminded us. He looked around at everyone and then he said, 'Remember, we know nothing for certain, and so to speak and act as if we do reveals more about ourselves than about what happened to Jeremiah.'"

"It was his tone, his manner...." Simon added. "He shut them up."

"To be fair, Lucia," Catherine said, "not many complained; there were just a few. And maybe it was the war. War can stir up the ugliness in people."

Simon snorted, disagreeing. "It stirs up the good as well, if it's present."

"He thinks I'm excusing them, but I'm not."

They ate together quietly for a while.

"You wrote me, Godmother, that there were strangers coming into the village. Aaron and I passed only a few people we didn't recognize."

"It's not so bad right now. But that professor, Aaron's friend—" Catherine began.

"Frederick," Simon interrupted.

"Yes. Well, Frederick says there will be more refugees because the war is going badly for us. He also says it's only a matter of time before villages like ours will be forced to give up our young men. I'm afraid for Aaron and the others."

Simon added, "Father Lawrence and Aaron have met with all the young men in the village and figured out who's opposed to fighting. Aaron has come up with a plan for hiding those who don't want to fight. Some of the young men are already storing food in a secret place in the forest – not only for themselves, but for the village as well, in case soldiers demand our food. "

"I would like to help," Lucia said.

Simon slapped the table again. "And so would I, but the wife says no."

"I only say so because of your health, Simon. You know that. You've had your day and your fight. It's time for the younger people to step up."

"Just when I see more clearly what is right and good, and what makes a man, I can't act on it."

"It's not like you to feel sorry for yourself," Catherine said.

Simon opened his mouth to say something, and laughed loudly instead.

Lucia sought out Father Lawrence the following day. He was patching a wall of the church. They sat on a stone bench.

"Why aren't other people helping you?" Lucia asked.

"People have offered, but this is something I feel I need to do.

I like working with my hands." He stretched out his hands, palms up. "They're teaching me things."

A fox appeared, curious. Lucia gazed at it until it trotted away.

"I love Aaron," she said quietly.

"I know. And he loves you. May I ask…will you marry soon?"

"I don't know. Aaron wanted to when we were still at the shrine, but I wanted to be wed here. When we spoke about it on our way home, he said he had thought about it and wanted us to have our own house before we got married. I think he's also worried about the war and what might happen."

"What about you, do you think it's better to wait?"

"I would like to marry as soon as we can."

"Ah. Well it's for you and Aaron to decide. I shouldn't get in the middle of it. So tell me whatever you wish about your time in the mountains."

Stories gushed from Lucia, one after another in a steady stream. She told him about Judith and Richard, about what Richard wrote about the goddess. She told him of her experiences at the shrine, of the dream she had that night after she had bathed in the spring, and how at the end of it she had seen Sophia, and how Sophia had told her to try and understand and become like the Woman so that she could bear everything. And she told him about her experience on the mountain after Nicholas came with his message. Father Lawrence listened without speaking, his eyes closed for most of it. When Lucia fell silent, he looked at her.

"You went looking for Her, Lucia, and it appears you found Her."

"What about you, Father? Have you been looking for Her?"

"I told Sophia I would, and I've kept my word."

"Who is She, Father? You said I found Her, but I don't feel like I have. Everyone says different things about Her. The church calls Her Mary, the Virgin Mother. Judith's husband called Her the goddess and Sophia called Her the Woman Without a Name. Aaron told me that Frederick calls Her Wisdom — and Jeremiah, I think, saw Her as Eve."

"She's a mystery, isn't She? I've reflected on what scripture says about Her and what Sophia said, but I'm still at a loss. I sense She will open up my understanding of Christ, but I don't know how. And as soon as I start thinking about Her, She utterly eludes me. Perhaps She has to show Herself to us for us to know Her."

"When I was on the mountain feeling the pain of all those people, Father, I think that in the end, She was that Presence that gave me so much bliss. She showed Herself to me, but She is still elusive. In my dream, Sophia told me to learn from Her and to become like Her, and I want to with all my heart, but I don't know how to do that."

Father Lawrence shook dirt off his hands. "Ah, but you have begun to realize it is possible! I have been pondering something that young scholar said — I mentioned him to you in my letter. He said that it was essential for us to align our outer being with our innermost self and that because the inner self knows what is true, it has to gauge and direct the outer. He said that was the way to the queendom of God. I think, Lucia, that you are already on that path. Just speaking with you, I sense I'm moving closer to Her."

"In speaking with you, Father, I feel the same. Why is that? Is it just because we are sharing like this with each other?"

"That could be, Lucia."

"We're trying to understand something together. And its like She's there, but I can only see Her out of the corner of my eye. When I try to look at Her directly, She's gone."

"So maybe the secret is to see without seeing — that's how Sophia saw Her, isn't it? When you try to see Her, you're looking for something outside of yourself and separate. Perhaps She isn't like that at all….This is wonderful, Lucia. We'll have to talk more about this. I'm sure Aaron and Frederick would want to be part of the conversation."

"I would love that."

"Frederick is looking forward to meeting you. You will be impressed by him."

When Lucia was introduced to Frederick a few days later, he took her hand in his very large one and bowed his head. Helen had invited him and Father Lawrence to dinner.

"After what I've heard from Aaron and Father Lawrence, I've been looking forward to meeting you, Lucia," Frederick said simply.

"And I've looked forward to meeting you," she said. Frederick was, as she had imagined him to be from Aaron's description, a large, solid figure whose face and bearing were intimidating, but whose gentleness of manner put her immediately at ease. When they were all seated around the table, Frederick asked Lucia about her impressions of the shrine and what had occurred there. He shared that he had heard about it from many sources, but had actually never been there. Lucia began by telling him about Richard, his letters, and the room full of goddesses, and noticed how intently he listened.

After the meal, they took their chairs and sat by the hearth, where a fire was blazing. Lucia was asked to continue, and she spoke about the time she had experienced others' suffering as if it were her own, and about what had happened to her after Nicholas had given her Aaron's message. Although Frederick was a relative stranger, she felt no hesitation in divulging the intimate details of her experience. During her long narrative, Lucia was moved by the tenderness in Aaron's countenance as he looked at her, and it increased her already great endurance for storytelling. But eventually the late hour, the wine, and the food caught up with her, and she had to stop talking.

"Thank you, Lucia," Frederick said. "You've given me a great deal of food for thought."

"Aaron has told me how much you made *him* think! I would've liked to have been one of your students!"

"We'll have ample opportunities to teach each other in the future. It seems I'll be here for a while. What I will say now is that there are people searching for meaning and purpose, something that will make them fully human. I call what they're looking for 'Wisdom,' because there is historical precedent for doing so. And that is a word more acceptable to philosophers like myself who have the religious impulse, but have soured on religion.... Pardon me, Lawrence."

The priest gave a little wave of his hand.

"Do you think Wisdom is a woman?" Lucia asked.

"The word does have a female association in many cultures."

"Do *you* think Wisdom is something womanly?" Lucia asked.

"I sense you do," Frederick said, smiling. "And when you put your question like that, I would probably more agree with you than disagree." Seeing Lucia's quizzical expression he added, "I see you are not yet accustomed to the cautious evasiveness of philosophy." Frederick laughed.

Aaron's mother, Helen, jumped in. "If Wisdom is a woman it's because She grows life within Herself and sees to everything, even the smallest things."

Frederick nodded appreciatively. "I was going to add that in my experience women tend to understand the nature of Wisdom more easily than men. Thank you for illustrating my point, Helen."

Helen glowed.

"Professor, I've told you some of my story, what about yours?" Lucia asked this with a half-questioning, half-coaxing tone.

"I think what you're most interested in is my attraction to Wisdom." Frederick looked at her for confirmation. Lucia nodded her head. Frederick continued, "In that case, I will have to tell you some things about myself to give you some background. I was an only child, raised mostly by my mother and grandmother. My father was a judge and was seldom at home. We were a wealthy and influential family and I was as spoiled a child as there ever was. From my earliest years, I had the habit of teasing others mercilessly. I was always trying to prove that I knew more. My poor tutors! How I made them suffer for their efforts to educate me. My grandmother and mother and even my father rebuked me, but I think they were also entertained by my eviscerating comments about my teachers. They tried to be more consistent when it came to other offensive behaviors of mine — like my choice of friends — but they were never successful.

"When I was a young man, I met a handsome, hard-drinking man from a poor family in a tavern we both frequented. My father thought he was a rogue and had no inhibitions about saying so in his presence. I fell in love with this man. He was everything I was not, for though I was brave enough in speech, I lacked his physical courage and daring. When he joined the army, I joined it too. I hated the military, but I wanted to be with him. And I wanted him to admire me. He had risen quickly from the ranks and talked about making a career out of soldiering.

"I was grateful that he wanted me around and was always asking my opinion about things — how to dress, what to think of particular men. I thought he needed me, which gave me great pleasure. When it seemed he was losing interest in me, I started drinking more and became more scathing in my observations of others, trying to amuse him. I started giving him money under the pretense that I was loaning it. Both he and I knew I would never ask for it back. It was a sordid affair. I lacked the strength to break free and was too ashamed to seek the advice of others. I was probably incapable of following it in any case.

"When war broke out, another young man from a good family named James joined our group. James hardly spoke, but after a few weeks I rarely saw my lover apart from him. He would say James was only a friend, but I knew otherwise. I didn't understand the attraction, until one morning in my rush to tell him some news I burst into my lover's room and saw James helping him dress. James's servile manner and demeanor shocked me. I left the room without saying anything.

"That evening at dinner, my lover laughed it off before I could ask him about it. A week later, he invited me over to his room for a drink, and when I knocked on his door, James answered. James never looked me in the eye. He got us our drinks and busied himself brushing my friend's clothes. After a few drinks, my lover was in a foul mood. And when he pulled his glass away too soon when James was pouring and the wine spilled, he stood up as if he was having a fit and struck James across the face. When

I asked him what he was doing, he told me without apology or remorse to mind my own business. I remember remarking that James was not a servant — he was from a good family. My lover said that James preferred being treated so, and that I shouldn't interfere.

"I regret that I didn't try to intervene after that. I was with my lover on at least three other occasions when he struck or kicked James. And then we were sent off to the front. Because of my family's wealth and position, I was given the rank of captain. I was above my lover, who because of his seniority, was above James. Even though I had grown to hate myself and considered the man I was besotted with to be monstrous, I unfortunately continued to try to win his affection by making sure he received special privileges. Not surprisingly, the morale among my men was very poor.

"And then one evening after a full day's march, we were ambushed and I was wounded. The man who had held me enthralled was killed before my eyes. He fell without making a sound, as did the enemy soldier who had shot both him and James. It all happened so quickly. James was clutching his stomach and blood covered his fingers, but he dragged himself to the enemy soldier and began stabbing that man's chest repeatedly although the man was already dead. Then James crawled over to the body of the man we both had clung to and shot himself in the head."

"How terrible," Helen exclaimed.

"Yes, it was." Frederick was quiet for a time. "As I was losing consciousness I told myself I was not going to die, and I knew I was meant to live differently than I had been. I was unconscious for three days. When I had barely come to, I heard a voice — a beautiful, resonant, deeply masculine voice chanting something extraordinary. Please excuse me," Frederick's voice quavered. "I can't do what I heard justice, but I want to try."

Frederick collected himself, took a deep breath and began to chant. His voice was sonorous and drew its listeners in:

"Rise, stand up my brothers.
You know She exists.
Don't listen to putrefying thoughts
Or be commanded by sightless fears.
Hear Her summons with your hearts.

Rise, stand up my brothers.
Strike out into this day's desert.
You know She waits for you.
Claim anew Your manhood and very self
Through meeting Her.

Don't faithlessly flee the emptiness
Or tremble before desolation.
They are merely Her instruments.
She is refining your senses
Shaping you for Her service
Tempering you for the keenness of Her bliss.

Go out to meet Her, my brothers.
If you think heaven a wisp of fancy
Earth an insatiable and lonely hell.
If You feel we are only doomed survivors,
She will show you otherwise.

See with your hearts, my brothers.
You know the world is finer than it looks
And that eternal separation is not earth's destiny.
Knowing this is Her gift to you.
She is the future and the love you already bear for it.

She has not forgotten us, nor ever deserted us
She feels the suffering we endure in earth's making
The struggles we must face in becoming men.
And still She firmly urges us on
Knowing the glory in our pain.

Enter Her realm, my brothers.
Listen, She is calling you.
She is your paradise, your bond
She has birthed your very self
And from you draws the fullness of love."

When Frederick was finished, he appeared spent.

"After all this time, it still moves me... the unknown man chanted this in several languages. When I first heard it, I was stunned, disoriented. I still didn't know where I was and that voice...those words...I soon found out I was a prisoner, interred in a camp with hundreds of others. Many were soldiers like myself, but some were being detained there for other reasons. Thinking at first that I had possibly dreamt the whole thing, I said nothing about what I'd heard and slipped back into sleep. But early the next morning I heard the same voice, singing the same thing, and I knew I was fully awake and not hallucinating. I asked someone who was tending my wounds about the man who sang.

He told me the man's name was Jacob and that he was a Jewish cantor. He said that Jacob sang the same thing every morning and that I should have heard him when his voice was stronger. When I asked him who he was singing about, the man shrugged his shoulders and said he didn't know, but that it didn't matter. All the men felt better, listening to him.

"When I had somewhat recovered, I sought Jacob out. He had an illness and was not much more than skin and bones, but his eyes and manner revealed a strength and integrity that made me feel weak and false by comparison. Being in his presence was like a sobering slap to the face. I told him that I wanted to thank him for his singing and that I had a question. He guessed that I wanted to know who he was singing about and said he would tell me if I was patient and listened to a fairly long story.

"Jacob wasn't raised Jewish. His family was Christian, not out of conviction, but because it was more convenient and had become a generational habit. When he was still a very young man, he began to sing and it was obvious to all who heard him that he had a special gift. His parents and older brothers and sisters worked hard to see that he received lessons from the best teachers. By his early twenties, he had become famous. He sang professionally, on all the major theater stages. He loved the attention and the acclaim, and became very rich. One evening after a performance, there was a dinner in his honor. Twenty doting people were at the table, but there was one, a self-contained young woman, who did not seem interested in flattering him at all. She was the one who intrigued him. Her name was Rachel and she was the daughter of the theater's owner. Jacob said she was lovely beyond words. She had dark, wavy hair, lustrous eyes, pleasing features, and a well-proportioned figure. But Jacob said that later, when he had

gotten to know her, her most captivating quality was her sensitiv-
ity. She seemed moved by things that other people didn't even
notice. He was completely entranced!

"By honest and more devious means, he found out about
more her. She was a devout Jew, neither married nor betrothed,
and the eldest of four children. She was especially drawn to the
Shekhina. Jacob did not know what this meant and began to research it whenever he had time. He asked his Jewish friends what
this Shekhina was, and paid for translations of esoteric texts.
He discovered that the word is a Hebrew noun made from the
word, 'shakhan,' which means the act of dwelling. The idea of
the Shekhina had evolved over time in Jewish mysticism, and was
loved as a feminine aspect of God. She was the cloud and the fire
that had gone before the Israelites when they wandered in the
desert. She was the Sabbath Queen and the mystical community
of Israel. She was the door to the Divine, the mother of the soul,
and she could be experienced directly.

"In the Shekhina, Rachel saw her own life's purpose. Her intention, one that she frequently renewed, was to make the Divine
visible through all her deeds. Jacob said that though Rachel never
wrote a book, completed a painting, or composed any music, he
had never met anyone so imbued with the spirit of art. Jacob
knew that Rachel's intention would include their relationship, and
that her hope was that their marriage would manifest Shekhina's
union with another more heavenly aspect of the Divine: the
Tif'eret. Jacob told me that the union between the immanent
Shekhina and the transcendent Tif'eret was what gave birth to
the human soul.

"Jacob said he was not discouraged by finding all this out.
Quite the contrary, he was even more fascinated. He converted

to Judaism. He let Rachel know that he was willing to give up his career and anything else necessary in order to live as a devout Jew. She was duly impressed. He did leave the stage and began working as a cantor in a large synagogue. Soon after, they married. When he had decided to convert, he chose to rename himself Jacob – that had not been his Christian name. He chose it because it was the name of a man who also loved a Rachel. This man had spent seven years working for the right to marry her, and because of his great love, considered it no more than a few days.

"Jacob and Rachel were very happy for ten years and had two healthy children. And then Rachel got pregnant with their third child. From the beginning, the pregnancy was difficult and Rachel had a feeling she might not survive the birth. She told Jacob she was praying for the child and for him to the Shekhina. She wanted Jacob to be strong no matter what happened. The birth *was* difficult. Both Rachel and the child died. Jacob said he was inconsolable, and afterward, he couldn't sing. He told me his adopted faith seemed as fragile as the paper upon which its stories were written, and his surviving children seemed like strangers.

"One morning he took a walk and came to a bend in the road. Light was filtering down through the trees. He said he suddenly found himself listening with the whole of his being to something and realized it was music. Its quality was such, that by comparison, the most sublime music he had ever heard was a mere playing of scales — and that done poorly. He said he didn't hear the music with his ears. It didn't vibrate through the air. Everything had become Music. There was nothing outside of it: everything was included, the visible world as well as invisible ones. He heard the connections that exist between beings as the most ineffable harmony, and was awed by its intelligence and beauty. And then he saw how Rachel was a note in this Music, as was he. He saw that she had moved up to another octave, but that they still existed in harmony with each other. He also knew that his experience had been sent him as a gift by his wife. There, in the bend of the road, where the light filtered down through the trees, his heart began to sing.

"When he returned home, the voices of his children and the sounds coming from the kitchen seemed extraordinary to him. He felt himself eased back into the world. Jacob told me that the Shekhina had answered his wife's prayer in a manner so surprising and exquisite that every time he remembered it, he would be overcome. He had composed and sang many songs for the Shekhina since. Sometimes, he said, it seemed that he was not creating the music, but was only singing or transcribing what he was hearing.

"I was so astonished when Jacob shared this and was deeply ashamed when I compared my life to his. I shared this sense of shame with him. Jacob asked me questions about myself, and I told him all that had transpired. I remember what he said: 'You are a man like me. You, too, are capable of deep devotion. You erred only in your choice of object. Find a worthier one, then all will be well with you.' Although I thought that Jacob saw my situation too simply, what he said meant a great deal to me. We had many conversations afterward, but not as many as I would have liked, for Jacob died of his illness after a few months.

"By the time I was released, I had a new sense of myself. For a short time when I was meeting with Jacob, I had thought about becoming Jewish, but I quickly sensed my way was different. What I was better suited for was approaching the more hidden aspects of existence on the more meandering paths of reason and reflection, and I soon discovered that these were most effective when applied to personal experience. I knew there were other people who might benefit from approaching life and experience similarly and that eventually I would have something to offer them. Wisdom has many children, as Lawrence tells me."

"It is something Christ said," Father Lawrence added.

Frederick gave an acknowledging nod and continued, "I went to a university and eventually became a professor. I met a good man, a potter. He was a careful and creative craftsman and tried to teach me that there is wisdom in the body and in the earth as well as in the human mind. He told me he would have these impulses to create something, and then a feeling would come and then a vague image of something. Then his hands would begin moving as if they were intelligent and autonomous beings. And as his hands worked the clay, he would be amazed by how the clay came alive and willingly partnered with his hands and the changing image in his mind. He said he felt the clay reimagining itself as it yielded to his hands working it, and that the clay's reimagining gave a more distinct and concrete form to his original inspiration. Based on his personal experience, he believed that a true work of art was never a product of mental invention alone. He believed that art came from a partnership of an imagining mind, an imagining body, and an imagining world — that we had lost the sense of that.

"I loved him dearly and we lived together for two decades, despite the objections and interference of others. But always, ever since that time in the camp, my true passion has been for helping people enter the depths of their experience. There is something immanent in experience that calls forth our selves, and this has become the most worthy object of my devotion. For want of a better name, I call it Wisdom."

Frederick paused and looked at the faces of his listeners. "Now perhaps we should say good night. The hour is late."

Lucia piped up, expressing the feelings of the others. "If we have to say good night, sir, it's only because we believe we will have an opportunity to speak again."

Chapter Thirty-Four

Uncertainty about what would happen next, and when, permeated the village. Though its arduous past had taught the villagers something about the ephemeral and temporary nature of peace, their sober assessment of the nature of politics had never entirely squashed the expectation that peace, or some semblance of it, would eventually return. Their feelings were different now. Though they were still relatively undisturbed by the war, many villagers felt something was coming that would mean the loss of all that they knew and held dear. The news of the war was less the cause of their worst fears than it was their validation. Several of the villagers took Father Lawrence to task for the lack of urgency in his sermons and suggested that his manner did not adequately reflect the nature of the times they were living through.

Of the four men who had left the village to join the army, only one returned; he seemed incapable of caring about anything. For hours he would sit and stare at nothing and then would suddenly rant about the end of the world. Jude and another young man had been killed in combat. The last young man was still at the front and was deathly ill. The fate of these four made the other young men reconsider any plans they might have had for soldiering. They sought Aaron out for his opinion and the rest of the village was glad to see it, for they did not want to lose any more of their able-bodied men. As it was, their food supply was dwindling. There had been too few to plant and harvest. Even though the women had stepped up, illness had laid low many villagers and the summer had been abnormally cool and wet.

Lucia was not immune to the fear and uncertainty in the village and this was largely due to the fact that Aaron was gone five, sometimes six days a week. He had found employment as a bookbinder in a town a half day's ride away. When Lucia observed that there was plenty of work to do in the village, Aaron explained that the situation was only temporary, the pay was very good and he was better able to keep informed about the war. He told Lucia that someone had to sound the alarm if soldiers were approaching the village. Lucia knew he wanted money to build and furnish a house, and that he was trying to do his part to protect the village, but was never comfortable with his decision. As soon as he left for work, she would have a sense of foreboding, of impending loss, and would begin grieving for him as if she was certain of his death.

She kept her feelings from Aaron, not wanting to trouble him. She knew he had many responsibilities and worried about Frederick. The professor was staying in contact with several of his students and with prominent people who were working against the continuation of the war. Aaron feared that Frederick's letters would be intercepted, that the messengers he paid would betray his location if bribed or pressured. While Lucia thought she spared Aaron by her silence, she soon discovered she was making things unbearable for herself. She realized she had to talk to someone.

She thought of Catherine, but her godmother was worrying about Simon's health, and even if she had no such worry, Lucia assumed Catherine would overreact to her disclosures. She did talk to Father Lawrence who told her that her fear was natural, given all the losses she had experienced. He reminded her that Aaron would be cautious, that he had learned to judge risk more prudently. Lucia felt a little easier and lighter after sharing her feelings with him, but on the whole, was not much helped by what Father Lawrence said.

Not long after this, Lucia formed a friendship with a young woman named Miriam. Miriam, her young son Samuel, and her father had been recent refugees from an occupied border town. Miriam's husband had been killed trying to ward off looters. She and her father had chosen the village to settle in because they had a relative living there whom they could stay with. When Lucia heard that Miriam had carried books of poetry across hundreds of miles, she knew Miriam was a person she wanted to become better-acquainted with.

Lucia took over some leaves for tea and introduced herself. Miriam was a little older and taller than Lucia. She had a round and pleasant face with prominent cheekbones, fine skin and thick hair, and was a hopeful and energetic person despite all she had been through. Her son was polite but lively. Lucia was impressed by both of them. Miriam had also taken an immediate liking to Lucia, calling her the sister she had always wished for. Lucia told her what she felt when Aaron was gone and Miriam encouraged her to tell Aaron what she felt, but without making demands on him. "I will pray to Christ's mother for you," Miriam had added.

Lucia followed Miriam's advice and was surprised by how responsive Aaron was. He took her in his arms, kissed her, and tried to reassure her. But the most helpful thing he did was tell her that he would work outside the village less. Lucia trusted he would keep his word, and he did.

Father Lawrence weathered the times as if he were made for them. Though he never took on the prophetic role that some had urged upon him, the villagers began seeking him out more frequently for comfort and advice. A few confessed to him that they feared and even hated the displaced strangers that were coming into their village and admitted they had denied them food, or had threatened them if they didn't move on. Most of the villagers genuinely, if sometimes half-heartedly, wanted to respond with a more Christian attitude and Father Lawrence would try to guide them. Many asked him if he thought it was the end times and if God would protect them. He told them he had no answers. He said that he did not believe that they were living in the last days, but that perhaps people were sensing the end of an era. His guidance often took the form of drawing their attention to the beauty and goodness still present in their lives. He would remind them to do what was needed moment to moment, and for the rest to trust in God.

Most of the villagers were grateful to him, but he noticed that their appreciation was not as necessary to him as before. He discovered in himself a vast, if secretive joy that did not seem to depend on outer circumstance. This causeless joy he treated with reverence; he tried not to be too possessive of it.

Meanwhile Frederick was immersing himself in writing and would have been content living a fairly quiet and relatively solitary existence, but Lucia had made it her mission to introduce him to the other villagers. To that end she would ask him to accompany her to the market, and more often than not he agreed.

During his first trip with her, he made the mistake of offering to help the women haul up their buckets from the well. Lucia had tried to warn him off, but he rolled up his sleeves and went ahead anyway. After the third bucket, he heard the women titter and caught more than one rolling her eyes. He suspected it was because he was too slow. He rolled his sleeves back down and looked around at them.

"A smart man acknowledges when he is less able. It took me only three buckets to figure that out. Logically then, I must be a smart man."

The women laughed good-naturedly. One of them said, "We know a lot of men that aren't as smart as you." That incident, which was soon widely known, his compliments on their crafts and produce, his courtesy and his genuine interest in how things were made and grown, earned him the villagers' goodwill.

Wanting uninterrupted conversation with him, Lucia asked if she could sometimes accompany Frederick on his daily walk along the river. At least twice a week they began taking walks together; she would point out various wildflowers and would draw his attention to birds and small mammals. He told Lucia that she reminded him of his companion, for he had done the same thing. He shared that his companion had often chided him for ignoring his senses. Placing himself under Lucia's tutelage, Frederick began paying attention to things he tended not to notice before, and found it refreshing. Nature had previously been a mere backdrop for his thinking; now he saw how everything spoke. The natural world wordlessly expressed ideas, principles, and relations. It was truly wondrous.

After a few months of such walks with Lucia, Frederick began sitting in the open door of his little house without a light or a book in the evenings. He would smoke his pipe, look out at the night sky, and enjoy the currents of air and the orderly display of the stars. Ever since he had woken up in that prison camp, he had felt compelled to think. Over the years, thinking had become a safeguard against sensual indulgence and selfishness. But life moves on, and perhaps he was at a point where balance could now be achieved. He listened as the leaves moved around their slender stems and felt a buoyant delight, such as he had experienced occasionally in childhood.

Aaron was torn between providing a sufficient life for Lucia and wanting to be near her. Frederick had asked if he could contribute toward the construction of their home, saying that it was the least he could do to thank him for his hospitality, but Aaron's pride made it impossible for him to accept more than a few small sums for food. He reminded Fredrick that it was with his help that he had purchased Thunder, and that Frederick had nursed him back to health. What he did not mention was that he felt he owed Frederick a debt he would never be able to repay, for it was his carelessness which had led to Frederick's beating.

At times, Aaron's responsibilities weighed heavily on him. He looked forward to the half-day trips on Thunder to and from his employment and felt lighter when he was on the road. He only wished Lucia was with him. Sometimes he remembered his days as a student and would imagine himself back with his fellow students and professors. Whenever he caught himself doing this, he would try to stop. Calling up such memories seemed a waste of time. *The past is past,* he would tell himself.

With the young men in his village and with some of the middle-aged ones as well, Aaron developed a warning system. Together they decided to create additional hiding places in the village in case they did not have enough time to make it to the forest. The hiding places in the forest were now fully stocked.

When Catherine and Simon heard that Aaron was looking for hiding places in the village, they offered him Simon's workshop. Aaron looked it over with Simon, who suggested a place where they could start digging a hole in the floor. Aaron asked permission to dig one large enough for two men to sit in comfortably, and Simon agreed. For several weeks, Aaron would spend his evenings with Lucia, digging. She would help him carry the dirt to the garden. Simon told him that he and Lucia were having a strange sort of courtship, but by the sound of it they seemed to be enjoying themselves. Aaron told Simon that he was right.

"I'm digging holes again," Aaron told Simon. "I thought I would never dig another hole."

"At least these holes are for the living," Simon answered.

"Lucia says that I will miss taking the dirt out of her hair and her eyes — that maybe we should continue digging holes together even after the war." What Aaron didn't tell Simon was how Lucia would splash him when they were cleaning up and then run off, and how he would take off and try to catch her, and when he did she would alternate between squealing and laughing. She would then try to slip away again and he would have to wrestle her without hurting her. Afterwards they would walk or lie together, watch the stars and talk. She was always open with him and he loved listening to her. The lying together was sometimes hard for both of them because their desire for each other was so strong and because they had agreed not to have intercourse again until after they were wed. But however difficult it was, lying together was not something either one of them wanted to give up.

On one of her walks with Frederick along the river, Lucia asked if he would be willing to share more about his experience in the camp.

"Is there something in particular you wanted to know?" Frederick asked.

"Yes. I was wondering if it was your talks with Jacob that changed you."

"They were very important to me, definitely. But you're correct if you're thinking that there had to be another cause as well. No one changes only because of another's influence. When I woke up in that prison camp, I was very happy to be alive, and probably like many other people in similar circumstances, I knew I had never fully appreciated life until then. Tasting life in that manner was intoxicating. But that experience didn't last long. Life was demanding something of me and I had no idea what it was. And I doubted that even if I did comprehend it, I would be able to measure up. I could only remember how I had been living, and that now appeared loathsome to me. Frankly speaking, I found myself repulsive. When I told Jacob what I was feeling, he counseled me to temper the harshness of my judgment. His instruction must have had some beneficial effect, because I was able to reflect on my experience with a little more calmness and objectivity.

"I noticed that my revulsion and loathing paralyzed me. I felt great stirrings of life, but could not act. That had never happened to me before. A part of me had always known when I acted perversely and stupidly, but previously that knowledge had not put a stop to my behavior. Now, however, it did. I wondered why. Was I seeing what I had always known, but only more clearly? Did coming close to death inevitably change a man's feelings? As I thought about these questions, I would have a fleeting sense of how much of my intelligence remained unused. Then I would try to explain to myself how I could sense that.

"When I told Jacob about all this and about how difficult it was for me to understand what was going on, he said I might not know it then, but I was blessed. Then he suggested something: 'Don't try to figure all this out, just keep listening and looking with your heart.' When I told him I didn't know what that meant, he came closer and pressed his fingers on the center of my breastbone. He closed his eyes and kept the pressure there for several moments. Something opened up in me below or behind that spot. I began weeping. 'In there lies what you are seeking, and the knowing of it,' Jacob told me.

"So did you see and hear with the heart after that?" Lucia asked.

"I did when I was talking with Jacob. It took some time to develop a regular habit of it. I think the turning point for me occurred when I felt again how much of my intelligence remained unused and I asked myself how it was possible to sense such a thing about oneself. But instead of immediately thinking about it, there was a moment when I simply looked and listened. And I had a glimpse of an intelligence — one broader, more active, and more beneficent than my own. And yet it *was* mine. I saw that too. As I tried to describe this experience to Jacob as accurately as I could, I realized that this intelligence was mine and not mine simultaneously. This was not a logical or rational conclusion. However, it was a true one. That experience showed me that while reason had its place, the deeper forms of perception came from a different place."

"Do you call the intelligence that you saw, Wisdom?" Lucia asked.

"Yes. You employed a good use of logic just then," Frederick said, smiling.

As soon as she could, Lucia shared this conversation with Aaron, Father Lawrence, and Miriam. They were as eager as she was to hear more. Lucia planned a dinner and invited them all so that they would have an opportunity to question Frederick further.

"Frederick," Aaron began after passing him the potatoes, "Lucia told us about your conversation. I think we are all curious about what you told her about Wisdom, how it is us and not us."

"Ah," Frederick said, holding a spoonful of potatoes suspended over his plate. He glanced at Lucia. "You did warn me that I might have to sing for my supper." Frederick dished the potatoes onto his plate. "Well, I'm willing. This looks like a deserving repast."

"Miriam helped," Lucia said.

"Well, my thanks to you both then."

"Thank you, Professor," Miriam said. "I *am* very curious…"

"It is a paradox," Frederick began, "something contrary to expectation. But rather than sticking with the word paradox, I like the word indeterminacy. After I had more training in attending to my experience and had become privy to the experience of others, I realized that indeterminacy was not an uncommon phenomenon. For many, the past at times can be more immediate and real than the present, and what is cause and what effect, on closer inspection, are not always clear. Things have more fluidity than what the logical mind proposes."

"What does indeterminacy have to do with Wisdom?" Lucia asked.

"That intelligent fluidity is Wisdom. Music is a form of intelligent fluidity, and Jacob's experience of music after his wife, Rachel died was, in my opinion, an experience of Wisdom. Wisdom is an exceedingly active and very mobile intelligence." Frederick looked at Aaron. "From what you've told me, Aaron, I think you experienced that aspect of Wisdom the night we met."

"It's true, Frederick. I felt a Presence moving quickly through everything. But that Presence also had an absolute stillness about it. Another example of indeterminacy, Professor?"

"Yes, stillness and movement existing simultaneously. The rational mind naturally recoils when faced with such seeming contradictions. It strives to keep things singular and separate, to hold them to their first appearances."

"Is there any danger in what you call indeterminacy?" Father Lawrence asked.

"Yes. I have been giving that much thought lately. It is likely that a mind more naturally accepting of indeterminacy, and lacking training in attention and good judgment, may be overwhelmed by it and collapse into mental passivity and inertia. For minds that overvalue reason, indeterminacy can seem identical to chaos. Such people may despair of ever having solid ground to stand on. Everything may appear meaningless and insubstantial to them. Even the self may seem nothing more than an illusion.

And there is another danger. I can also foresee the possibility that some might see indeterminacy as a rationale for seizing upon and molding human nature itself to their liking."

"Those are terrible risks, Frederick," Father Lawrence said.

"They are. But indeterminacy will also bring many benefits. Judging others will seem less sensible, and we may be better able to recognize our common humanity despite our differences because those differences will no longer be viewed as being absolute. Indeterminacy may give us the capacity to rethink and reimagine everything in this world."

"What is indeterminacy exactly, Professor?" Miriam asked. "I'm still not quite sure what it is."

"It's good to own our lack of clarity. It is often the first step toward deeper understanding," Frederick replied. "I think indeterminacy is an effect of the forming of a new organ of perception. This organ will not obliterate the rational mind or the senses. I believe it will find a way to work with them. However, it is something distinct and represents an entirely new realm of possibility."

"I've never heard anyone speak of this new organ before," Miriam said.

"That's not surprising. How often do you hear people talking about the marvelous fact of vision, of how our two eyes work together to create one, seamless view? The absence of talk about something does not mean it does not exist or that it is not important. So it could be true that even though we are paying little attention to it now, a new organ of perception is beginning to form."

"What would it be like to see the world with this new organ?" Lucia asked.

"When it is better-formed? I think we will notice Unity much more readily than separate forms. And when Unity becomes evident, it will allow for an ever greater fluidity and change, without losing that felt quality of coherence and order."

Lucia, Aaron, and Father Lawrence had not touched their food in a good while. They were too astounded to eat.

"Have you experienced this new organ?" Lucia asked.

"Yes, I think I have...once...at a friend's funeral. It was as if everything had gone through a bath. Violence of every sort was washed away from every crack and crevice of the world. I recognized the presence of grief, but it did not dominate. And fear was gone. Those were the changes I noticed. Otherwise, I realized everything was as it had always been: whole, golden, beautiful, clean...sweet beyond words. I just hadn't seen it." Frederick stopped and closed his eyes momentarily. "Innocent...that was how I could describe it.... I wish I could say more, but I am not a poet."

"You described it well," Lucia said.

"What will happen to religion with this new organ of perception?" Father Lawrence asked.

"All I can say is that it will change many things," Frederick answered.

"People will fight it then," Aaron said.

"Is that why many are feeling that we are living in the end times?" Father Lawrence asked. "Is this forming of the new organ what people are really sensing?"

"That could be," Frederick replied. "Perhaps people will fear the change less, if they have some idea of what it means, if they are more prepared."

As he said these last words, Lucia felt her heart, mind and will stretching as if they felt the billowing action of an adventurous wind. She caught Aaron's eye and reached for his hand under the table. He entwined his fingers with hers and in the touch of skin and in the gentle pressure of muscle she sensed he knew what she was feeling.

Chapter Thirty-Five

Father Lawrence and Aaron were taking a break from repairing the church's roof.

"It's done. The roof was the last thing that needed fixing. Thanks for your help, Aaron."

"You're welcome, Father."

"Are the hiding places in the village finished?"

"We have three now, and there are two in the forest near the ruins."

"Good."

"I'm thinking of talking to Lucia about planning our wedding. Do you think it's premature?"

"Premature? No."

"We would have spoken of it sooner, but I wanted her to have her own home. I know she works hard and is used to making do, but I wanted to begin our lives together with our own place." He added in a hesitant tone, "I accepted a gift from Frederick."

"A gift I'm sure he was happy to give."

"I didn't want to take it. But he was insistent, and Lucia and I want to be together…"

"It was the right decision….You're very responsible, Aaron.

But don't make the mistake of thinking you were meant to carry everything alone. Burdens are best carried if they're shared."

"Not all, Father."

Father Lawrence studied him.

"Do you mean Timothy?"

Aaron looked surprised. Father Lawrence cut some cheese and handed Aaron a piece. "I know what happened to Timothy still weighs on you."

Aaron said nothing and ate distractedly. When he was finished, he looked at the priest.

"Aaron, Timothy was there that night by his own choice. He knew the risk."

"I know. Frederick said the same thing.... I thought I had come to terms..."

"Don't be too hard on yourself."

"That's not it, Father."

Father Lawrence noticed Aaron's jaw clenching, knew he was fighting back tears. He wondered whether he should encourage him to say more, or if he should let him be.

"It's not just, not fair," Aaron said.

"What's not just?"

"One moment of carelessness..."

"It wasn't that one moment of carelessness, Aaron. That wasn't the cause. There were many circumstances, nearly all of them outside your control."

"But there was that one thing that was in my control, Father, and Timothy...." He could not go on.

"Would you accept forgiveness?"

"I know you're trying to help, Father, but you don't understand..."

"Tell me, then."

Aaron visibly struggled with himself. "I'm angry. I know the world isn't evil, but it seems that way at times and when it does, I can't accept it. I can't accept a world where one misjudgment carries such a price. That is *too* cruel, Father."

"Do you hold God responsible? Do you still believe in Him, then?"

"I don't know. After what I've experienced, I know there's something greater than us at work in this world, something incomprehensible, something that binds us together, something that brought Lucia and me together...."

"You have reverence for life, then. That's what's essential."

"I don't know."

"This something greater that binds us together.... Is it *that* you can't forgive?"

Aaron appeared confused. "I don't know, Father. I don't know what I mean exactly."

"Does Lucia know what you're feeling?"

"Most of it."

"Not the anger?"

"No. It's too poisonous."

"You're trying to protect her..."

Aaron stood up. "Please Father, let's finish the roof."

While Aaron and Father Lawrence were repairing the roof, Lucia was visiting with Miriam. They were spinning wool together. Miriam was singing.

"You have such a lovely voice," Lucia said, "the most wonderful voice I have ever heard. Would you sing at my wedding?"

"I would love to," Miriam replied. "Just don't ask me to sing the traditional song to Mary. I used to like it, but now it seems too bloodless to me, too acquiescent. Mary was a lioness…a blazing sun. I would like to sing her own hymn, her 'Magnificat.' Would you mind?"

"No, of course not," Lucia said.

"I will make up my own melody, if it's all right with you."

"Sure. Go ahead."

"So you *are* finally planning it, Lucia. Since when?"

"We haven't yet, but we will soon, I think."

"Well good for you. It's about time."

Lucia bent her head down over the toothed device in her hands.

"What is it, Lucia? You looked sad just now."

"It's been difficult, waiting…and I have this fear…"

"It's not easy…is it?"

"What's not easy?" Lucia asked.

"Being a woman. Living in these times — and I'm not just talking about the war. Things are changing between men and women. I think for the better. I see it with you and Aaron. But the old ways are still there. It helps if you remember that." Miriam laughed. "My husband and I both thought that we preferred the new way."

"What do you mean you 'thought'?"

"Well, the old ways were sticky. My mother told me something that made sense. She said that for hundreds, maybe even for thousands of years, a woman felt that if she couldn't keep her husband's attention, it meant that her social standing, if not her very physical survival, was at risk. We women competed with each other, connived, despaired, raged, and tortured ourselves trying to appear more beautiful — all to keep a man's attention.

My mother said that in every woman there is a strong memory of the old ways and that if I kept that in mind and was patient with myself and my husband, things might not be as difficult....And they weren't. It helps knowing what's going on. That's why I'm telling you. And men? They say they like the new way, but there are some things about the old they find very hard to give up! It can be such a muddle! You have to keep combing through the bad feelings. Remember your first meeting, and all you felt then."

The day before their wedding, Aaron and Lucia walked nearly five miles into the forest to the largest ruin. Lucia wanted to see it.

"Well, what do you think, Lucia?"

"How long could you stay here...if you needed to?"

"At least a month. There's plenty of food and water."

She took his hand and traced the scar. "This might get you into trouble."

"I'll be safe. Please don't worry."

They ate some bread while sitting on a crumbling, moss-covered wall. Lucia ran her hand over the broken stones. "Jeremiah said that these were part of an ancient city."

"I remember the story." He got down off the wall and knelt in front of her.

"What are you doing?"

"I'm kneeling before Beauty in her earthly form."

Lucia laughed hard, holding her belly. And then she remembered how Jeremiah had called her the delight of his eyes and the joy of his heart. She suddenly felt ragged, as if something about her relationship with Jeremiah was still torn and unmended.

The night before their wedding, rain fell in spurts, but by the morning the sun was holding steady in a blue, untroubled sea. Aaron arrived at the church before anyone else and when he heard Lucia speaking to Catherine at the back of the church, the sound of her voice thrilled him. Catherine came in a little later, along with several other women, carrying flowers. And then Father Lawrence was near the altar, finding the passage in the Bible he wanted to read. Many villagers were making their way into the church. Helen and Frederick sat down next to Aaron, and when Catherine was finished arranging, she joined them with Miriam in tow. By that time the church was full and people had begun crowding around the door.

In the midst of the bustle Aaron sat quietly, amazed by the level of expectancy he sensed in his fellow villagers and slightly awed by the enormous goodwill that seemed to envelop him. When Father Lawrence gave him a nod, he stood and walked to the altar. He was only there for a few moments when everyone's attention focused on Lucia as she entered the church. Calmly and protectively, Simon walked by her side. Some of the women made approving and delighted sounds as Lucia approached the altar, or made comments about her gown and hair. Aaron was too overwhelmed by Lucia's radiant presence to notice any particulars except her smile. When she stood near him, he took her hand and it seemed to him the entire village took joy in it. For a brief moment, he felt of one mind and heart with everyone assembled.

Silence descended and in the silence everyone was aware of witnessing something deep and true and beautiful. Father Lawrence addressed the villagers and the couple, and then stepped back while Lucia and Aaron declared themselves husband and wife. Afterward, the priest blessed them and then motioned for everyone to sit down.

"It is not customary for a priest to say much at weddings. On this wonderful day, however, I will make an exception. If I seem long-winded, you may blame this newlywed couple, for they have provided much of the inspiration for what I am about to say.

"I want to tell you about another Bride and Groom. I want to speak of the relationship between Wisdom and our Lord Jesus Christ, for it is their loving union that illuminates what we have been privileged to witness this day.

"Yesterday, in preparation for this wedding ceremony, I read the first two chapters of Saint John's gospel. I read how John the Baptist told his disciples that he was not the bridegroom, only the bridegroom's friend. John said that it was Jesus who was the bridegroom. Now this intrigued me, and I wondered why John felt like that. Why didn't John see *himself* as the bridegroom? And, I had another question: Who is the bride John is talking about?

"We all know that John the Baptist lived a pure and holy life. He had few possessions and did not desire power for himself. He lived in a harsh and barren desert, praying, fasting, and waiting for God. Many people were drawn to him, but he never did anything to make sure people liked him. He continued to speak the truth as he saw it. He challenged everyone to cleanse themselves of everything that was ungodly. But despite all of this, John knew he was not the bridegroom. When John told his disciples this, they were probably confused and wondered what he meant. However, for John it was very simple. John knew he wasn't the bridegroom because he couldn't see a bride. But John knew he had been with and spoken to someone who did see one, and that person was our Lord Jesus Christ.

"What do I mean by this? I mean that when John looked at the world around him, he saw violence and cruelty, selfishness and greed. John saw how the world had forgotten the spiritual and how unfaithful it was to God. It led him to believe that most people had grown nearly insensible to any higher feeling and understanding, and the only hope for human society was in the purifying fire of judgment. Jesus, on the other hand, while not blind to the present condition of the world, interpreted it and experienced it quite differently. Jesus heard the world calling him. He heard the world summoning forth all his strength, all his energies, all his capacity for feeling and understanding. As a woman can call forth what is the best and deepest in a man, Jesus heard the world calling forth the divine that was in Him."

"I asked myself how the world could do this if it was something unholy, and realized that it couldn't. The world has to be something holy. And that holiness is what Jesus could hear and see and feel and what He responded to. That holiness of the world has a name and we find that name in scripture. That name is Wisdom. Jesus perceived Wisdom's presence in the world. He saw the world as Wisdom's form. He heard Wisdom in the sounds of the world. And Jesus knew it was God's will that He respond utterly and completely to Wisdom, to Wisdom in Her earthly form. This may seem like a new idea, but it isn't. In the Book of Wisdom we learn that the Master of All has always loved Wisdom and that He loves only those who dwell with Her. My friends, Jesus was clearly a lover of Wisdom.

"As our teacher, Jesus Christ, responded to Wisdom's call and attraction, He discovered that he was bringing forth His deepest and truest Self. And Christ learned to offer that Self to Wisdom to make Her call to us something more readily heard. In his public life, and with His disciples. He imitated Wisdom's generous and humble gestures of invitation. Our Lord and teacher had found that His deepest and most hidden Self was essentially a gift, a gift offered on behalf of the divine to all that was, had been, or ever would come to be, a gift that humanly expressed Wisdom's unstinting and gracious benevolence. Jesus realized that He was the individual form and expression of Wisdom's love, that His very nature and essence was love and gift and that if we followed Him, the same would be true of us. We too were called to enhance all the flavors of the earth and provide light for men.

"All this is why Jesus worked his first miracle at a wedding in Cana and why we celebrate the wedding of Aaron and Lucia, today. It is through the fullness of love between a man and a woman that we catch a glimpse of the depth of Christ's response to Wisdom and Wisdom's surrender to Him. We in the church have always focused on Christ's sacrifice, on His giving, and we have neglected to say much about Wisdom's generosity toward Him, or Wisdom's love of Christ. But Jesus was always experiencing it and trying to convey it to us, 'Seek and you will find,' Jesus said. 'Knock and the door will be opened to you.' What he encouraged us to do, He had already done. These words are echoes of others in the Book of Wisdom. In that book we find these words: 'By those who love Her, She is readily seen, by those who seek Her, she is readily found. She anticipates those who desire Her by making Herself known first. Whoever gets up early to seek Her will have no trouble, but will find Her sitting at the door.'

"I want to return to what I said in the beginning about how John and Jesus saw the world very differently. I want to be clear about something. Jesus was not naïve about the state and condition of the world, and I believe John knew that. Jesus was aware of what was in the hearts of men and he probably would not have disagreed with John's observations of people or of society. However, Jesus saw a depth and breadth in the world, a meaning that was imperceptible to the physical senses, to the rational and pragmatic mind, and even to the moral sense. While John could not see as Jesus did, he was great enough to admit his own vision was more limited. John publicly declared that Christ's capacity for perception and response completely surpassed his own — so much so that he felt unworthy even to untie Christ's sandal. John recognized and acknowledged that Jesus lived in the world and experienced it at a much higher level than he did himself.

"Now it seems to me, my friends, that this story of John and Jesus is calling us to make a choice. Are we disciples of John, or are we disciples of Jesus? If we are disciples of John, we believe that the world and ourselves are separated from God and that we are not even worthy to approach Christ or touch Him in any way. If we are disciples of John we believe that what has begun between Aaron and Lucia and is being celebrated today is something doomed to fail, something that must be propped up by prohibitions, something that is a breeding ground of compromise and impurity. If we are disciples of John we believe that in every marriage the wine of Divine love will sooner or later run out, as it had for the couple in Cana.

"If, on the other hand, we are disciples of Jesus, we do not believe that God and the world are separate. If we are disciples of Jesus, we know we have been invited to a divine wedding. If we are the disciples of Jesus, we see that what has begun between Aaron and Lucia is something eternal and that the love that unites them is of such a nature that it could never run out because everything they will experience can be changed into it. For as long as Aaron and Lucia realize that their relationship flows from the love of Christ and Wisdom, this will remain true. For the love that exists between Christ and Wisdom is stronger than all the forces of death and evil combined. In the presence of that love, even death and evil are changed."

Hearing these words, Lucia was stunned. She marveled at how Father Lawrence's thoughts had been developing and she felt a profound gratitude to him for sharing them with the village on her wedding day. She turned toward Aaron and saw that he was also very moved and surprised.

During the celebration that followed at her godparents' house, Lucia overheard comments about how Father Lawrence's sermon was different than anything they had ever heard before. People were wondering if their priest's strange words would be considered heretical if heard by other priests or by the bishop. A few wondered how relevant the sermon was. Lucia asked Miriam what she thought and Miriam said it was delightful and refreshing, and several young women standing nearby agreed, but found it difficult to explain why.

As they ate together, Aaron couldn't keep his eyes off his new bride even when she turned from him to speak to a guest. Simon came up behind him and clapped him on the shoulder. Aaron jumped. "Lovely, isn't she?" Simon said. He lowered his voice. "Catherine put some flowers in the house and turned down the bed. The rest is up to you." He laughed when he saw Aaron's ears reddening.

When the eating and dancing were winding down, Miriam stood up and got everyone's attention.

"I have been asked by the bride to sing something for her wedding. I'm not going to sing the more traditional wedding hymn to Mary. With the bride's permission, I'm going to sing Mary's own song, her 'Magnificat.' When Mary was pregnant with Jesus she went to visit her cousin Elizabeth, who was also expecting. As soon as Elizabeth heard Mary's greeting, the child in her womb leapt for joy and Elizabeth was filled with the Holy Spirit. Elizabeth felt her unborn child and the whole of her body coming to life. She was filled with power. And all of this was simply because she heard Mary's voice. Elizabeth didn't keep all this to herself. She immediately shared it with Mary and when she did, Mary could recognize more fully what God had done for her. She was so overcome with feeling and so overflowing with joy that she said her 'Magnificat.' Friendship between women can be like this. Women can do what Elizabeth and Mary did for each other." Miriam looked pointedly at Lucia before lowering her head and closing her eyes.

The guests quieted. Slowly Lucia's friend raised her head and a soft, spiraling sound came from her mouth and grew in strength. The sound soon bore words and the words a spirit. Suddenly it was as if a bright, self-assured, self-aware, almost fierce young woman had entered their gathering. She carried the memory of all their hardships and burned with a steady, unstinting hope:

My soul magnifies the Lord
and my spirit rejoices in God my Savior,
for He has looked with favor on the lowliness

of His servant.
Surely, from now on
all generations will call me blessed;
for the Mighty One has done
great things for me,
and holy is His name.
His mercy is for those who fear Him
from generation to generation.
He has shown strength with his arm;
He has scattered the proud
in the thoughts of their hearts.
He has brought down the powerful
from their thrones,
and lifted up the lowly;
He has filled the hungry with good things,
and sent the rich away empty.
He has helped His servant Israel,
in remembrance of His mercy,
according to the promise he made to our ancestors,
Abraham and to his descendents, forever.

As Miriam sang, Lucia was reminded of how Jeremiah spoke of Eve, how he made Eve alive to her as Miriam was now making Mary alive. She remembered how he had said that Eve had reached out for the not yet. Mary was different. Mary agreed to take the possible into herself. She received the divine-human in its embryonic form, exulting in its presence, giving her substance, her life to it, despite the great pain and suffering it would cause her and Joseph and eventually so many others. Suddenly, Lucia knew that her own desire for adventure, for a greater life, linked her to Eve and Mary. *I am the daughter of Eve and the daughter of Mary and the daughter of my mother, Sophia,* she thought. *And they all came from Wisdom, and Wisdom from the Woman without a name. These are the ancestors of my soul, of my inner self. They are the ancestors of all the women I have ever known and loved. We are joined because we give life and because we bring forth the possible from within ourselves.*

For several moments after the singing had stopped, Lucia felt the sound of her friend's voice vibrating in her own chest. She held out her hands to Miriam, expressing her feelings of being given a great gift. Miriam smiled and blew her a kiss.

After the feast, a small procession wound its way, under a canopy of stars, to the couple's new home, not far from Helen's. Catherine and Miriam slipped in to light the candles while the others were saying good night to Aaron and Lucia. When they stepped out, Aaron and Lucia thanked them, then the couple went inside. Lucia had never been inside her new home and Aaron had never seen their home fully furnished. The group that had accompanied them began singing a traditional wedding night song, their voices becoming softer as they walked away.

Lucia slowly moved through the small three-room house and took in everything. She was delighted with the flowers and the candles. Above the hearth, she noticed her statue of Isis, and on the bed, a coverlet she knew Judith had sent. What took Lucia completely by surprise was the small rug in front of the hearth. She recognized it as one of Sophia's.

"Do you like it, Lucia?"

"Everything is so lovely! Where did you find the rug?"

"That's a long story. It will take a long time to tell it. We'll need to lie down for it."

Lucia laughed as Aaron scooped her up in his arms and laid her on the bed....

The sun shone through the curtained window in their bedroom. Lucia remembered waking up long ago in Sophia's house, remembered the smell of the room and the bird, singing. She turned in bed and watched Aaron sleep. His bare skin glowed and he had the clean smell of air just before a rain. He was breathing deeply. Lucia nestled in his arms and for the first time felt the possibility of being at home in the world.

Chapter Thirty-Six

Aaron was away at his bookbinding job and Lucia and Miriam were sitting in Lucia's home on a summer's evening, working on their mending. Samuel, Miriam's son, was practicing his writing. Lucia began sharing stories about Sophia and Jeremiah with Miriam. Miriam listened as she sewed, only diverting her attention from time to time to offer Samuel encouragement or correction.

"Since my return to the village, I've wanted to do something to express my love for my mother and Jeremiah," Lucia told her friend. "And now an idea just came to me."

"What is it?" Miriam asked.

"I want to have a meal in the meadow where Sophia and I walked and where Jeremiah and I met to create poetry. A meal under the stars. A whole night under the stars with you and Aaron, Father Lawrence, and Frederick. What do you think?"

"I think it's a wonderful idea! I could help you cook and my father could watch Samuel. Would you tell us more stories about your mother and Jeremiah?"

"Yes. And I think I would like to show all of you something Jeremiah showed me, something about Sophia."

Lucia and Miriam chose a time, told the others and enlisted the additional help of Catherine and Aaron's mother. The four women spent an entire day in Catherine's kitchen, preparing. Aaron borrowed Simon's larger cart and packed it with their table, chairs, utensils and blankets. Simon had also contributed two lanterns and a couple bottles of wine. Aaron told Lucia that Thunder knew something was up for he neighed insistently and would paw the ground whenever Aaron was near. On the evening planned for their gathering, Aaron hitched Thunder to the cart. Lucia drove and Frederick sat up front with her while Aaron, Father Lawrence, and Miriam followed on foot.

As they were unloading and setting up under Lucia's direction, Frederick whispered to Aaron, "What is that wife of yours up to?"

Aaron shrugged good-naturedly. "I have learned to go along and not ask too many questions."

While Miriam set the table and arranged the food, the men collected wood for a fire and Lucia picked up small branches which she dropped in a separate pile. She also looked for and found a larger, more pointed branch. When they were done with their various tasks a thin, rosy line of cloud, like a vein, stretched above the trees. Crickets chirped and frogs, working their bodies like bellows, announced their humid pleasures. Before they started eating, Lucia asked Father Lawrence to bless the food. He deferred and suggested that she say the blessing, since it was her inspiration that had brought them together. Lucia began bowing her head over the table, but then pushed back her chair, stood, and raised her wine goblet. The others followed her example.

"We thank the earth, our Mother, for this food and drink, and we wish to bless all those who have brought our Mother's work to such tasty completion."

They touched their cups, smiled at each other, and then sat down. Lucia began passing the fresh bread, which was followed by roasted chicken and lamb, a vegetable salad, and cheese. Conversation flowed as easily as the wine. With the coming of the blue-black twilight, Aaron lit the lanterns. After dinner, he and Father Lawrence got a fire going and the rest drew up chairs near the stone where Lucia and Jeremiah had often sat. The group was silent, warm, and content with wine and food, until Lucia spoke.

"After my mother died, Jeremiah and I met again at this spot. I have told all of you about Sophia's vision. When I told Jeremiah about it, he wanted to help me understand it. He used little sticks." The other four watched as Lucia drew a circle in the ground in front of them with the branch. She then stood over the tangled pile of sticks she had collected earlier. She reenacted for them what Jeremiah had shown her. She stooped down and, taking a twig, poked around the pile, telling them that most of the time when we used words it was as if one word was searching for its mate. Then she placed a stick just outside the circle she had drawn in the dirt and stretched out on a blanket on the ground facing it.

"Jeremiah said that his best moments as a storyteller and as a poet were when the words seemed to come from nothing. The circle I have drawn represents the nothingness. Jeremiah told me that it wasn't really nothing, but he couldn't describe it better. The nothingness made him appreciate words like the darkness helps us appreciate the stars."

Following Lucia's previous instructions, Miriam took a white flower from a cup on the table. "Now I want to show you what

Jeremiah showed me when he was trying to explain what happened to my mother," Lucia said.

Lucia leaned her body above the circle. Miriam knelt down and slowly raised the white flower toward Lucia, just as Jeremiah had done.

"Jeremiah said that Sophia was leaning into the nothingness and that there she heard nothingness express itself in one word, 'Woman.' That word was like a flower whose meaning could unfold until it comprehended everything."

"Incredible!" Frederick responded. "What a simple but profound manner of teaching."

Lucia stepped out of the circle. Miriam handed her the flower as Jeremiah had done. Aaron went over to Lucia and took her hand. Frederick and Father Lawrence stood up and moved closer to them. The group of five stood quietly, forming a small circle. The fire and lanterns were going out, but no one stirred to rekindle them. The company was bathed in the light of the stars and the half moon. One by one, they raised their heads and looked around and it was as if the universe had just begun. They looked long at the sky, contemplating a beauty that ennobled them; then, lowering their eyes, each one gazed into the faces of the others while the stars moved in a deep hush across the sky — and the others ceased to be others. When weariness overtook them, they spoke softly together about sleep. Aaron made a new fire. They laid blankets on the ground and put straw under them for padding.

Lucia could not sleep. She felt the urging of a power she could not explain or resist. Leaving Aaron's side, she got up and walked to the circle she had drawn on the earth. After only a moment's hesitation, she stepped inside. Raising her arms, she felt lifted up. Everything dropped away. And then it was as if nothingness had a body and was lovingly embracing her, and it was as if she had a body of nothingness which received the embrace. But she saw it was actually only one body giving and receiving. Then a sort of gate opened above her, releasing a flood of power which descended upon her like a mighty waterfall. The power lit up the multitude of tiny beings that seemed to make up her physical body. They had been hidden, dormant, forgotten seeds which in a moment exploded into full and radiant bloom. Lucia was awake and bursting with power, life, and bliss, and knew they could not be borne alone and separate. Inspired, she willed they pass through her physical body and pour themselves out on everyone and everything.

Slowly, peacefully, she returned to her usual sense of self. And as she did, she knew that the embrace was always taking place in everything. It was the very ground of life which, for some mysterious purpose, remained hidden. Wisdom, the beloved Bride, had revealed Herself in her. And Lucia knew *she* was the Beloved as was every other human being, as was everything that existed. Being a Bride was the secret of the individual and of the whole. She stepped out of the circle and lay back down next to Aaron. He asked if she was all right, then wrapped his arms around her.

As she was falling asleep, Father Lawrence was dreaming that Lucia was lying in the house where she had lived with Sophia. The house was burning. He was rushing in to save Lucia, when a younger Sophia met him at the door and would not let him enter. He begged and pleaded with her, but she would not budge. "Why?" he asked Sophia. "Why won't you let me in?"

"Fire cannot consume what is indestructible," she said. "The flames will only brighten it."

In the morning, they cleaned up and repacked the cart. While Aaron was hitching up Thunder, he glanced over at Lucia. Her beauty made him ache. He knew he would never possess it; it would never be his. He saw that clearly. She did not belong to him. She was not an addition to him. Rather, she stripped him bare. Even the love he felt for her was not his.

Chapter Thirty-Seven

Two months after their festive gathering in the meadow, Lucia began suspecting she was pregnant. She wanted to tell Aaron right away, but he was away at work and not due back for a couple of days. When Helen, Aaron's mother, invited her over to lunch on Saturday, market day, Lucia wondered if she somehow guessed her condition. Helen insisted on serving her and would steal careful glances at her. It was an awkward lunch; Lucia was eager to share her news with Helen, but wanted Aaron to hear it first. When they were nearly finished, Frederick came in and sat with them. Helen had gotten up to get him some food, when Aaron stepped through the door. Thunder could be seen not far away.

Lucia was so glad to see her husband that she did not ask why his time away had been shortened. However, she did notice the restrained urgency of his manner and Thunder's sweaty lather.

"What is it, Aaron?" Aaron's mother asked.

As soon as Helen asked the question, they all heard the church bells.

"Are the soldiers coming?" Helen asked, concerned.

"Yes. I have to go." Aaron went to Lucia and, bending down, kissed her. He quickly straightened and turned to Frederick.

"Hide all your correspondence, whatever you are working on, everything. If anyone asks, you are my mother's brother. Keep an eye out for Lucia and my mother. Most of the young men are already in the forest."

Lucia stood and embraced him, wanting to tell him her news, but knowing it was not a good time. He kissed her again. "I'll be back as soon as they're gone. There's an official and ten soldiers. I don't think they'll be here long."

He left quickly, but turned to look at them all when he was just outside the door. Lucia ran after him and watched him leap on the horse. "Please take care, Aaron."

"I will. You take care, too. Don't go in the forest. Stick close to the house."

By late afternoon the official and the soldiers rode into the village. They were in the market looking at the produce and helping themselves to the tastier-looking wares, when Father Lawrence sauntered by, as if being at the market at that time of day was a regular habit. He asked the official how the war was going and was told that their army was being pushed back and that the enemy, along with its new allies, had invaded their homeland. Looking around at the nervous villagers, he raised his voice and said, "This is the time for sacrifice. It's time to give back to your country in its hour of need."

Several of the villagers standing around wanted to ask what their country had done for them other than taxing them and taking their young men; however, they had been warned by Father Lawrence not to say anything that could be construed as sedition or uncooperativeness. So they said nothing. They simply waited to see what would happen next, expecting that the sacrifices they were supposed to make would be made clear to them fairly quickly.

Father Lawrence said nothing and began selecting produce.

"Father, we need places to stay. We noticed one on the road. It had a workshop in the back."

"That's the home of Catherine and Simon," Father Lawrence said noncommittally.

"Could we put soldiers there?"

"I wouldn't want to speak for them, sir. It's not our way."

"Are you saying we have to go door to door?"

"As I said…"

"Ridiculous! Aren't you the priest?"

"It doesn't make a difference here. My parishioners worship their independence nearly as much as they worship God." Father Lawrence shook his head as if he, himself, had been similarly inconvenienced on numerous occasions.

Catherine and Simon were not happy to have soldiers in their house. As the three soldiers they were forced to board walked across their threshold, Catherine had every intention of making their stay miserable no matter what Father Lawrence said. But as they stood around in their smelly uniforms, hats in their hands, waiting for directions, Catherine noticed they were all very young and unsure. She felt a tug at her maternal instincts.

When the official accompanying the soldiers left, Catherine put her hands on her hips.

"Young men, we'll feed and board you, but we expect you to keep yourselves presentable and be respectful. First thing, you need to wash those uniforms. My husband, Simon, will get you some water and soap."

"Madame," one of the soldiers said, "we thought you would wash them."

"I will feed you or wash your uniforms. What will it be?" Catherine asked. Simon smiled, amused by his wife's regal nonchalance. He left to fetch water and soap.

After a couple of days, Father Lawrence went to check on Lucia, Helen, and Frederick.

"I don't think the soldiers will be here much longer," he told them.

"How's Aaron...any word?" Helen asked.

"There's no word. But that's what we agreed upon, unless there was trouble."

"Do the soldiers suspect something?" Lucia asked.

"They've noticed how few young men are in the village. We told them that we've already lost men in the war and that many of our young men are gone because they have had to go look for work in the valley. Two more of our young men have volunteered for the army and they are compelling one of the older men to leave too. That was a surprise. And they'll be taking several horses and enough food to last them for a while. They've purloined Simon's cart. All in all though, it has gone as well as one could hope — but the official told me that more soldiers will come and if any man was caught evading his duty, he would be punished."

The official, the soldiers, and the three village men left two days later. Before the young men in hiding returned to their homes, Aaron met with them. They made plans to replenish the food they had eaten, discussed improvements to the warning system, and then decided to celebrate how well things had gone by consuming large quantities of ale. It was late when Aaron arrived home. He stole in quietly, undressed, and slipped into bed. Lucia woke and greeted him.

"I'm so glad you're back."

"Me too."

"Do you want to hear some news?"

"Is it good?"

"The best...I think I'm pregnant."

"What?"

"I think I'm pregnant. It is early yet, but I feel I am."

"Oh, Lucia! I'm so happy." He kissed her. "Does anyone else know?"

"I wanted to tell you first. It's been so hard...."

Aaron lifted up her nightclothes and kissed her stomach. Then he tenderly placed a hand on her belly.

"I don't feel anything."

Lucia laughed. "It's too soon, silly."

That night, Lucia had a dream. She watched as a flaming star fell through the night sky. Cupping her hands, Lucia held them out to catch it, but the star passed through her hands and disappeared into the ground. Trying to understand what had happened, she stared at her hands and was surprised to see that the star had burned holes through them.

She woke up, disturbed by the dream, and shared it with Aaron when he woke. Although his words were reassuring, she saw fear flutter in his eyes. She wondered if she should have told him. He still had a great deal on his mind. The next few days, whenever she was not concentrating on something, she thought about the dream and hoped it did not mean she would lose her

WOMAN WITHOUT A NAME

child. Catherine and Miriam had both talked to her before the wedding about the possibility of miscarrying, and how that did not mean a woman would not eventually have a child. Catherine told her that she, herself, had miscarried twice before she had her firstborn, and she reminded Lucia of the other women in the village who had miscarried, most of whom went on to give birth to several healthy children. Lucia knew what might happen, but she sensed that everything was as it should be with her pregnancy. So what was the dream about? She wondered if her morbid imagination was at work again. She had had premonitions of something bad happening to Aaron whenever he left the village to work, but nothing horrible had ever occurred.

Soon after the soldiers' departure, Frederick approached Aaron about having Lucia help him with his correspondence. "Many of my students are asking for personal advice and I don't have time to answer them all. When I've asked Lucia's opinion about their various difficulties, I have often been struck by her intuition and her ability to articulate difficult matters. I could use her help. However, I will accept it only if I am allowed to pay her for her work."

"She would like helping you," Aaron said. "And I'll worry less knowing that she is not physically overdoing it or out in the forest collecting plants. We would be grateful for whatever you wanted to pay."

"I will discuss payment with Lucia, if that is all right with you."

"Please, go ahead....Is the hiding place for your papers large enough?"

"It's adequate for now. I may need another space in a month

or two. If I need help I'll let you know. I'm doing a great deal of writing."

"I'm grateful to you, Frederick, for keeping an eye on Lucia and my mother."

"Father Lawrence also seems to keep an eye out. He comes by quite a lot. I find that I enjoy his company very much. And from how he speaks of you, I believe he thinks of you as a son."

"Unfortunately, like many sons, I fear I disappoint."

"Not in this situation, I'm sure. Fear often has no rational basis. As I say this, though, I am reminded of how professors fear disappointing their students. Such fear of disappointing seems a common thing. I imagine even priests experience it."

Lucia enjoyed helping Frederick with his correspondence. He would read all his letters and then put those with more personal questions in a separate pile. She would write a letter responding to the personal questions, first explaining that she was a student of Frederick's and was assisting him. Frederick would read her response, add something in his own hand, and then she would seal the letters. They usually worked together in Helen's home for Helen enjoyed their company, but would not disturb them. Frequently, hours went by and Frederick and Lucia did not say a word to each other, but on some mornings Frederick wanted conversation or he was mulling over something he was writing about and would ask Lucia, and sometimes Helen, for their ideas.

When Lucia told Catherine, Helen, and Miriam that she was pregnant, she unleashed a fury of womanly planning. The women put their heads and hands together and refused to show Lucia what they were up to, saying it was a surprise. Lucia enjoyed their scheming. She enjoyed many things at this time and felt vastly content. Being pregnant agreed with her. Her morning sickness was short-lived and Aaron was in good spirits. Every night when he was home, he would lay his head on Lucia's belly and talk to their child about what he did and saw that day and how much he loved his wife. He would tell his unborn child how fortunate he or she would be to have Lucia for a mother and how he, the father, would always be there.

Lucia found great pleasure in working with Frederick and having her mind stretched, although some days thinking felt like the last thing she wanted to do. As Lucia went about her other chores in the afternoons, her hand would slowly curve around the slight bulge of her belly. She would hum or even sing if no one was around. And she would remember all the ways Sophia had mothered her.

One evening when Aaron was away, Father Lawrence came to visit. He asked how she and the baby were doing. He told her that he and Frederick had begun exchanging letters as a way of clarifying and widening their thinking. Lucia was surprised by this and wanted to ask him more about it, but Father Lawrence seemed to be deciding something. She took up her darning and waited.

"How's Aaron?"

"He's looking forward to the baby. He's a little nervous about being a parent."

"He'll be a good father....Does he ever mention his time in prison or in the army?"

"Not very often. Why, Father?"

"I was just wondering."

"He's told me it's hard for him to practice what he did in prison. He can't let go of everything from one moment to the next like he learned to do there. He says the hardest thing is letting go of responsibility. It's not just the responsibility for us — his mother and myself and the baby. And it's not just Frederick and the young men in the village. I think its Timothy. He can't let go of feeling responsible for what happened to Timothy – not completely."

"Do you think there is anything I could say, anything I could do to help him?"

"No, Father. I tell him he's too hard on himself, but that's not all that is going on. I know he gets angry at the world, at how it is. I talk to him about it, but it really doesn't change the way he thinks and feels about things. Letting go…that is going to have to come from inside of him. I think it will, but I don't know when."

Father Lawrence gazed at the young mother, awed by her wisdom. He was reminded of Sophia and thought how delighted she would be if she could see her daughter now.

Chapter Thirty-Eight

It was a cool, crisp morning. Smoke from household fires hung in the air. Aaron, working at his bookbinding job, had been gone for two days. As she walked the short distance to Helen's house, Lucia's hand lingered on her belly. She was looking forward to a full morning working with Frederick. Helen would have breakfast ready for them.

Nearing Helen's, she saw someone cloaked and hooded standing uneasily by a tree not far from the door. When the figure turned toward her, Lucia saw that she was a young, rough-looking woman, a stranger. Rather than evade her gaze, the woman stared back at her defiantly, her lips twisting upward, sneering. Lucia knew something horrible was happening. Her senses sharpened; her attention both widened and grew more intense. There was the sound of wood breaking and a heavy thud from behind the door. She moved quickly, but the young woman was faster and stood blocking her way to the door. Lucia tried to get around her, but the woman stood her ground and managed to force her back. Powerless, terrified, and not knowing what else to do, Lucia started screaming. The young woman struck her on the mouth with her fist and then went around Lucia and pushed her through the unlocked door and into the house.

Shock, the blow, and the dim light made it impossible for Lucia to see anything. She heard a wet sound coming from the floor near her feet. She was pushed from behind again and lurching forward, she grabbed onto a chair to steady herself. As her eyes adjusted, she saw two men with iron rods beating someone who lay in a pool of blood on the floor. She heard the sound of metal striking yielding flesh. The air was so dense she gasped for breath.

Awareness contracted around the two men who were now staring at her. Behind them was a low fire. One of the men was wiping his face with his sleeve. She wanted to move, but could not. It was as if there was no longer any room in the world for her.

The men had stopped briefly when she came in, but now they took several more swings. She heard them talking but could not make out what they were saying. They stopped and drank something. The young woman asked for her share and was telling them to hurry, that someone might have heard Lucia screaming. Then the two men were bullishly pushing her aside and making for the door. Lucia fell to the floor, landing hard on her backside. She was momentarily stunned. While she was trying to orient herself, she heard the young woman yelling coarsely at the two men. She continued to berate them as the three left the house.

Turning her head, Lucia saw Aaron's mother lying on the floor only a few feet away, her eyes open in a frozen stare. She scooted toward her and closed her mother-in-law's eyes. Then she scrambled to her feet and stumbled toward Frederick who lay on his back, his face unrecognizable. She knelt by his side and placed a finger where there once had been a nose–she felt no breath. She laid her head on his broken chest, feeling Frederick's blood moisten her skin and stick to her hair. Lifting his hand to her mouth, she kissed it.

She heard the boots of the men when they returned, watched them raise their rods as they approached her. She put out her arms to deflect the blows and heard a crack. She was hit once on the head and twice on the shoulder before she collapsed to the floor. She hoped that it was over, that her unborn child was still safe, but then the men began kicking her, aiming their blows at her belly. She tried to curl up. She entwined her fingers across her stomach. She wanted to scream, "Not my baby! Not my baby!" She heard the young woman again, as if from a great distance. And then everything was still.

She became intensely aware of how she was witnessing everything. It was like that time in the barn during the storm. She had the impression she was surveying the whole of her life from beginning to end and that she was aware of everything that had happened to her. And what stood out, like a mountain peak, was her love for Aaron. Fear and pain fell away. Then her vision narrowed and Aaron was an image floating on the surface of water. When a viscous darkness descended, his image disappeared. She was a pool of blood and water and felt herself too wide and deep for the earth to sop up. She knew she was dying. That knowledge was accompanied by utter peace and calm. She knew no more....

IV.

A New Birth

A New Adventure

Chapter Thirty-Nine

Father Lawrence picked himself off the church floor, and though he faced the crucifix he could not focus on it. He had not been able to pray. He could not think. His body was a dead, immovable weight he was forced to carry. He knew only one thing: he had to go to Aaron. He had to give Aaron the news and he had to stay with him while it sunk in.

It felt impossible, but he put one foot in front of another until he was out the church door. He circumvented his own will, ignored the pressure of his emotions, and used duty and loyalty as his only guides. Skirting the village, he went around the meadow, not wanting to run into either the soldiers or his neighbors.

As he walked through the trees, everything seemed unreal. He lost track of time and was surprised when he came upon one of the hideouts. He hoped it was not the one being used, but it was. He saw some of Aaron's friends talking and slowly approached them.

"I have very bad news for Aaron. He's going to need all of you. Don't let him out of your sight the next few days. Do you understand?"

The young men looked at each other, dismayed. "What is it, Father," one asked, "what happened?"

The priest ignored the question. Another young man said, "Of course, Father."

"Where's Aaron?"

The young men pointed to a small clearing. Father Lawrence headed in that direction and the young men followed at some distance. Aaron was sitting on the ground, leaning against a tree, reading a book. His peace was palpable and spread outward, filling the space around him. The priest stood rooted to the ground, unable to move closer, fearing that such a moment might never be Aaron's again. After a few minutes, Aaron looked up. He saw the priest and he saw his friends behind him. Looking more closely at Father Lawrence, Aaron saw that he was not himself. He closed his book, stood, and walked toward him.

"What is it, Father? You don't look well."

When the priest looked down and put his hand over his eyes, Aaron staggered as if from a blow.

"You have bad news. Tell me!"

"Your mother and Frederick are dead."

"What!" Aaron rocked on his feet.

"They're dead."

"And Lucia. What about Lucia?"

"We don't know yet. She's alive but barely breathing, and she's lost a great deal of blood.... She lost the baby."

Aaron spun around. He took a few steps, then fell to his knees. Leaning over, he started beating his head against the hard ground and clawing the dirt with his fingers. A prolonged, deep and hollow sound came out of him. His friends, who were standing too far away to hear what Father Lawrence had told him, were shocked and frightened by the sound Aaron made and by his be-havior. Father Lawrence waited a few moments, then went up to Aaron and knelt down beside him. As Aaron was raising his head to beat it again against the earth, Father Lawrence seized it in his hands. "No more. Don't hurt yourself any more." Aaron jerked his head away and wailed. Father Lawrence continued kneeling next to him and after several moments took him in his arms. Feeling Aaron's tears on his neck, the priest's heart broke.

Aaron rocked back and forth within the priest's arms and then pushed himself away. "Where is she now?"

"She's at Catherine and Simon's and is being well-cared for. An army doctor, a surgeon, has treated her, and a well-known healer has also come. You can see her in a few days."

"A few days!"

"You're too distraught to see her now. You will get yourself captured, and put the rest of the men here in danger. If the soldiers don't leave soon, I'll come up with a plan for you to see her. Until then, stay here. Do you hear me?"

"Yes."

"Your friends will hold you to your word," Father Lawrence said quietly.

"What happened?" Aaron stammered.

"No one knows who was involved or why they did it. It must have happened around the time you came back to warn the village about the soldiers. I don't think they were the ones who did this."

"Were they after Frederick? Did they find anything? His letters?"

"I don't know. His place was torn apart too. Perhaps they were only looking for money. Your home was untouched."

"Frederick?"

"He was horribly beaten. Your mother had her throat cut. She probably died very quickly. Your child....I saw it was a girl, though she wasn't quite fully formed. She was lying in blood," Father Lawrence forced himself to finish. "I wrapped her in a blanket and buried her next to Sophia and Jeremiah. We will bury your mother and Frederick close by."

Aaron started retching. Father Lawrence motioned the waiting friends for water. One ran to get some and handed a cup to the priest, who offered it to Aaron. He thrust it aside, spilling the contents. Another cup was procured and offered. "Drink, Aaron."

Aaron absently took a few sips, then looked at the priest. "Why, Father? Why did God allow them to suffer and die like this? Why did He take my child? What did Lucia or my mother do to anyone?"

Now that he had delivered the news, Father Lawrence was empty. He could not answer Aaron. Instead, he stood and gestured, offering to help Aaron up.

"Give me an answer, Father. Give me a word."

"I would give you a word even if it killed me, if I had one to give."

"There's only hell, then. That's the end. That's the last word on this bloody earth – not love. Isn't it? Isn't it?" Aaron said progressively raising his voice.

The priest shook his head, but grief had seized his throat and was constricting it. Shocked, he watched Aaron clench his fists and narrow his eyes. His face darkened. His breathing grew shallow. He was an animal about to pounce. The priest backed away.

"You're a priest. How can you not know? What good are you?"

"I am only a man, like you...."

Aaron trembled with a barely restrained rage. Without saying another word, he walked away. Father Lawrence was shaking. He was surprised his heart had not given out again. After a few moments, he walked toward the young men. He told them briefly what had happened and reminded them with a broken voice to keep a watchful eye on Aaron.

That night, Father Lawrence wearily climbed the hill above the church overlooking the village. For a time, he saw the images of Helen with her throat cut, and of Frederick, beaten beyond recognition. He saw Lucia and all the blood, and the child. And then his uselessness to the man he loved more than any other seized him like a hostile demon. He fought with this demon of absolute uselessness the rest of the night, trying to keep himself from succumbing to despair, forcing himself to think of what he might do for or say to Aaron, but nothing came to him. In the early morning light, he knew he was lost, entirely defeated. He could not summon up anything helpful, anything that would push back the darkness. He felt like he was striking rock so compact and hard that not only did nothing within his grasp make a dent, but every attempt to chip away at it shattered him. His utter weakness was completely exposed and Father Lawrence waited for what he assumed would follow: judgment and condemnation. Time passed. The judgment and condemnation he feared did not come. It grew colder, quieter.

Just before dawn, he noticed a slight warming breeze. The gently moving air seemed a blessing. And when the sun rose, it appeared as if a great being was hailing him across the silent expanse, inviting him to soar. Slowly, Father Lawrence realized that he had been wrestling not with a demon, but with an angel, perhaps with Christ Himself, and that his utter defeat had been the beginning of a victory he could not yet understand.

When Aaron walked away from Father Lawrence, one of his friends, seeing his bloody head and fingers, offered to bandage them. Aaron kept on walking as if he neither heard nor saw him. He sat down on one of the ruin's crumbling walls with his hands on his knees, his head bent toward the ground. After a while, he got up and strode deeper into the forest. Three of his companions, seeing what he was doing, followed him.

He walked for over a mile and then knelt down facing a young, newly sprouting tree. He put his hands around it and then began shouting Lucia's name over and over again. His friends moved closer together as if by their contact they could help each other stand the unrelenting anguish. Aaron gave no sign of knowing they were even there. For hours it went on. When evening came, one of the men went back for food and a lantern. By the time he returned, though Aaron was still calling out his wife's name, there was a new note in his raspy voice – one of pleading and loving tenderness. When the moon rose over the forest, Aaron finally let go of the tree, lay on the ground and fell asleep. His friends ate quietly together and kept vigil, as the priest had directed them.

After three days, Father Lawrence returned to the hiding place. As soon as Aaron saw him, he ran and threw himself at his feet. "Forgive me, Father."

Father Lawrence squatted on the ground, facing Aaron. "You did me a great service."

"You're not useless, Father. I was wrong…."

"But I am. I am nothing."

"I don't want you to feel that way, Father."

"You mistake my experience and underestimate its power. I am at last a free man."

Aaron gazed into the priest's face and saw that he was being utterly sincere. He did not entirely comprehend what Father Lawrence had just said, but felt absolved by his words.

"I feel forgiven."

"Not by me. Now can we sit somewhere?"

They found a spot in the sun, near a ruined wall.

"Lucia? Is she better?" Aaron asked.

"She mends slowly and is not conscious yet. But her breathing is stronger."

"Is she in pain?"

"Not now. Not while she is in her condition."

"I have to see her," Aaron said.

"I know."

"How are Catherine and Simon?"

"They're holding up."

"Will the soldiers leave soon?" Aaron asked.

"I hear not for another several days."

"Can I see her before then?"

"I'll go with you tomorrow. Miriam's made a robe and a cowl for you. You'll pretend to be a religious brother come to visit his aunt and uncle in their hour of need. I hope you remember some Latin phrases. An inquisitive soldier with half a brain will see through the story, so it would be better if you didn't have to tell it. Simon will keep watch and will signal if there's trouble. If there is, you can slip out the back and hide in the shelter in his workshop."

"Thank you, Father."

"I want to share something with you, Aaron. A dream I had that night in the meadow. I dreamt that the house Lucia and Sophia had lived in was on fire again. I knew Lucia was inside and wanted to go in and save her. But Sophia came out and stood in my way. She told me she wasn't going to let me in because the fire could not destroy what was indestructible, it would only brighten it."

Aaron began sobbing, his chest heaving, like that of a person struggling for breath.

"Was I wrong to tell you?" Father Lawrence asked.

Aaron could not say anything, but he vigorously shook his head, no. Father Lawrence sighed and was turning away, when Aaron grabbed him and the two embraced.

That evening Aaron took his share of food and moved away from the other men. They left him alone. The priest had said it was all right. After eating, Aaron somehow found his way back to that same young tree which he had wrapped his arms around. That night there were no stars, and the moon was veiled behind a curtain of cloud. He squatted on the ground and wished that he had some token, some reminder of his mother, of Frederick and of his daughter, some tangible objects he could hold over his heart. But he had nothing. He had not even knelt before their bodies or buried them in the ground. He desperately wanted to sense their presence, but saw clearly that the dead were not meant to be conjured up for his consolation.

He held out his empty hands and then put one hand over the other. If that was all he had: nothing — well, that was what he would place next to his heart. That would be their token. He lay on his back on the ground and held his empty hands cupped over his heart; and then he sensed her, his unborn daughter. He sensed her pure, sweet, unconquerable love for him. And somehow she impressed upon him that her going was for her mother's good. He wept and his daughter seemed to be touching him through his own tears.

When he had begun burying the dead, he had felt he was being initiated into something. He had that feeling once more. Something shifted in him that night – a center of gravity; it moved from his head to a vast space behind his heart. Life stirred again — a powerful, fluid, supple force filling his body. He felt life tug and sweep at the dense tangle of his emotions, loosening them, unsticking them from each other. They were a real but flimsy barrier against the flow.

Father Lawrence came the next night with a robe and cowl as he had promised he would. As Aaron donned his disguise, the priest sensed a profound change in him. He told himself he would ask Aaron about it later. Aaron told Father Lawrence that he wanted to stop at his mother's house and Frederick's to check things out.

"I don't think that's a good idea."

"I have to look around, Father. If those men who beat him took his letters, it means others might be in danger and would need to be warned."

Although the villagers had removed the broken furniture, and had patched and scoured the walls and floors, when Aaron stepped into the house where he was raised, it felt like the house of strangers. It seemed to him that he and his mother had never lived there.

"I found a few of Frederick's letters in here," Father Lawrence said. "I hid them until I could talk to you."

Next, they went to Frederick's place. Aaron immediately went to the fireplace and reaching up, removed some stones and dragged out two large iron boxes. When he opened them, their contents appeared untouched. Aaron sighed with relief and re-placed the boxes and then the stones. As the sun dipped below the hill, they arrived at Catherine and Simon's.

Catherine opened the door at Father Lawrence's knock. She took Aaron's face in her two hands and looked into his eyes. "She's sleeping well tonight. I know it'll make a difference, your being here. You'll do her good."

In a moment, Simon was at the door, shaking his head as if he still could not believe what had happened. "Prepare yourself," he told Aaron.

Father Lawrence put his arm around Aaron's shoulder and guided him to the room where Lucia lay. Aaron went up to the bed. Lucia's red and golden hair had been closely cropped, her head was stitched, a sling held an arm in place. Her eyes were closed. One was swollen. A cheek, bruised. Her face was so pale. A smattering of light freckles spread across her nose, more prom-inent than he remembered. Father Lawrence placed a chair near the bed for him, and Simon set down a candle, and then both men left the room.

Aaron sat down on the chair. "Lucia…. I'm here." He took her free hand gently in his. It was swollen and had a large black bruise. There was no loving pressure returned, no sign she knew he was there. He bent down and kissed her hand. She seemed withdrawn far into herself and that frightened him. He knew she was close to death.

"I love you so much, Lucia. You must get better. Don't leave me. I need you. We have work to do, you and I."

He wiped his tears away quickly with the back of his hand. She looked frail, broken. He had the fleeting thought that she did not belong in such a savage world, but that was quickly followed by the thought that he was part of that world. He was capable of rage and hate, even against the innocent. He had almost struck Father Lawrence, of all people.

Suddenly, an astonishing thought came to him. The thought was accompanied by power and certainty and had the vividness of an image. *I can call Lucia back from death.* He began sweating profusely as if the thought was a high fever his body was fighting. Agitated, he got up off the chair and began pacing around the room. He wanted Lucia to live, but the risk in admitting such power was terrifying to him. He felt himself torn in two, love and fear in opposition, battling each other. The thought came again with renewed force. It came from above his head and was intentionally pressing down upon him. There was a strange physicality about it — as if he was being pinned to the ground under a crushing weight. Believing that to yield would mean the death of his own willing, he became singularly bent on resisting it. But all his intensity and purpose, next to that imperative weight and steady intention, were completely impotent. He staggered, awed by the will and strength of something that clearly was not human. He had to yield. Grabbing a bedpost, he went to his knees.

Another thought pressed down upon him. *I have to accept everything.* There was power and certainty in that thought too, and it seemed connected to the first. Feeling stronger, he stood up. It was as if some of the force that had pressed upon him had entered into him by his simply perceiving it. The thought came again that he could call Lucia back and this time he did not resist it. But he knew that to call her back, he had to call everything back: the violence, cruelty, lies, senselessness; everything about the world and himself that he loathed, despised, and had tried to distance himself from. He had to embrace it all. Nothing could be excluded. He could not pick and choose anymore – that was the unrelenting condition.

Aaron surrendered and worshipped in a single, liberating deed that altered not only his mind and heart, but his physical body as well. His body felt expansive and weightless as if it were made of streaming light and yet at the same time it felt like a pillar of concentrated and radiating strength. He planted his feet solidly on the floor, and with his legs slightly apart he raised his arms. With the palms of his hands angled in a welcoming gesture he said, "I accept everything."

All the old habits of grief, the long sorrow that inevitably follows the quick dissolution of dreams, the rending, persistent pain of obstinate isolation — he felt them enter into him. But there was no sense of burden. They had changed because he had. Something new was unfolding. He felt he was at a beginning, a place where understanding and mastery were possible. Lowering his arms, he moved back to the chair at the side of the bed and sat down. With one hand he took Lucia's free one and with the other touched her face. "Lucia, come back," he softly commanded her.

She made noises and moaned a little. Aaron urgently called for Catherine and when she stood, flustered, at the door, he told her about the sounds Lucia was making.

"She does that sometimes," Catherine said. Aaron felt she was disappointed.

"Is she waking up? Can she hear me?"

"I don't know. Keep talking to her. It will do her good."

"I want to stay the night, but I'll leave before the sun comes up. Can you tell Father Lawrence?" He closed the door and went back and sat by the bed. Throughout the night Aaron continued calling out her name. He would alternate that with telling her that he loved her and so did little Sophie. Periodically, he would pace the room and then would go back to the chair. The thought that Lucia might not live still flitted about, but never settled in his mind. An hour before dawn, he left the house.

Chapter Forty

Lucia knew she was waking up, but time and place were too vague for words and even her physical boundaries were uncertain. She had the clear sense that she had forgotten who she was, as if her memory of herself was dawdling behind her awareness. She felt something touching her, but could not figure out where; and heard something that agitated her, but did not know what her agitation meant. There was a vague impulse, a strong movement forward without knowing how to shape or direct it. Suddenly, she was aware of excruciating, overwhelming pain. It sharpened her attention, and swiftly her thoughts began organizing themselves into half-formed questions. But before what she wanted to know clarified itself, she fell back asleep.

It was Catherine who was there when Lucia opened her eyes for the first time. She was carefully wiping Lucia's face with a warm, damp cloth when she was suddenly confronted by a look of pure inquisitiveness. Catherine pulled back, surprised.

"Catherine?" Though Lucia seemed confused, her voice was strong.

"I'm here, Lucia. You're safe now."

"Where's Aaron?" Lucia asked. Catherine could tell by her question and her tone that Lucia was alert and focused, nearly back to her old self.

"He was with you all night. He had to leave before it got light…to be safe. He'll be back tomorrow."

"What time is it?"

"It's close to supper. Do you want to eat something?"

Lucia looked around the room and then down at the sling. With her free hand she reached for her abdomen. Catherine put her hand on top of Lucia's.

"Where's my baby?" Lucia asked, the muscles around her eyes twitching as if they already knew the answer.

"She's gone," Catherine blurted out. "She's with Sophia and Jeremiah, now."

"I lost our child?"

"You didn't lose her, Lucia. God took her."

"My baby was a girl?"

Crying, Catherine nodded her head. She used the cloth she had been wiping Lucia's face with to wipe her own.

"We were going to name her Sophie," Lucia said quietly. She closed her eyes and became very still. Catherine wondered if Lucia had lost consciousness until she saw tears squeezing out from underneath her lashes.

"I'm so glad you're here, Lucia. It's a great mercy. It would've broken Aaron's heart if you had died."

Lucia opened her eyes and looked at Catherine. "Does he know about little Sophie?"

"Father Lawrence told him everything… about his mother and Frederick too." Catherine stopped herself from saying more.

"They're dead," Lucia said. "I remember." Through her sobs

she said something to her godmother, but Catherine could not make it out. Catherine decided not to ask her to repeat it.

"Aaron's left you a letter. Would you like to read it?"

Lucia weakly raised her free arm, and Catherine took the letter out of her apron pocket, unfolded it, and placed it in Lucia's hand. The effort Lucia had to make to read what Aaron wrote gave her an excruciating headache. She handed the letter back to Catherine. "Please, read it for me. I can't make it out."

Catherine tried not to appear disturbed by Lucia's request. She took the letter and began:

My dearest Lucia,

I love you so much. I will be with you as soon as I can. I know our daughter, Sophie, loved you. I felt her love and I want my love to become as great as hers. Thank you for bearing our child and for trying to protect her.

I believe you know this already: my mother and Frederick are also dead.

Catherine stopped reading. "It's too terrible, what's happened!"

"Is there more?"

"I'll read it later."

"No.... Now."

Catherine nervously cleared her throat.

Father Lawrence arranged for our daughter to be buried near Sophia and Jeremiah. My mother and Frederick are also buried nearby. I did not feel their presence as I felt our daughter's, but I know they are with us and we will always be with them. And we will be together, you and I.

Do not worry yourself about me. There is no need. I have been given a strength I could not imagine possible. I have accepted everything.

We have work to do, Lucia. So get well.

I love you so much,
Aaron

Lucia murmured, "I have accepted everything," as if it were a prayer not yet fully hers. She fell back asleep.

Several days went by. When Aaron came again, Lucia was awake. They kissed awkwardly; he leaning over, trying not to hurt her. He took her free hand in both of his and they wept and kissed again, tasting each other's tears. She asked him what he had meant in his letter about being given strength and about how he had accepted everything. As best he could, he told her what had happened the first night he had come to her, and about his experience with little Sophie. While he hoped what he shared with her would give her strength, he noticed that it seemed to have the opposite effect. As she listened to him her face softened, her eyes filled with tears, and she appeared even more vulnerable.

"I'm so sorry, Aaron. Your mother.... And Frederick. I saw them beat him," she sobbed. "There was nothing I could do. I didn't remember everything I saw and heard until today. The blood, the awful smell...."

Aaron sat on the bed, on her good side.

"I saw your mother's eyes when she was lying on the floor.... They kept kicking me... I lost our baby."

Aaron was about to place a tender hand on her stomach, but sensed it would unleash more sorrow and so only caressed her hand.

"What if I can't have other children? Sophia couldn't."

"She didn't try.... And she had you." Aaron took Lucia's hand and placed it over his heart. "How are you feeling?"

"Weak. Catherine had me walk a little today and Miriam kept me company.... I have such a headache."

"Should I let you rest?"

"No. Stay with me. I have this headache *all* the time.... Why are you dressed like that?"

"The soldiers are still here. It's safer like this. How's your shoulder?"

"It hurts. Who found us?"

"Father Lawrence."

"Father Lawrence? He saw everything?"

Aaron nodded. "I'm grateful it was him." He told her about Father Lawrence's dream, how in his dream Sophia had stood in the priest's way and wouldn't let him save her, how she told him that fire would not consume her because there was something in her that was indestructible.

"I don't feel that way."

"Tired?"

"Very. Can you stay here till I fall asleep?"

"Of course," Aaron said. "Will it hurt if I lie down next to you?"

"Let's try."

Aaron gently scooted Lucia over and lay down next to her. He took her hand and held it over his heart, as was his way.

"Your heart is beating so fast, Aaron. It's so strong," Lucia said.

After ten days, the soldiers left and the young men returned to their homes. The villagers were grateful for the return of relative normalcy and for the fact that the soldiers took less than anticipated. Father Lawrence's intervention had something to do with it. An old man, notorious for his nosiness, had overheard the commanding officer telling his men that since the war was almost over, he was sparing the village the full tax. His men had argued with him. One eloquently pleaded their case, "Showing mercy to this village is being cruel to us. We've served under you, these people are strangers. You know we haven't been paid for months and we have wives and children to feed too."

The officer heard them out. "We'll talk about this again tomorrow," he told them.

The nosy man rushed to report this to Father Lawrence, explaining how unhappy the soldiers were and how they would probably be up to mischief. The priest immediately talked to as many villagers as he thought would be willing, convincing them to voluntarily turn over more food supplies than had been requisitioned, but less than the village had originally expected to pay. "A goodwill offering at this point will serve everyone's interest," he explained. Despite a great deal of grumbling, the villagers grasped the wisdom of Father Lawrence's suggestion. And so that very evening, Father Lawrence and a few of the other villagers brought a wagon of foodstuffs, candles, wool, and woven cloth to the officer, saying that it was for the soldiers' families since they had endured hardships even greater than their own.

Grateful, the officer invited the priest to join him for dinner. Father Lawrence politely declined.

"Have you completed your investigation? Have you found out who murdered my parishioners?"

"I made careful inquiries, Father. It wasn't any of my men. They were all accounted for when the incident occurred. And it's not my duty to hunt down and prosecute criminals. I *am* sorry for your losses."

"I'm sorry for yours, Officer," Father Lawrence said, looking the man in the eye.

The officer grimaced. "It's the devil himself who's running things, Father. Soldiering and religion won't save us, now."

As Father Lawrence had hoped, the soldiers left soon after the villagers made their voluntary donation. Several villagers, those who took the time to imagine what might have happened, thanked the priest for his advice. He told them that the meddling villager had made his action possible and that they should thank him. The villagers did not take up his suggestion; they could not forget the grief the man had caused in the past. However, though the nosy man received no thanks, a note of affection crept into the villagers' continuing complaints about him.

The villagers felt grateful to Aaron and Lucia for reasons they felt vaguely ashamed of because they bordered on superstitious. The unlucky couple had taken the full brunt of a lightning strike, sparing them. The villagers were relieved because evil like that was unlikely to strike so close again for a while. A few men offered Aaron work, so he would not have to be so far away from Lucia. Aaron sensed the guilt that partially motivated the offers, but it did not lessen his gratitude or keep him from accepting their offers.

After the soldiers left and the village had settled down, Father Lawrence announced that there would be a mass for Helen, Aaron's mother, and Frederick and little Sophie. The church could not hold all that came. Many stood outside in the chilly autumn air; snatches of the priest's sermon had to be relayed to them by those standing close to the door.

Aaron, Lucia, her godparents, and Miriam and her father arrived at the church early. Lucia wore one of Miriam's scarves over her shorn head. She walked on her own, but because of her frequent dizzy spells, Aaron and Simon held her gently under the elbows. Lucia heard very little of Father Lawrence's sermon, for her head was hammering, her vision blurring, and she was sick to her stomach. Afterward many villagers came up to her and Aaron, expressing their sympathy. Lucia found this torturous, but tried for a while to be gracious. She was grateful when Catherine told Aaron to take her back.

That evening she said she wasn't hungry and went into the bedroom to lie down. Aaron got up and followed her. He helped her undress, pulled the covers over her, and then curled up next to her. Lucia fell asleep fairly quickly and dreamt that she was standing in front of the house Aaron had built for her. She knew a child was in there and all her things, but it was as if the house was no longer hers and she could not go inside. Jeremiah appeared at her side. He was clean, handsome, and dressed in a shirt and pants the vibrant color of leaves in early spring. He led her to the river, to the spot where he had taught her about desire.

She was going to find a stick to throw in the water, remembering that he had asked her to do that before. He said there was no need and waded into the river. He let his legs go and then his arms until he was floating on his back with his arms and legs outstretched. Lucia walked into the water. Too frightened to surrender herself to the river and awed that he could, she touched his naked foot and felt waves of light and joy down to her toes and out to her fingertips. He began floating away, but his body did not bob up and down like she expected. It moved inseparable from the current, the sunlight falling on it as if it were water.

Chapter Forty-One

For the next several months, the continued pounding in Lucia's head made it difficult for her to keep her eyes open for more than a few minutes. Light was often intolerable and movement made everything spin. Her arm and shoulder continued to throb with a deep bone ache. And at any time, she would suddenly imagine Helen lying at her feet or the bored, contemptuous look of the young woman. Various sounds would make her jump: the opening of a door anywhere in the house, footsteps, or Catherine's thumping the rugs when she cleaned them.

Most painful of all was the loss of little Sophie. Where her daughter should be, there was only emptiness, and as time went on, the emptiness penetrated everything. She tasted it in her food, felt it in her dreams, saw it in the faces of those she loved, heard it in words others spoke to her. She wondered how life could hold so much emptiness. When Lucia reminded herself of Aaron's experience – how he had felt little Sophie's love – it helped, but not for long. She wondered if her dream of Jeremiah floating away was about her own imminent death. Had he been teaching her how to meet it and that death was nothing to fear? But she was not willing to leave Aaron and sometimes felt there were things she still needed to do.

Every day was a struggle: a struggle to get out of bed, to walk, eat, fall asleep, and talk. Over and over again she said how sorry she was for her sharp, impatient words, her requests to be left alone, her unstoppable tears. Aaron and her godparents would try to reassure her and did everything they could to keep her spirits up as well as their own.

One morning, Lucia noticed that the pain in her head and shoulder had eased; and after three days of feeling better physically and emotionally, she thought the worst might be over. However, her reprieve did not last. One afternoon as she was resting, she felt a slight touch of terror. She did not think much of it, but for the next several days, the moments of terror multiplied and lengthened. Lucia could not figure out what was causing them and hoped they would pass. She said nothing about it to Aaron or her other loved ones, for they had been heartened by her recent progress.

One evening, while she was having dinner, her food suddenly became tasteless. She looked at Aaron and her godparents trying to follow their conversation, but they seemed thousands of miles away. The terror returned. She put down her fork, said she needed some air, and left the table. She went and stood outside under a tree near Simon's workshop, and when Aaron came to check on her, she sent him back inside, saying she was fine. When he left, though Lucia's heart sank, she knew that there was nothing he could have done or said that would have comforted her. She stood there, alone, while the emptiness eclipsed everything: all she knew and loved and all she had thought and experienced. It was as if there had never been anything but this emptiness, nor would there ever be.

After several days and nights of this, Lucia decided if she

wasn't to go mad or worse, she needed a long deep sleep at the very least. She was about to ask Catherine for something that would induce it, when she noticed something nudging her inside. She was gently being pushed to do something. As she was trying to sense what it was, Lucia heard these words: *Take in the emptiness. Eat and drink it. This is also Me.*

Lucia was shocked. She would not have been able to accept those words if she had not simultaneously had the recognition they were coming from a mind much greater than her own. And besides, the words were not like an ordinary suggestion. They communicated the near completion of a tremendous deed, a deed that awaited only her complete assent to be fully accomplished.

Lucia did assent and immediately was able to do exactly what the words had said, though she would find it impossible to describe how she could to anyone. And when she had taken in the emptiness she saw how grossly she had previously misinterpreted it, for the emptiness seemed now a space, and the space a womb, and the womb held everything. It held little Sophie and all of little Sophie's possibilities. It was not a womb that held anything static or confined. It was a womb that nourished freedom and the power to move about in ways she had not imagined previously. This freedom and power seemed the very taste of the divine. Lucia could hardly believe the gift that had been given her. She remembered what Aaron had said about little Sophie leaving for her sake, and she wept.

Over the next few days, Lucia savored the experience of freedom and movement. She felt as if she was living within an infinite and intelligent spaciousness capable of endlessly delighting her. Sometimes it made her feel as if anything was possible while at other times the spaciousness seemed nurturing and restorative. Her body and mind were healing within it, of that she was certain. When she told Aaron what had happened, she said she thought it was the Woman Who had told her to take in the emptiness. "Only She could have known about emptiness that way," she said.

From that moment on, though she appeared more distracted, Lucia's health and mood dramatically improved. Aaron was very relieved, but after a short while he realized he was bone tired, exhausted to the core. When he fell asleep at the dinner table, Catherine told him to go to bed and not get up until she said. He slept for nearly eighteen hours. When he woke, Lucia was lying next to him.

As she grew stronger, Lucia helped Catherine around the house. She swept, dusted, and did the dishes. Aaron could hear her laughing at her godmother's embroidered tales about the various happenings in the village. Simon heard her, too. "It's good to hear laughter in this house again," he whispered to Aaron one evening.

One morning, Aaron snuck up on Lucia when she was doing the dishes and kissed her on the neck. She squealed, turned around and flicked water in his face, and then grabbed for his hand to keep him from doing the same, but he was too quick and strong. He dipped his hand in the water and flicked drops at her. They nearly emptied the basin, flinging water at each other, and then they kissed. When they drew apart, Aaron looked into her eyes and saw she was ready to go home. He was glad of it, but there were things he knew he needed to take care of first.

He had offered Frederick's place to Miriam, her son, and her father. That was an easy decision. They were still living in cramped quarters with their relatives with whom they had no affinity. Frederick's place was small. However, they had money to add other rooms and Lucia would be comforted having her friend close by.

The decision about what to do with his mother's house had been more difficult. As with the other villagers, thrift was second nature. The habit of carefully managing what he owned kept him from doing what he had felt like doing for many months. Now he was certain that his feelings were the better guide and that he had to act on them. It was not right that anyone live in that house or use what was in it again.

On a cold spring morning, he set fire to his mother's house with all its furnishings still inside. He kept adding fuel until the blaze maintained a destructive momentum and then stood back and watched everything burn to the ground. The flames attracted several villagers who stood around, arms crossed over their chests. No one said anything.

The next morning, he went back with a cartload of dirt and a shovel. He broke up the embers and mixed dirt into them. Some children came by and offered to help. "There'll be grass here and flowers," a red-headed girl said. "And then it'll be better." Father Lawrence arrived when they were nearly done. He gave the children sweet biscuits and then he blessed the charred earth with the holy water he had brought. When Aaron told his wife what he had done, she kissed and thanked him. On their way home several weeks later, he showed her the spot. There were tiny shoots of grass already poking through the bare earth.

Chapter Forty-Two

Among the tasks Aaron had given himself was going through Frederick's writing, including his voluminous correspondence with his students. Consulting with Lucia, Aaron discovered that several letters were still unanswered and that quite a few mentioned Frederick's anticipated return. Aaron faced the daunting task of informing Frederick's students that he was dead, and that Lucia, whom many were beginning to know through her letters, was still unable to write to all of them because of her injuries. And then there was the question of what to do with the large sum of money Frederick had left. Aaron knew that Frederick had no children, and that his parents were dead. He knew of a brother, a niece, and a nephew, but had no idea where they lived. Aaron went to Father Lawrence about it.

"I think Frederick would want you and Lucia to use whatever you need to get on your feet again, and use the rest to continue his work."

"The students *are* starting to meet again. They say so in their letters. They beg Frederick to return and say they are hoping that Lucia and I will return with him. There were some letters from you, Father, among Frederick's things. Do you want them back?"

"Do you want to read them?"

"I *am* curious. Lucia told me that you and Frederick had begun a correspondence."

"Keep them then, and I will give you the letters Frederick wrote to me."

"What did you think of him, Father?"

"I never met a more intelligent man, but what most impressed me was how his mind followed his heart and how open both were. He was a fearless man, and I found myself becoming more fearless when I was around him."

"May I ask what you spoke about at your last meeting?"

"He recalled the experience he had at his friend's funeral. He brought it up again because we had been discussing how forcible attempts to create unity never work and how they are always destructive. We agreed that political tyranny is only the most obvious example. Frederick said that at his friend's funeral he had found himself in a world of unforced Unity and that it seemed a world permeated by Wisdom, and he said again that it was a world completely devoid of violence. Frederick said that experience became a window through which he saw how violence permeates even ordinary perception and common and accepted behaviors, and that the repropagating roots of oppression and absolutism of every kind can be found in all of us. He believed that as long as we perceive ourselves as separate and imagine that evil is the doing of others, human society won't fundamentally change and nothing it constructs or organizes will be innocent."

Aaron had been listening attentively. "He was right, Father."

Aaron told Father Lawrence about the night he first saw Lucia after her beating, told him about his struggle against a power that was more than human and how he had to embrace everything. The priest listened, honored that Aaron would share such things with him. "So you see, Father," Aaron concluded, "all that time I had wanted to change the world, I was probably only adding to its misery."

"Maybe you saw yourself as separate, Aaron, but you also desired the world's good. You must own the nobility of that desire as well."

Aaron gave the priest a slight smile. Father Lawrence caught the meaning of it and knew Aaron was being too dismissive of his own goodwill. *Perhaps I was too disparaging of it in the past as well,* the priest thought.

"Was innocence the last thing Frederick talked about?" Aaron asked.

"No. A young woman, one of his students, had sent him a medallion of the Blessed Virgin. When he asked me about her, I reminded him of Miriam's song at your wedding. I told him that Miriam had been quoting a passage found in the gospel. He expressed a desire to read it. He had read the New Testament only once, as a boy, when he was forced to by a tutor. I told him I would bring him a copy."

"Did you?"

Father Lawrence shook his head sadly. "I was taking it to him that morning."

"*That* morning?"

"Yes."

"When I told Lucia you were the one who found her, she said how terrible it must have been for you. She felt…. She knew. But the way I treated you…what I said…I remember you backing away from me….”

“There is no need to bring it up again,” Father Lawrence said quickly.

“Please hear me out,” Aaron pleaded.

“I’m sorry….Go ahead.”

“I’ve never thanked you for telling me what happened. You saw them first and then you had to tell me.” Aaron’s voice cracked. “I know it was a hard thing for you to do because you love me. You’ve always loved me like a father.” Aaron paused, trying to collect his strength. “Your love and your opinion of me have mattered more than you know. I’ve always wanted to be your son. I’ve wanted you to be proud of me.” Aaron softly beat his chest, overcome with emotion.

The priest took him in his arms. He too was overcome, but struggled to speak. “Never has a father been more proud of his son or learned more from him.”

Kneeling in the church that night, Father Lawrence felt awash in grace. At some point, to ground himself, he got off his knees, went outside, and climbed the hill behind the church. He sat on the earth, barely noticing how cold it was. Thoughts of his mother came to him, of her illness, and death, and how helpless he had felt. He stretched out on the ground and watched the stars until sleep overtook him.

He dreamt he saw an immense female bird. Its breast was a luminous, deep black while the feathers on its head were multicolored and brilliant. The bird’s eyes were sharp and penetrating. Slowly it unfolded its vast wings until they were completely outspread. The feathers on top of the wings were a blinding white, and on the bottom were the color of flame. He stood underneath Her — a helpless hatchling sensing the true power of its mother for the first time. The giant bird began beating its wings as if preparing to fly, their down and up thrusting movement warming him till he caught fire, strengthening him for the ascent. He knew that in the shadow of those infinitely protective and fearsomely commanding wings, he would come to know who he truly was and what the world was.

When he woke, stiff and chilled to the bone, it was almost dawn. He made his way down the hill, and while standing for a long while before the graves of Sophia and his other friends, he recognized that an intention had been born in him. No matter what the cost, he would continue to break the church's long silence about the Divine Mother. He had taken the first tentative steps at Lucia and Aaron's wedding. Now, it was time to begin in earnest.

Chapter Forty-Three

Summer arrived. Though the war was officially over, its effects lingered. Food was scarce and more refugees were passing through the village. Some wanted to stay, too exhausted and dispirited to go any further, knowing that they had nothing to go back to. Aaron organized the willing and able-bodied to help build homes for those who had small children or elders with them. A few paid them, many could not. Father Lawrence went around encouraging other villagers to open up their homes. Catherine and Simon took in two sisters who had lost their husbands. The influx of people strained the already dwindling food supply and people's generosity. Helping the villagers strike a balance between caring for their own families, and assisting the unfortunate strangers, was a delicate, ever-shifting task for Father Lawrence.

Aaron would come home late, exhausted. He was still working on a couple of farms as well as helping the refugees. Lucia would cook him dinner, using what she had grown in her new garden. They would talk while they ate, and then Aaron would collapse on their bed. After several months of this, Lucia told Aaron he had to pace himself, that she missed him too much. Aaron decided to take Father Lawrence's advice and began using Frederick's money. He quit working on the farms. Father Lawrence, knowing how he was, told him it was the right thing to do.

The harvest was a good one. By the feast of St. Michael in September, things were improving in the village. Strangers were still passing through, but not nearly as many. Although there was a push to build homes for those still without before winter came, Aaron was coming home earlier. In the evenings, lying in bed together, Lucia would read to him some of the letters from Frederick's students and her letters in response. She had been corresponding with the students for several weeks. Though most knew what had happened, many still wrote, wanting to stay in touch with her and reiterating their wish for Lucia and Aaron to join them. The students also wanted to know what Frederick had been thinking about during his time in the village and wanted to see a copy of his latest writings. Lucia had found notes for two books Frederick had been working on and some of his unfinished letters. Father Lawrence had also given her the letters he had received from Frederick. Lucia had begun copying these out and was sending them to the students. She would share with Aaron what she felt were the most striking passages. One evening she read to him a letter addressed to Father Lawrence.

You asked me to say more about Unity, how it applies to human experience, which seems so diverse. I will begin with a basic and fairly common experience, (and therefore one easily ignored), the experience of being one united self, a single, unitary subject. This experience persists in a manner that defies reason. I think of the young boy I once was. How different that boy is from this older me, and yet I believe the boy is me and it was I who was that boy. And I have also observed that I have many aspects, many unknown parts, and even personalities that I have experienced at different times. I have said and done and felt things that surprised myself, and yet recognized these things as myself. And finally, though I have such little knowledge or control of the workings of my body and all its aspects (some even say our bodies are a congregation of many living organisms), my experience is that this body is mine and not another's.

When I first began observing these things, I was frightened for a brief time and then I became curious. I have given much thought to these phenomena over the years and attempted to formulate an explanation for the durable and enduring unity and coherence that seems to be essential to the sense of self. I came to the conclusion that the self, perhaps because it is more fundamental or more encompassing than the mind, cannot be fully comprehended by it. While accepting this, I could not let my questions rest. I wondered if there might be another method I could use to investigate the nature of the self, a method not constrained by mental constructs. A solution came to me one morning when I was waking up: I simply needed to allow myself to become more aware of my experience. Over time, I discovered that the best way to train myself to do that was to sit quietly and observe whatever I was experiencing, to simply be a container for it, and only after a period of time to allow myself to reflect on it. I found that, after years of practicing this, I could observe myself while I worked and met with others.

I discovered that when I felt particularly intense emotions or a notable surge of vitality and remained still, allowing myself simply to become more aware of them, my inner experience was one of transformation or of see-ing something I had no idea of previously. Paradoxically, these experiences strengthened simultaneously a sense of being an indivisible unity and of being completely permeable and open. These experiences, and those I had observing my more typical emotional and vital states, led me to two important questions: How are awareness and the sense of unity connected, and where is the self in this?

For years I sat with these questions. Whatever I came up with, I would check against my experience. How many formulations had to be discarded as being unequal to experience! I am now at the point where I see these three: self, unity and awareness as fundamental, inseparable "forces" that are "behind" and directing human experience, but sense that behind these three, and holding them together is a body of Wisdom.

It takes all my attention to contemplate such matters and when I manage it, I sense how far I am from understanding and inhabiting even my own being. But how could I sense this if I did not in some way already know and inhabit? And so I am back to a question similar to the one I had when I was a young man in prison. Then I wondered how it was I could see so clearly my own stupidity and lack of integrity. I came to the conclusion then that an intelligence I later called "Wisdom" was nearer to me than my own self, that it was more my "self" than anything I had previously identified with. The conclusion was similar in this case, also. "My" life is only fully understood and inhabited by Wisdom — as is every life — and it is offered to me as being fully understood and inhabited, as a continual gift.

Lucia paused.

"What do you think?" Aaron asked.

"It's a wonderful letter, but one that you really have to hear rather than think about. Do you know what I mean?"

"I think so. His students need to see it."

"I've already copied it out for them…. Aaron, what did you feel when I read the letter to you?"

"I felt like I was watching an intelligently designed building going up stone by stone. Maybe that's because each of Frederick's experiences seemed to build on the ones that came before."

"And each experience was really a meeting with Her, with Wisdom."

Aaron leaned over and kissed her. "I like that. Did you want to read something else?"

Lucia picked up different pages and scanned through them. "Listen to this. It's the letter Father Lawrence wrote back."

Frederick,

You have the gift of putting what I thought unspeakable into words. Few have ever been able to point to the mysteries of our existence has have you. As a man of religion, I am deeply surprised by how without a religious tradition for support, you have drawn near to the deepest mysteries.

I gave much thought to your last letter. And I have also been reflecting on what Sophia, Lucia, Jeremiah and Aaron have all shared with me. I have come to believe that the church, my church, has been desperately trying to survive despite a weakened and failing heart. We have been trying to understand Christ while resisting seeing what He saw or loving what He loved. I am referring to Wisdom. How strange it is that a man and a teacher who is not a Christian has helped me more than any other understand and identify with Christ. I feel a fire burning inside of me, a fire I had once given up hope of ever experiencing again. I know the fire burns because I have found my path. How simple everything is. Though it is sometimes hard going and painful, the path is right beneath our feet. The path is our experience fully lived and attended to for in every experience Wisdom is inviting us.

"It took courage for Father Lawrence to write that," Aaron said. "He has to know he's beginning something that might cost him everything."

"We are beginning something too, Aaron, and it might cost *us* a great deal."

"What are you thinking?"

"Father Lawrence is going to try and get the village and the church to see Her. I feel I am being called to do the same, but not here. I sense a need to join the students…at least for a while. Do you feel the same?"

"I was thinking about going back with you, but wasn't sure if that was the best thing. Are *you* certain?"

"I'm not certain about anything, Aaron, but I feel it's the next step. I don't see another right now. I want to serve Her. I want to make Her known, even though I don't know what that means yet. But that's all right. Somehow, I think that not needing to know pleases Her — maybe because it's more adventurous!"

Winter came and then spring, and with spring's arrival both Lucia and Aaron felt more keenly that their time in the village was coming to an end. When Lucia suggested inviting Father Lawrence to dinner to discuss things, Aaron readily agreed. They both knew the priest had been sensing something important was going on; he had hinted as much.

Lucia cooked two rabbits and there were mushrooms, pota-toes, and fresh bread. Aaron had splurged on a bottle of wine. Father Lawrence said a blessing and they began eating.

"Is there something you two want to tell me?"

Aaron and Lucia looked at each other.

"You tell him, Aaron. Go on."

Father Lawrence thought it strange that Aaron would be the one announcing Lucia's pregnancy, but then, they had always done things differently.

"How did you know, Father?" Aaron asked.

"I've known the both of you since you were children. I knew something was up. When will it be?"

"We thought Midsummer's Eve."

"You know the exact day? It seems a little soon."

The priest noticed that both Lucia and Aaron appeared confused. Suddenly Lucia burst out laughing.

"He thinks I'm pregnant."

"You do, Father?"

"I did." The priest laughed along, but quickly sobered. "What *did* you want to tell me?"

"Lucia and I are thinking of joining Frederick's students…"

Lucia interrupted, "They've been asking us for some time. They've formed a small community…"

"Would you be part of it?"

"We're not sure, Father," Lucia answered, "but we both feel we need to be there at least for a little while."

"They're not sure themselves about what they're doing; they have no plans," Aaron added.

"Does anyone else know about your leaving?" Father Lawrence asked.

"You're the first," Aaron replied.

"I will miss you both, of course…. I had hoped we could do something together, something to honor Her here in the village. I was looking forward to it."

"Maybe we could do something before we leave, Father," Lucia said. "I would like that very much."

"But would that be fair to you, Father?" Aaron asked, concerned. If there are consequences… if something happens afterward, we would not be here with you."

Father Lawrence put a reassuring hand on Aaron's shoulder. "I'll be fine," he said and as he spoke he had a bodily sense that his words were true.

On Easter eve, Catherine and Simon pulled together a large, festive meal for two of their children and their grandchildren, and invited Father Lawrence, Aaron, Lucia, Miriam, her son, and Miriam's father to join them, as well as the two sisters who were still boarding with them. Aaron was sent out to the workshop to fetch Simon when he arrived with Lucia.

"You know, don't you, that Catherine suspects something," Simon told him. "She will try to wheedle whatever it is out of you. She thought at first Lucia was pregnant, but now she thinks it's something else."

Aaron laughed, amused. "You're a wheedler yourself, Simon. I think you are trying to get information out of me before she does."

"Maybe I am."

Aaron stood quietly, deciding. "Lucia and I are going to join Frederick's students."

"Leaving, is it?" Simon looked at Aaron. "You know what you're doing? What if she *does* get pregnant?"

"We've talked about it. We don't know what we'll do, Simon. Lucia says she has a sense we will be taken care of and says we have to trust."

"Well, I suppose women have babies wherever it is you're going. But it is going to be very hard to say goodbye to our god-daughter a second time. Catherine may put up a fight."

After Catherine and Simon's children and grandchildren went home, the two sisters gathered up the dishes and went into the kitchen. Lucia and Aaron told those who still sat around the table that they would be leaving and where they would be going. Catherine eyed Simon, and though Simon tried to look surprised, she could tell he had already been told. Simon knew he would have to answer for that before he went to sleep.

"What will you live on?" Catherine asked.

"At first, we will use the money that Frederick left," Lucia said. She placed a hand on Catherine's arm and when her godmother started crying she hugged her.

"What will you and Aaron do?" Miriam asked. "Will you be teaching? Will you be talking about Wisdom?"

"Maybe…I think so," Lucia answered.

"Seems a fools' errand, if you ask me," Miriam's father said.

"No one is asking you," Catherine said, shaking.

Everyone was taken aback by the ferocious tone of Catherine's retort, everyone but Simon. He knew she meant no harm; it was her protective instinct that had been riled.

"There are worse things than fools' errands," Aaron said, dispelling the tension, slightly. "Of course," Miriam's father said, wanting to mollify Catherine.

"We all have to do what is set before us," Father Lawrence added.

"What does that mean?" Catherine demanded, fixing the priest in her sights while still managing to blow her nose. "Are you leaving now too, Father?"

"No, Catherine. I have no plans to leave and there's something I must do here."

"If you need assistance, Father, the wife and I…we can help," Simon said.

"That might be difficult in this case," Father Lawrence said.

"What is it?" Catherine asked.

Father Lawrence looked quickly at Aaron and Lucia then gave his full attention to Catherine. "I'm going to preach the whole gospel."

"Isn't that what you've always done?" Catherine asked, impatiently.

"I've preached the gospel, but not the whole of it. And neither has the church."

Simon scratched his head. "I'm not following you, Father."

"What if someone asked you to tell your story and you left out Catherine?" Father Lawrence asked.

Simon guffawed. "That wouldn't happen. Even if I forgot to mention her — and I wouldn't — she'd set me right."

Miriam stirred in her seat. "You mean Wisdom, don't you, Father? You want to tell the village about Wisdom."

"Yes," Father Lawrence replied.

"Well, this Wisdom business must be something important," Catherine said to the priest. "You, Lucia, and Aaron seem to think it is, — and Miriam too. But I don't see it."

Lucia reached for her godmother's hand. Catherine turned toward her. "Why are you leaving us again, and you just healed?" she asked quietly as if she and Lucia were alone.

"Catherine, we've seen and experienced so many wonderful things and we have to find a way to share them. Aaron and I believe they belong to everyone," Lucia answered in a low voice.

"You sound just like Jeremiah," Catherine said. "He said things like that."

Lucia leaned away, surprised. "That's true. We *are* like Jeremiah." She leaned back toward her godmother and looked at her pointedly. "But we are different, too. We're not as alone as he was." She squeezed Catherine's hand.

"No, you're definitely not alone. You and Aaron have each other and you'll always have us. You have us too, Father," Catherine said, looking at Father Lawrence. "You do what you think you have to. It doesn't matter if it's something we don't understand. If anyone tries to give you grief, Simon and I will make them think twice about it. Won't we, Simon?"

All eyes turned toward the relieved-looking husband. "We'll make them shake in their boots, Captain," Simon said.

The whole company laughed heartily, but Aaron laughed longer and harder than the rest.

Knowing their time together was short, Aaron, Lucia, and Father Lawrence met often to discuss questions they were wrestling with. Conscious of the boldness and daring of their topics of conversation, sometimes one or the other would hesitate. They discovered it was better to talk about their doubts openly; if doubt was neither feared nor unexamined, it would usually broaden and deepen understanding. At one point Aaron said that he felt all meaningful questions were like the leaves, branches, and great limbs of a single tree and working even with one question with the whole of one's mind and heart seemed to give an intimation of the entire living tree. As the day for Lucia and Aaron's departure approached, the three spent more time discussing what could be done in the village to honor Wisdom.

One evening, Lucia shared the beginnings of a poem she was writing with Aaron and Father Lawrence. Afterwards, both insisted that it had to be included in whatever they decided to do. Lucia mentioned that she had also shared her poem with Miriam, and that her friend had offered to provide a wordless voice accompaniment if Lucia ever wanted to recite it aloud. This sparked something in Father Lawrence. He suggested that the finished poem be spoken on the feast of Pentecost after Holy Communion and that his sermon could be a preparation for it.

"Why that day?" Aaron asked.

"I'm not sure," Father Lawrence said. "It's a feeling I have, a sense that a new world was almost born then."

"What kind of world?" Lucia asked.

"Her world," the priest said simply.

When Aaron asked if this would be the topic of his sermon, Father Lawrence answered in the affirmative. "Well, Father, you and Lucia have your tasks. I'll make mine getting people to come, especially the younger men. The church *will* be full."

When Catherine heard about their plans from Lucia, she offered to give a feast on the evening of Pentecost. "You and Aaron would be leaving soon afterward," she said. "It will be your farewell dinner. If we hold the feast after the mass, you'll be able to hear what people think about Father's sermon and what they felt about your poem." Lucia told her it was an excellent suggestion. "The sisters will help me," Catherine added. "They're so grateful to you and Aaron for offering them your home. They won't stop talking about it."

On the Saturday before the feast of Pentecost, Catherine, Miriam, the two sisters, and Lucia went to the market to procure food for the farewell feast. Catherine had told Lucia she didn't need to accompany them, the dinner was after all for her, but Lucia had insisted. The crowd milling about was larger than usual. There were many people the women did not recognize.

While the rest of her company had moved on to the fruit and vegetable tables, Lucia lingered at the one displaying goat cheese and other goat products. She picked up a wrapped cheese, took a deep whiff. She was remembering a time when she and

Sophia were milking Malena and Maxine when suddenly, someone pushed up against her, jamming her into the table. She was a
little perturbed, but did not think much about it, for being jostled
and bumped was part of a busy market day.

"Pardon me," she heard a woman say without any genuine
feeling. Lucia turned to accept the half-hearted apology and saw
a young, hard-looking woman, somewhat taller than herself, with
a bruised, swollen nose that looked recently broken. She was
with an unpleasant-appearing man who strode on, unaware that
the woman had stopped. The woman appeared dumbstruck and
frightened. She backed away from Lucia as far as the dense crowd
would allow. Lucia's first thought was that the woman had mistaken her for someone else. She was about to introduce herself
when she suddenly knew who the young woman was. The young
woman, seeing that Lucia had indeed recognized her, began fran-
tically scanning the crowd for an opening, an unblocked passage,
and seeing none, began rolling her head and beating her temples
with her fists. Those nearest her shuffled away nervously, assuming she was mad and having a fit.

Lucia stood still. She remembered the feel of the young
woman's hands striking her, pushing her. Now, it did not seem
so important. The woman began screaming, dissolving in terror.
She continued to beat her temples and began shouting a man's
name. Moved, Lucia took a couple of steps forward and held
out the wrapped cheese that had evoked for her so many warm
memories.

"Here, take this," Lucia said. She had to repeat herself several
times before the woman calmed down enough to hear her.

"I'll take nothing from you," the young woman screamed,
looking away.

"You're not taking, I am giving," Lucia replied quietly and firmly, renewing her offering.

The young woman turned around. She appeared disoriented, bewildered. As if in a trance, she cupped her hands and stretched them toward Lucia. Lucia placed the cheese in them. Another village woman, seeing what Lucia did, approached and gave the young woman three wild strawberries, as she was still holding out her hands. The young woman stared at her gifts, unbelieving. Her unpleasant-looking companion suddenly returned, and seeing the strawberries, plucked them from the young woman's hand and ate them; then he pocketed the cheese. Without a word to anyone, he grabbed the woman's upper arm and dragged her away through the crowd.

Lucia watched the young woman go, saw her struggle to free her arm from the grip of her companion. Moved by something that felt like power and feeling together, she inhaled deeply, consciously taking the young woman into herself, allowing herself to experience the young woman's pain as her own. She suddenly felt defenseless, like a worm squirming and convulsing because it was exposed to too much light. She held her breath for a little while and then exhaled, consciously releasing the pain, freeing it to better understand itself.

The other villager, the woman who had given the strawberries, began railing against the rudeness and roughness of the young woman's companion. Lucia could not hear her. She was in the presence of Wisdom, now felt as Mother. Lucia saw how Her compassion was simultaneously a knowing, feeling, and acting, that it was never blind or impotent. It was a knowing/feeling power.

As the young woman disappeared into the crowd, the other

village woman was asking Lucia if she had ever seen her before. Lucia shook her head. She never told anyone the identity of the young woman or shared what had happened at the market. It would always seem an intensely intimate moment that belonged to Wisdom and the young woman — not to her.

Chapter Forty-Four

It was Pentecost Sunday. The day was warm and there was a noticeable softness in the air as if the lightest, silkiest imaginable cloth was touching the skin. As Lucia and Aaron approached the church, Lucia told him there was something she wanted to do. He guessed what it was and asked if she wanted him with her. "No," she said, "I'll only be a little while."

As Lucia went around the church to the cemetery, she saw Father Lawrence standing near the graves of Sophia, Jeremiah, and little Sophie. She walked through the cemetery until she stood across from him. Father Lawrence glanced at her. His manner told her she had been expected.

"I was just remembering that evening when Sophia told us about the Woman — the day you spoke to us for the first time."

"I remember how curious I was and how I said I wanted to see the Woman like she had."

"Yes. And remember how Sophia said she had never heard anything about the Woman in church? I knew she was trying to bait me and it worked. And here we are.... I know many people will not like what we are about to do, but I know your mother is saying, 'It's about time.'"

"It would have made Jeremiah happy too, Father. He would have been inspired to compose a poem or tell a story, or maybe he would dance."

Father Lawrence nodded and closed his eyes. "Yes, Jeremiah is here today too. He sees the beauty in what we are doing together…. Remember the circle of stones, the little twigs and the flower? What an extraordinary night that was! And how generous of you to share what Jeremiah had taught you! It's difficult for me to speak of what happened that night, how one I felt with you and Aaron and Frederick …." The priest wiped his eyes. "I will miss you both terribly. But this is not the time for goodbyes; it's a new beginning. Let's tell ourselves that even if we do fall flat on our faces, we will pick ourselves up and dust ourselves off and try again."

"We won't fall, Father. So many are helping us. Sophia is here and Jeremiah and Helen and Frederick and little Sophie…"

The priest held out his hand to her. She took it and came around to his side. He knelt on the ground in front of her. "I asked Sophia to bless me once and she did. Now, I am asking you, Lucia, to do the same."

Lucia smiled shyly, and placing her hands on the priest's white hair, gently pressed down. No words came to her, but love streamed from her hands and fingers. The exquisite tenderness of it made her weep. Father Lawrence looked up at her and she saw he also wept and his cheeks were flushed. He put both hands over his heart like a child. "She loves me," he said wonderingly. Lucia nodded, knowing who he meant. "And you," the priest added, "She loves you so much."

Though Pentecost was considered a major feast of the church, the villagers had never warmed to it. The story of Christ's disciples hearing something that sounded like a violent wind and then having a tongue of fire rest on them which drove them to start talking to people who spoke different languages seemed very strange. The villagers were not particularly fond of violent winds, distrusted visions, and saw garrulousness as a weakness, if not an outright vice. For these reasons the church was typically only half full on Pentecost, unlike Christmas and Easter. This Pentecost, however, was an exception. Today, even the young, single men were there, standing about in groups or with their families.

Aaron had spread the word that something memorable was going to happen at mass on Pentecost, something that any naturally curious person would not want to miss. As soon as the villagers saw Father Lawrence at the altar, they knew Aaron had been right. The humble priest had a majestic air. And when he read the scripture it was as if he was speaking aloud something he was creating in the very act of trying to fathom it. All of this intrigued the villagers and they found themselves listening very carefully. When the priest stepped up to give his sermon, his presence seemed to fill the whole church. To many, he seemed physically altered, both taller and wider than they remembered, and there was a light in and around him. There was not a sound in the church.

"My friends and neighbors, after Jesus died he descended into the underworld and brought light to the dead. We also know, that after He died, He raised up His body, showed Himself to his disciples, and then ascended into heaven. But the culmination of his death, resurrection, and ascension was the feast we celebrate today. I never really understood this feast of Pentecost until just recently. I knew the particulars of the story. I knew that all the disciples had met together in one room after Christ had ascended into heaven and how, at one point, those men and women heard a sound that was like a mighty wind. And then tongues of fire appeared in their midst and rested on each of them. After that, the disciples were moved to speak to everyone and anyone, to all inhabitants of Jerusalem and to all its visitors, and the amazing thing was that they were understood even by people who spoke a different language. I knew this part of Christ's story, but I didn't know what it really meant, or why it was important. But things have happened that have made me listen to this story of Pentecost with greater attention.

"What was the wind the disciples heard? Wind is the sound of power and a sign of change. The Scripture says the disciples actually heard a sound like a *violent* wind. A great reverberating power filled the room and the disciples knew it meant something big. *But what?* They probably wondered. The answer was in those tongues of fire that first appeared in the midst of the company and then came to rest on each of them individually. Fire destroys. We all know this. So what was *this* fire destroying? This fire was destroying the walls that keep us isolated and ignorant of each other. It was destroying separation. And this fire was no mere vision, no image to treasure in private. It was a *tongue* of fire. It had to express itself, like material fire needs to burn. It was power and understanding and joy bursting into this world together, and it obliterated separation.

"But fire not only destroys, it also creates. It bakes our bread, cooks our meat, and forges our tools. It warms and sustains our bodies. Around its comforting light we gather in the darkness. So what is fire creating here? Here, my friends, fire is creating a new world, not a world where fire exists, but a world of fire — a world where everything speaks from its heart to everything else, where even the most insignificant bush is a tongue of fire, a world of fire, where the very stones cry out. Jesus desired this world with the whole of his being. 'I've come to cast fire on the earth,' he said, 'and how I burn until it is accomplished.' Jesus was speaking of the fire that destroys the old separations so that we can really hear each other, the fire that clears a space so everything can speak its deepest truth, freely. Everything…"

Father Lawrence paused. As the villagers waited the tension grew. Everyone in the church felt as if he or she was poised on a narrow ledge where flight and falling were both possible.

"I've been wondering what it must have felt like to be there, to be a disciple in that room on Pentecost, to see and feel that fire. When I left this village to recover my health, I lived near the ocean. I remember watching a little creek run down from the hills. It joined another and then with greater force emptied out into the even greater power of the sea. I think the moment of Pentecost was also a joining like this. The disciples were being drawn to complete strangers and found that differences did not separate. A new Unity was coming into being and expressing itself through the disciples. Everyone sensed it. Men and women who had come from many different countries and spoke many different languages could hear what the disciples were saying, 'each in his own language,' and they began wondering together what it all meant.

"That was the moment when a new world, a new human race, was almost born — and we were no mere passive spectators of this birth, we were wholly participating in it. But then our fear and lack of understanding made this new world stillborn. Some who heard the disciples began speaking contemptuously of them. They dismissed the blissful power they felt streaming out of the disciples by saying it was due to drunkenness. They told the others that the disciples had lost their reason. In what they said, we can hear what they most feared: the end of the primacy of the rational mind. They thought, mistakenly, that the end of this reign meant the downfall of the human race, and of themselves particularly. That fear, expressed as disdain, gave separation a foothold again in this world. The new world began retreating.

"The contempt of bright and reasonable people likely frustrated and angered the disciples. They grew impatient. They knew the preciousness of what had burst upon them and wanted to protect it. And in thinking they were responsible for defending it against the ignorance of others, another step away from the new world was taken. The disciples began spending time and energy separating out who believed rightly from who didn't. They no longer communicated or expressed Unity. Christ's disciples began using Him as if He were a definitive test, even condemning those who would not acknowledge Him. When the disciples were making that step, the church was born and the new world retreated yet another step. And for centuries that new world has continued to retreat until the Pentecostal fire eventually shrunk to a few burning embers.

"This is why the church, to this point in time, has always been the reminder of what almost was and holds out the promise of what is to come, but it has never been able to bring about a new and truly united world. The evidence for that is all around us. To hide its failure from itself, the church has taught that the world is intractably dark and riddled with evil, as learned and clever men have hid their failure to surpass themselves by declaring the existence of absolute and binding laws in nature."

The people were stirring in their seats. There were gasps and mutterings. Some noisily left the church. Catherine was nervously fanning her forehead while Simon sat stunned. Lucia and Aaron listened to the people behind and in front of them. They heard a few say that Father Lawrence was possessed, delirious, or drunk. Some said that he was blaspheming and they could not bear listening to him. Lucia reached for Aaron's hand and Aaron looked around, studying people's faces. Many appeared shocked, but there were also quite a few who appeared animated and intrigued. The young were a majority among these, but there were also older people, men and women both, who looked alert and curious. Father Lawrence waited until the people who had wanted to leave had left and the rest had quieted down. He did not seem surprised or perturbed and even his sadness sat upon him lightly.

"This was how Christ, the Divinely-human man, the man of Unity, became a sign of contradiction and contention, and how His fire has nearly been put out…nearly put out, but not entirely. My good friend Sophia, whom many of you will remember, once told me that fire plays tricks with us. When we think it has gone out, it rekindles itself. I know from personal experience that this is true. I know from looking around and seeing what is happening in the world today, that this is true. The fire of the new world is reigniting everywhere.

"What Pentecost began was not completely lost. It was not lost because Pentecost was not only a glimpse of a new world, but of a new task. Pentecost presented us with a job. If you have work to do, but don't do it, it waits for you. It doesn't go away.

The broken fence or roof doesn't suddenly disappear or mend itself, and you cannot entirely forget it. Pentecost is like that. It's the work we had just begun and then left off, the task we've resisted. The longer you put off mending the roof, the more it drips, the more you are reminded of what you haven't done.

"What is this work I am talking about? My friends, I believe our job is to learn how to receive Wisdom's many gifts. I believe our task is to ask us to show us Her ways, our task is to invite Her to begin the work of our healing. *But we have Christ,* you might be saying. True. But who of us can say we understand Christ fully? Who of us can say we love Him as He deserves? I can't say that, my friends. But Wisdom can. She alone can. Wisdom understands who Christ is and what He accomplished for us. Wisdom loves Him as He deserves to be loved.

"As I am speaking to you now, I realize that those tongues of fire were Hers. Yes, that fire was Hers. And the words the disciples spoke — they were Hers too. And the initial listening and understanding were also Hers. Wisdom was bursting with the desire to sing of Her lover and to hear His praises sung. That was how the new world first approached us, my friends – as the force of love, as words of intoxicating love. Wisdom had to tell the world about Her Beloved even though it was not ready to hear Her. We erred and still err, in thinking that it is *our* words, *our* love, *our* understanding of Christ, *our* little fire that is so important when in truth it is only Hers."

The silence in the church after Father Lawrence stopped speaking had a quality no one had ever experienced before. It was full, bursting with energy and life, spreading like fire, creating a feeling that all things were possible.

After communion, Lucia and Miriam stood up without any preamble and moved to the elevated front of the church. People stirred, wondering what would happen next, not sure if they had the stamina to hear anything more. Standing in front of the church with Miriam behind her, Lucia sensed their unease and dread. She glanced at Father Lawrence, who nodded to her in encouragement. Miriam, observing this, began a haunting, soft, wordless melody that slowly gathered strength and felt like the opening of the heart. The villagers as well as Lucia found themselves surrendering to its beauty. And then in a clear, steady and impassioned voice, Lucia spoke:

Mother,
I know that I am
Because of You.
You have carried me within You
From all eternity
As You have borne
All things
All worlds
All experiences
All names
Even the names of God.
You are the self-creating womb
That nourishes everything with Your infinite substance
And makes each being the compassionate twin of all the others.

Because of You
I am the inseparable twin of the Earth.
I am the inseparable twin of the Sun.

I am the inseparable twin of the moon.
I am the inseparable twin of every plant and animal,
Of day and night.
You join me to all.

Mother
Mother Divine
I will speak of You.
I want to say your name over and over,
But You have no single name
For you are the bearer all our names
Even the names of God.
You are the Woman Without a Name,
Our Mother.
The Woman who can now be seen
By the power of not seeing.

Woman Without a Name,
I am among the limitless multitude
Who opened Your vast womb
And made You Mother.
You pushed me forth.
With the might of your spirit.
And though Your breath and substance remained in Me,
I lost the shared sleep of the All
And the feeling of Your bliss.
In entering time I came into a world
I did not recognize.
I found I had taken on a wide-awake and solitary emptiness
That ever frightened me.

How brave You are, our Mother,
How adventurous!
And hopeful —
To separate everything from Yourself,
To push each thing
Toward an infinite and conscious growth
Despite the risks,
To imagine each thing You ecstatically
And peacefully held within You
As being a mere seed of itself.

But what suffering Your labor and imagining has unleashed.
In You first, and then in us, and then in You again because of us.
What friction and hostility!
What greed and despair!
For each has striven to lay claim to all
And to grow only by being fed by all
For each thing fears and flees the truth
Of its bare solitude,
Not knowing the glory of it
Or how it begins the new Unity.

How unlike You, Mother,
We have all become.
You knew this would be and accepted it
As the price of birthing us
And You have not abandoned us.
Every name of God that would help us
You have assumed in time,

Ordering them all for our greatest good.
Making love the highest of all,
Making it the force that drives all the others.
Your compassion, Mother, is ever with us.

If we struggle to return to You
You are seeking us much more.

You want to heal and teach and guide us
In your unlimited Wisdom.
You invite us to bring forth our hidden Self
As our Lord Jesus did,
He loved you with a love that was not only human but also divine
And in loving You, united both conditions
making You Bride as well as Mother.

Mother,
The force of Your Compassionate Love
Moves in and around and through all things.
Eve and Mary and my mother Sophia
Were each uniquely imbued with it.
Everything feels it, though it is not yet universally recognized.
And everything is uniting because of it.
In this You have become a surprise to Yourself.
It is as if You are waking up to Your power.
You are discovering that in addition to being our Mother and Bride
You are also our Queen.
And though we are still limited in our understanding,

We are beginning to see this too.

I sing of You, my Mother, Bride, and Queen.
I sing of You, Woman Without a Name
Bearer and birther and imaginer
Of my name,
Of every name.
I love You with the force of Your love
Within me.
And I will sing of You forever
As forever I grow into Your likeness
For nothing less is worthy
Of who I secretly am.
Of what all things are.

Lucia's voice had remained steady until the last few words, which seemed to dissolve into silence. It made those present pay close attention. Lucia closed her eyes and felt the power that had carried the words being released into the world. No one moved, no one spoke, but she heard the sound of deep sobbing in the church coming from women. It was as if she and Miriam had touched an ancient grief, or had fulfilled a deep and hidden desire.

Lucia opened her eyes and saw Aaron looking restfully upon her. Catherine had hooked her arm around Aaron's and was weeping. Lucia did not see Father Lawrence sitting off to the side, but others did. Some said later that he glowed as if in fire-light, while others said he looked worn down, as if he had just accomplished a prolonged and difficult task. For a long while, he sat in stillness and no one rattled about with their usual end-of-mass restlessness. When he rose, they rose too and realized through the tremulousness in their legs that something had occurred that had both moved and frightened them. As they bowed their heads for his blessing, some found themselves doing it unwillingly. Thoughts about the unorthodox nature of the day's proceedings and what had been said quickly lined up in full battle array. Aaron felt the change in the air, and immediately after the service rushed to Father Lawrence's side as he stood outside the church, greeting people.

The priest knew what was in Aaron's heart and when there was space to do so, quietly said, "You are a David. But there are no Goliaths are here. Go. Be with Lucia."

Many women and several men openly expressed such warm gratitude toward Father Lawrence, Lucia, and Miriam that they were overcome. Women reached out to touch Lucia and Miriam and Father Lawrence, although they didn't know why they felt the need to do so. One woman told them, "For years I have accepted and forgiven many things about the church and felt I received so little in return, but today I was given a gift that outweighs everything. I will always remember it. Today, I felt the blessedness of being a woman."

An older gentleman bowed toward them and said, "I felt the presence of Christ."

Some men and women, however, voiced their strong misgivings. "We know you have not been well, Father, and sometimes illness clouds good judgment."

Father Lawrence raised his hand to stop them. "At the present time, my health is very good. What was said this morning was the result of long and careful consideration, not due to any clouding of my judgment. You have an opportunity to oppose what happened here, if you feel the need, but do it honestly. Don't trivialize it and don't deny it."

"We were only trying to be charitable," a man retorted. "What was said this morning goes against the teaching of the church. You must know that."

"Was it? Was it contrary to the message of Jesus?"

"The church interprets Scripture for us. Who are you, one lone priest, to think you can know the mind of Christ?"

"But I wasn't alone. I am not alone," Father Lawrence replied, and as he said this, he knew the truth of his own words once more.

That evening, Catherine opened up her home to anyone who wished to come by for a last farewell, and many did. There was food and music and inevitably talk of the morning's events. Aaron and Lucia were already packed. They planned to leave in a few days on Midsummer's Eve. Though it was out of their way, they had decided to visit the shrine of the Virgin Mother and visit with Judith and the others at the inn before joining Frederick's students. Beyond that, they still had no plans.

When most of the guests had left, Catherine shooed Lucia and Aaron to bed, refusing their offers to help with the clean-up. "There are hands here willing to help. You two go on."

Aaron and Lucia went to bed, but after lying there for a while and not being able to sleep, they decided to go for a walk. Hand in hand, they left the house and strolled through the village before heading for the forest. Lucia drank deeply from the well of memory, while Aaron thought of Father Lawrence and wondered what was in store for the priest he loved so greatly. It was

Aaron who first saw the shooting star speeding across the sky. He pointed it out to Lucia.

Lucia gasped with pleasure. "Sophia loved shooting stars. I remember her telling me that falling stars didn't have anything and this gave them the freedom to make incredible journeys."

As she spoke, Aaron was lost in the contemplation of the beauty, pain, and adventure that was a human life. *How far everyone has to go*, he thought, *even our child who died, unborn.* When he returned to himself and felt Lucia's hand in his, he wanted to be joined to her. Lucia, immediately sensing his longing, and longing for him in return, found a patch of soft ground under a moonlit tree, and laying herself down, she pulled him toward her.

On the morning of Midsummer's Eve, Father Lawrence was waiting for Aaron and Lucia near the church. He heard Thunder snorting, cart wheels bumping along stones, and Catherine's voice. He was surprised to hear another female voice, and soon recognized it as belonging to Miriam. The little group which had come in two carts also included Simon, and Miriam's son. While the others stepped down, Lucia checked to see whether the winged statue of Isis was still securely tied to the top trunk in the back of the little cart.

"Good to see you all this morning," Father Lawrence said.

With the priest leading, they all went around the church to the cemetery. Lucia and Aaron went to the graves of his mother, Frederick, Sophia, Jeremiah, and little Sophie; before each, they knelt and kissed the earth, lingering longest at the grave of their child. Then the entire group went into the church. As Aaron and Lucia knelt together before Father Lawrence, the priest laid his hands on them and prayed, echoing his blessing of many years ago when he had blessed Lucia after Sophia's death. This time he also called upon Eve and Mary and all the holy women of all the ages, to bless Lucia and Aaron, and he added, "May our Divine Mother light your way and bring others to you to help you in Her work."

Father Lawrence and Aaron embraced, weeping unrestrained and copious tears. "Don't worry about me, Aaron," he whispered to him, "and I will try not to worry too much about you. There is light in you. Let it shine before the world." When they parted, the priest approached Lucia and kissed the top of her head. "How you have honored Her! How much you have moved me," he said. "Sophia was there when you spoke on Pentecost. I felt her presence."

Miriam then hugged Lucia tightly. "I'll write to you. I may join you someday…someday soon."

Aaron and Lucia next wrapped Catherine and Simon in their arms and thanked them. "We're proud of you both," Catherine said, too overcome to say more.

And then, as if in a dream, Aaron was helping Lucia into the cart and they were driving off. Lucia looked back often and waved at those she was leaving behind. At some point, she turned around and facing forward, looked back no more. Without saying anything, Aaron briefly put a hand over hers before gripping the reins. "Those who love each other can never really be parted," he said to her.

The little group that remained behind continued watching the cart until it disappeared in the forest. Just before they turned back, the sun came up and a burnished light flashed out among the trees.

"What's that?" Simon asked, pointing at the light.

"The sun must be hitting that statue with the golden wings," Miriam replied.

The rest of the villagers woke soon after Lucia and Aaron's departure and set about their chores in preparation for the celebration of Midsummer's Eve. Finding themselves looking at each other throughout the day, they sensed something between them that itched to be noticed — something wonderful that had always been there. It was difficult to perceive or speak of directly, but there was more laughter that day, more help offered, more patience with the irritations of a shared life, and more heartfelt conversation.

That night the celebration of Midsummer's Eve seemed the loveliest of all celebrations the villagers could remember. When the festivities were over, many, unwilling to see the night come to an end, did not go home. Instead, they wandered close together in pairs or in small groups underneath the traveling stars. And as they roamed about, the elder told the younger the story of the village and how an angel in the guise of a man had once visited them. He had told them all that they lived in the shadow Beauty cast as She drew close to them.

Breinigsville, PA USA
06 November 2010
248799BV00002B/3/P